WHEN 9 TO 5 ISN'T ENOUGH

WHEN
9 TO 5 ISN'T
ENOUGH

by

Marcia A. Perkins-Reed

Hay House, Inc.
Santa Monica, CA

WHEN 9 TO 5 ISN'T ENOUGH
A Guide to Finding Fulfillment at Work
by Marcia A. Perkins-Reed

Copyright © 1989, 1990 by Marcia A. Perkins-Reed

Certain names in this book have been changed to protect the privacy of individuals who were kind enough to share their information in the hope of benefitting others.

Excerpt from *Living in the Light* by Shakti Gawain with Laurel King. Copyright © 1986 by Shakti Gawain. Reprinted with permission of New World Library, San Rafael, California.

Library of Congress Catalog Card No. 90-80052

Perkins-Reed, Marcia A.
    When 9 to 5 isn't enough: a guide to finding fulfillment at Work / Marcia A. Perkins-Reed. — Rev. ed.
        p.   cm.
    Includes bibliographical references and index.
    ISBN 0-937611-93-X (tradep.) : $10.00
    1. Job satisfaction. 2. Quality of work life. I. Title. II. Title: When nine to five isn't enough.
HF5549.5.J63P367   1990
650.1—dc20

ISBN: 0-937611-93-X

Interior Design by Teri Stewart
Typeset by Freedmen's Organization
Printed and Bound by Delta Lithograph Co. of Valencia, CA

90 91 92 93 94 95   10 9 8 7 6 5 4 3 2

First Printing, 1989, by High Flight Press

First Printing, Revised Edition, July 1990 by Hay House, Inc.

Second Printing, October 1990

Published and distributed in the United States by:

Hay House, Inc.
501 Santa Monica Boulevard
P.O. Box 2212
Santa Monica, California 90406 USA

Printed in the United States of America

To the pure flame of Life
which inspires the life purpose
in each of us

CONTENTS

vii

PART FIVE: KEYS TO TRANSFORMATION

Acknowledgements

Many people have contributed to the ideas and the production of this book, and I wish to thank each of them.

First, my ever-patient, loving husband for his endless encouragement as my vision has evolved into the message you read in these pages. His support has been a haven for me when my purpose appeared masked by discouragement.

I also gratefully acknowledge my college psychology professors and the writers who so powerfully influenced me at that impressionable time in my life, including Erich Fromm, Abraham Maslow, and Daniel Yankelovich, to name a few.

When the student is ready, the teacher appears. And at each stage of my development, a spiritual teacher was there to guide me to the next level. I thank the late Lynne Lowe, Mary Fox, and Mary Boggs, who ministered to me in person, and so many others that affected me through their writing: Sanaya Roman, Marsha Sinetar, Shakti Gawain, Ram Dass, Ken Keyes, Tom Johnson, and Tony Robbins, among many others.

I especially wish to thank Lynda Falkenstein, without whom this book may never have been written.

And finally, I thank my employers for what I have learned about work in each new situation, and the associates in my business who have encouraged me and made it possible for me to devote the time and energy necessary to make this book a reality.

Introduction

This book is for you, me, and each of us who wants more out of our work than just a 9-to-5 routine. It is the product of my experiences in the radically changing workplace over the past two decades, as well as the work I have done with clients as a career consultant to facilitate their journey to career satisfaction.

It began when I was in college studying psychology and picked up an excerpt of a book by Daniel Yankelovich about the quest for fulfillment at work. That article struck a chord with me, since even at that early stage in my life I had worked in jobs that were fun—and others that were not so enjoyable. I had noticed that some people truly enjoy their work, and others just put up with it. Was it really true that there was a massive trend away from just working day after day with one eye on the clock and the other on retirement? Did other people besides me really want to be fulfilled in their work, and to accomplish something in their life?

I had sensed since I was a child that my life had a purpose —a mission, if you will—and that there was something important for me to do. I knew intuitively that it had something to do with my work. But for many years I did not know what my purpose was.

My life wove its path through various kinds of jobs, many years of education and ultimately law school, and many different spiritual teachings. Throughout this process of education, jobs, and relationships, I continued to seek my purpose. And I discovered that others were on a similar quest.

Then, just three years ago, while I was in the midst of practicing law and working on my personal growth, the awareness of my purpose became clear. I was to assist in the transformation of the workplace by sharing with others the concepts I had learned about right livelihood, experiencing fulfillment through work, and enjoying each day. This book is a part of the ongoing unfoldment of my life's purpose, as are the seminars on increasing fun and satisfaction at work that I now present nationwide. It will help you to discover your own purpose and bring a sense of meaning to your life that may have been lacking in the 9-to-5 routine.

Whether one is in career transition or not, all of us want more from our jobs than we have been experiencing. This book contains suggestions that will lead you through this transition, help you overcome fear and other unproductive beliefs, and expand your personal vision to its highest possible level.

You will find references to metaphysical concepts and spiritual truths sprinkled liberally throughout the book. These principles have made a marked difference in my life and are rapidly growing in acceptance during this time of spiritual awakening. If you do not agree with those portions of the book, I encourage you to simply overlook them for now and gain from the book the ideas that do benefit you. There is something here for everyone who desires greater fulfillment at work.

How to Read This Book: I recommend that you read the book from beginning to end, rather than skipping ahead to the sections that are of particular interest to you. This is because each of the chapters builds on the concepts introduced in the previous one. If you skip ahead, you will miss out on the foundation laid in the previous chapter.

Read the book through once, to glean the essential concepts it presents. Then, go back to the Action Steps in the chapters where you need particular work in your life, and do those steps that assist you with your issues. You may then wish to use this book as a handy reference whenever a specific type of belief or situation arises—you can simply turn to that chapter and remind yourself of the concepts that will assist you with that issue, doing the Action Steps if desired.

The Appendix of *18 Commonly Asked Questions* will also give you a brief overview of common issues, and will refer you to the chapter(s) that deal with that issue.

It is my sincere desire that this book be a tool for transformation in your life, and that it assist you in being absolutely the best you can be in your work and life. It is written in a conversational style, as though you and I are having an extended discussion about these important concepts. I invite you to continue the conversation by sharing with me your impressions as you read the book and do the Action Steps, and your experiences as you use the concepts in your work. You can write to me at 921 SW Washington, Suite 805, Portland, Oregon 97205.

And now, let's get on with the process of finding fulfillment at work!

PART ONE

Why 9 to 5 Isn't Enough

1

Transformation at Work

"Toto, I don't think we're in Kansas anymore,"
said Dorothy.

—*The Wizard of Oz*

TODAY'S WORKPLACE IS not what we expected it to be. The companies in which we work are being transformed before our very eyes. New jobs and careers are created every day. Values, structures, and lifestyles that served our parents well are no longer viable. And we are not prepared.

The 9-to-5 work routine was the most one could expect in generations past. "Put in your time, don't complain too much, and be grateful for a raise now and then," people were told. "If you are lucky enough to get a job you like, consider yourself fortunate."

It sounds a bit like a prearranged marriage, doesn't it? Our family, friends, teachers, and counselors urge us to make the "sensible" choice, to think of the future rewards rather than satisfaction in the now moment.

In the past the motivation for working was not love of the job, but obligation. The need to "make a living" and "get a steady job" became the paramount considerations. Often children joined the family business, not because they necessarily wanted to, but because of family pressure or lack of other options.

Thankfully, we are beginning to awaken to other choices. If our relationship becomes unfulfilling, we leave our mate and find a new one. If we want to live somewhere else, we move. If we don't like our job, we go to work for another company—or start our own business! In short, we are becoming more mobile in our activities — and more conscious in the choices we make.

Now that this mobility in relationships, jobs, and other parts of

3

our life is accepted, many of us fall into a trap: we often change the experience, but we fail to change the cause. The result? Even if we change jobs, we remain unhappy—and often repeat the experience we had in our last job. If we change mates, we still don't feel they treat us properly.

The only way to get out of this trap is to change the cause *behind* the experience. That is, we must work to change the beliefs within ourselves that are causing us to create, over and over again, the same external experiences.

In the context of our job and career, this inevitably means discovering what I call our life's purpose—and fulfilling it through our work. We will discuss what life's purpose is and how to discover it in the next chapter. (You may also need to overcome some internal fears, excuses, and other blocks—but more about that in a later chapter.)

Before we explore life's purpose further, however, we must understand why the structures, values, and lifestyle taken for granted by previous generations are no longer enough. What has changed? How are you, the worker of today, different from the worker of yesterday? And why aren't you satisfied with the 9-to-5 routine?

Changing Values

CASE STUDY—"Jim"

Jim, now 47, has been working at a local manufacturing firm since he graduated from high school. Beginning as a production line worker in 1957, he knew that he would work at the company for the rest of his life. He married his wife shortly afterward, and they have raised three children. His wife stayed home with the children when they were young. Jim has gradually worked his way up both the pay scale and the scale of responsibility in the company, and is now a manager in charge of one of the company's largest divisions. He looks forward to retiring when he turns 65 so that he can travel and enjoy life and pursue his hobby of collecting antiques. He doesn't think much about whether or not he enjoys his job—it is just part of his life.

Jim illustrates the values of what I will call the "Old Worker." Often described as the Puritan Work Ethic, the Old Worker's values require that the worker swallow his frustrations, suppress his impulses to be creative, and instead, be loyal and do what is expected of him. Others' needs come first. Tradition for the sake of tradition, institution for the sake of institution, is the norm. This worker lives to work. His life focuses on his career. And the worker is most typically a male breadwinner, with a wife and children to support.

This Old Worker is motivated primarily by job security, a steady income, and periodic raises. The entire society for which the Old Worker was prepared was based on manufacturing, originating from the Industrial Revolution. This context required conformity, and left little room for creativity or ingenuity.

Jim and other Old Workers are more and more uncomfortable in today's society. Contrast the case of Lisa.

CASE STUDY—"Lisa"

Lisa is a computer software consultant with a five-person firm. She and her four partners started the firm two years ago after becoming dissatisfied with the management philosophies in the Fortune 500 companies for which they had been working.

Although none of them believes that their new company will necessarily be a lifetime venture, they are all excited and motivated to contribute to its growth now, and for as long as the arrangement works for them both personally and professionally. Their compensation is not limited to a salary and periodic raises. Rather, they each participate in the profits, have a flexible benefits program, and fill their receptionist function with a job-sharing arrangement. Lisa is now 34, divorced and the mother of one child, who has been in day care since she was one year old.

Lisa typifies the "New Worker." She has discarded the view that steadfastness and hard work always pay off. Indeed, the number of workers who still believe in that Old Worker philosophy fell from 58 percent in the 1960s to 43 percent in the 1970s, according to Daniel Yankelovich in his book, *New Rules: Searching for Fulfillment in a World Turned Upside Down*. A study by Yankelovich's firm in the 1980s showed that 40 percent of the work force had adopted, at least in part, the belief that work ought to be personally satisfying, rather than valuable for its own sake. In short, the New Worker works to live, rather than lives to work. I call this new philosophy the Fulfillment Ethic.

The Fulfillment Ethic embraces the principle that life is to be lived and enjoyed for its own sake. Self-expression is key, as is creativity. Thus, entrepreneurship is booming, and firms like Lisa's are being formed every day. Increasingly, business owners and employees are women. By the year 2000, fully one-half of the businesses in the United States will be owned by women.

Rewards today are immediate, not postponed. What motivates New Workers is not stability and security, but the opportunity to be rewarded in proportion to their effort and contribution to the company; to express themselves creatively in their work; to continually grow and develop personally and professionally; and to be able to have input into company management—ideas that are listened to and acted upon.

What has caused these dramatic changes? One factor has been the shift in the focus of both society and the economy from manufacturing to information. Information processing and its companion, the computer, are the mainstay of business and work today. This change in overall focus has created new needs and values among today's workers.

I mention these changes in values and in society's focus to help put our career dissatisfaction into context. Once we understand these changes, we realize that we are not alone—the changes we are experiencing are shared by many others. We are not unusual for feeling the way we do. And we are not placing unreasonable demands upon the workplace by expecting to fulfill our inner needs through work.

The transformation to the Fulfillment Ethic not only affects our jobs, but the very way we manage our lives. In fact, the changes are so intrinsic that they are transforming the structure and operation of today's businesses.

Changing Structures at Work

In previous generations, businesses were typically structured as hierarchies. There were layers upon layers of management, each of which told the level below it how the work was to be performed. Decisions were not questioned, and traditions were upheld solely for their own sake. There was a strongly ingrained value of loyalty to the company and having only one career for life, and this imposed management was accepted as an integral part of the employment "contract." It also served the needs of the manufacturing-oriented society.

The information age has changed all of that. Information, by its nature, requires people to think to process it, and to apply it creatively. Innovation and teamwork are critical. The old hierarchical structures have been sloughed off like an old skin as this new focus emerges. Today, quality control groups and decentralized management have developed to meet the needs of the information-oriented society.

Businesses today commonly consist of a number of autonomous groups, each responsible for its own budget, quality control, working relationships, efficiency, and production levels—and often for developing new products as well. Though the groups interact with each other and serve a common company mission, they are often not subject to the dictates of one CEO or president who has the final word. The emphasis is now on quality, customer service, and excellence—not just on who has the highest profit margin or produces the highest volume.

Furthermore, this transformation is not merely limited to management structures. Businesses are recognizing the changing needs of their employees and are changing their benefit packages and employee incentives accordingly. Benefits offered to employees are no longer standardized, regardless of age or family status. Rather, cafeteria benefits, flextime, job sharing, and other innovative arrangements are offered to the New Worker. Workers who perform well are rewarded not just with increased compensation (which today may be tied to increased overall profits), but with added responsibilities and opportunities to contribute to further company growth. Today's parents expect to work while their children are young, which means employers must be prepared to accommodate the demands of children's illnesses and school activities.

Creative options such as these are increasingly available in many companies today. Is it any wonder that many, if not most, of us are dissatisfied with companies who continue to adhere to the old system? We now want to express ourselves creatively, to have our family obligations recognized, to be allowed to experience ongoing growth both personally and professionally.

New Challenges for Employers

These changes create some very new challenges for today's employers. On the one hand, they want their employees to keep their skills up to date. It is said that an engineering degree has a "half-life" today of eight years. That means that if an engineer with a new degree does not keep his skills current through continuing education, he will be obsolete in 16 years (or less, with the current information explosion causing unprecedented increases in the total amount of information available). With degrees in computer skills and information technology, the half life is even shorter.

On the other hand, the employer is concerned that the investment it makes in its employees may be "wasted" if the employee then goes to work for a competitor. What must be remembered is that employee turnover is an accepted part of business. It will continue whether the company trains its people or not.

Employers *must* train their employees and offer other innovative benefits, particularly in today's "seller's market." Employers are rapidly seeing the market transform from the baby boom, where there were many qualified applicants for every opening, to the baby bust, where companies must scramble to meet their basic needs. During the 1960s, 56.6 million "baby busters" were born, whereas 72.5 million "baby boomers" were born during the late 1940s through 1950s. This means that a record low number of workers are entering the job market for the first time. By 1995, the number of 16- to 24-year-old workers will have dropped to 14.9 percent, from 24.1 percent in 1975.

These baby busters have less incentive to work 80- or 90-hour work weeks and overachieve to succeed than did their baby boomer predecessors. Their high self-confidence, coupled with the seller's market, results in a strong desire for balance in their lives. To attract these increasingly scarce workers requires that employers sweeten their benefits package, decentralize their management, and treat their employees like fully functioning human beings, rather than as cogs in a wheel.

This is true not only for highly skilled and professional positions, but even for entry-level jobs. It is now common to see signs in East Coast hamburger stands and other food establishments offering college scholarships, wages at twice minimum wage, and other incentives to attract dependable servers.

How does all of this affect you? As a job seeker or career changer in this context, you are likely to find your prospective employer more willing than ever before to accommodate your desire for growth. Finding fulfillment in today's workplace is no longer just the "luck of the draw," but is a recognized, legitimate expectation. In short, you *deserve* to be fulfilled at work—and today's employers will often assist you in achieving the fulfillment you desire.

Indeed, your desire for satisfaction and fulfillment at work reflects another type of transformation—a spiritual awakening that is growing in ever-increasing dimensions.

Spiritual Awakening

More and more of us are beginning to view life in a new way. We are now coming to realize that we are, at our essence, spiritual beings. All that goes on in the outer world— including our work, our relationships, our health challenges, and how we handle our money —are just vehicles through which we learn and grow spiritually.

This awakening is reflected most dramatically in the rapid growth of what is referred to as the "New Thought Movement" over the past two decades. This movement includes the increasing number of metaphysical churches that encourage us to be all that we can be, to rely on our inner urgings, and to change our thinking if we wish to change our lives. Ever since their inception approximately 100 years ago, the exponential explosion of these churches in recent years is astounding.

Quite simply, these New Thought churches, as well as other experiential and counseling organizations (including the various groups designed to deal with substance abuse and other addictive behaviors, such as Alcoholics Anonymous) have emerged to meet the precise needs of today's Fulfillment Ethic. They provide a nurturing environment in which we can increase our awareness of ourselves. They accept as a basic principle that each of us has the inherent right to experience fulfillment in all aspects of our lives. Abuse of substances is simply a counterfeit method of attempting to experience fulfillment and peace of mind. These organizations provide us with tools to change our lives to be who and what we want to be—without imposing a system of dogma that has been so stifling in the past.

This awakening process has a dramatic impact on our values and on our approach to life. For example, we no longer view life's issues as black and white, right or wrong, in an absolute sense. Rather, we see shades of gray. Similar concepts are embraced by the relatively new field of "spiritual psychology."

In the days of the Puritan Work Ethic, the rules were concrete and absolute, and it was socially unthinkable to vary one's behavior or expectations from the rules. If a woman divorced her husband, it was scandalous. If the third son in a family of doctors had aspirations to be an artist, he was ordinarily not allowed to pursue his inner urgings.

Now, by contrast, we are learning to operate from our internal guidance, our essential spiritual Self, in making decisions and choosing actions. We trust ourselves and our inner voice more. We have fun with life and work—instead of waiting for a "greater later"to finally enjoy ourselves. We are internally driven, not externally focused.

This does not mean that we are entirely self-centered and uncaring, however. In the "Me Generation" of the 1970s and 1980s, the awakening process took on a selfish appearance. But that was just the first stage of the awakening. Now, in the 1990s, we are evolving into the "We Generation." Commitment is once again an important value. In this context, New Workers recognize the need for intimacy with others and demand that their relationships, including those at work, be genuine and meaningful.

This is a predictable evolution in awakening. It is only through discovering the splendor of the Self that one can truly reach out to others from a sense of fullness, and experience true intimacy. Indeed, one of the most remarkable characteristics of the baby bust generation is its concern with social issues. More and more often the baby busters are choosing careers in the service professions, such as teaching, nursing, and the like. This a natural outgrowth of their focus on balance in their lives and their healthy self-confidence.

As we awaken to our spiritual essence, we begin to reevaluate every aspect of our lives. One of the first areas of our lives that demands reassessment is our work. We wonder why we do the work we do, and how it fits into our life purpose and spiritual path. We can no longer justify spending the majority of our waking hours punching a time clock and performing tasks that lack meaning. We want more from ourselves, as well as from our work. And these changes are transforming not only our own lives, but our workplace and the world in which we live.

Whether or not you consider yourself to be on a spiritual path, you demand more from your work than did your predecessors. And you are living in the rapidly changing context we have just explored. That being so, you may well wonder how you can enjoy your work more on a daily basis. The beginning point is discovering your life purpose — the subject of our next chapter.

But first, read the following list of Old World/New Age comparisons to see how these transformations are changing your world.

The Old World vs. The New Age

Old World	New Age
Puritan Work Ethic: If I am loyal and work hard, it will pay off in the long run, even if I don't like my job. Supporting myself and my family is more important than personal satisfaction. Loyalty is key.	Fulfillment Ethic: I choose the career(s) I wish, which give me the greatest personal satisfaction. I am a better person, and therefore a better family member. Creativity is key.
Only intellectual, rational left-brain approach accepted.	Intuition accepted as companion to rational mind.
Rewards are postponed: gold watch at retirement, pension benefits, periodic pay raises.	Rewards are immediate: work is its own reward, creates enthusiasm that results in increased pay, creativity, and fulfillment.
God is "out there" somewhere, not a part of me; need intermediary to access.	God is within each of us, expressing as us; each of us can directly access.
Management philosophy is hierarchical, very structured, centralized; red tape is common.	Management is participative, person-centered, less structured; decentralized.
Fringe benefits are the same for everyone: no accommodation of different employees' needs.	Fringe benefits are often tailored to employee needs (e.g., cafeteria plans).
Large corporate structures dominate business world.	Entrepreneurs dominate business world.
Society structured around manufacturing industry.	Society focused on information and technology.
Individuals must fit existing job "molds"; little room for creativity.	Individuals encouraged to be creative; new jobs and career areas created daily.

Dualistic philosophy: work and play are separate; good vs. bad; labor vs. management; etc.

Holistic philosophy: work and play are one; shades of gray in values; labor and management united; etc.

Action Steps from 9 to 5

Think for a moment about your current job or occupation. If you work for someone else, ask yourself whether the philosophy of your employer is centered primarily in the Old World or the New Age. Then look at your own values and viewpoints, particularly your desire for greater satisfaction in your work. Do you subscribe primarily to the Old World or the New Age philosophy? Does your philosophy match your employer's? If not, you may have discovered an important key to the reason for your dissatisfaction.

If you are self-employed, analyze how you have been approaching your business. Have you been trying to use an Old World approach in the context of the New Age? If so, consider how you might include more elements of the New Age concepts into your business to enhance your own development and that of any employees you may have.

2

What Am I Here to Do?

My object in living is to unite
My avocation and my vocation
As my two eyes make one in sight.
Only where love and need are one,
And the work is play for mortal stakes,
Is the deed ever really done
For Heaven and the future's sakes.

—Robert Frost

THE MOST IMPORTANT DISCOVERY we can make is the discovery of our life's purpose. Once we make this discovery and begin to design our life around it, we finally begin to *enjoy* work. And that is no small accomplishment—a recent national poll found that 95 percent of us do not enjoy our work!

My personal philosophy is that each of us has an inherent *right* to enjoy our work. After all, we spend eight or more hours each day working—why shouldn't it be fun? I have discovered an important principle in my personal journey, as well as in working with others in their career search. It is simply this: We can achieve maximum enjoyment at work when we know our life's purpose and are fulfilling it through our work.

Each of us has come to earth to accomplish something. You may have had a sense since you were very young that your life had a mission, a purpose. But what is it? If you are unhappy in your career and have not yet discovered the answer to that question, know that the two issues are related. The answer to one provides the answer to the other.

14

What is Life Purpose?

Life purpose can be simply defined as a calling, a mission, or an overall theme for your life that transcends your daily activities. It is the quality you have come to earth to develop, the type of service you are here to render, the segment of the planet you have come to enhance or improve or heal. It is much broader than one job or career; it pervades your entire life.

Each of us shares one overall life purpose, in that we are each here to awaken to who we are and to express our Self to the fullest extent possible. However, the life purpose we are discussing in this chapter is more specific than that. It is something that is unique to you. No one can fulfill your purpose better than you can—once you discover it.

Characteristics of Life Purpose

Many people believe that if they set out to accomplish their life purpose, life will become too serious, boring, or tedious. They think of "mission" as what people do when they go off to the wilderness of a far country and live a meager existence. In truth, it is only through discovering and fulfilling our life purpose that life can become exciting, fun, and playful. Following your life purpose is the most satisfying way to live your life.

A woman in one of my seminars on increasing satisfaction at work was plodding along in a government job, anxiously awaiting the time when she could retire (which was still 10 years away). Meanwhile, she spent every spare moment looking at travel catalogs and planning trips she would take when she had the time. The hours passed quickly when she was doing her travel planning. She eventually learned that her life purpose is fun and joyful, rather than serious and tedious. She began to realize that a career in the travel field would fulfill her life purpose and bring her more joy than her government job. She then had the courage to make a career change.

A career change is not always necessary in order to fulfill your life's purpose. However, it is often the natural "next step," especially if you chose your current job out of convenience, or necessity, or for any reason other than to fulfill your life's purpose.

When you are fulfilling your life's purpose, you are completely absorbed in your activities. You do not notice the passage of time; the activity completely occupies you. Abraham Maslow, the noted psychologist, called these times "peak experiences." The Buddhists call them times of one-pointed thinking. Whatever they are called, these experiences are characteristic of the self-actualized, fully functioning person—and of you, if you are aligned with your life's purpose.

Your life's purpose will not only fulfill you personally; it will also serve others in some way. It will enable you to make a contribution to the planet that makes the world a better place to live.

Life's purpose can take many forms. For some of you, it will be the accomplishment of a particular activity, such as writing a book on a particular subject or working at a particular kind of job. For others, it will be a quality that pervades all of your life activities, such as raising the consciousness of others about environmental conservation, adding to the level of peace in the world, or serving others in some way. It might also be a cause, such as freedom and equality for women or minorities, which in turn spawns multiple activities that contribute to that cause.

Whatever form it takes, your life's purpose fits you perfectly. Discovering it often comes in an "a-ha" experience: you suddenly realize that "this is it." Other times, it comes into your awareness more gradually, as though it "ripens" over time.

In summary, then, these are some of the characteristics that define life's purpose:

- fun
- joyful
- absorbing
- energizing

- creative
- unique
- fulfilling
- perfectly fits you
- can be a quality or an activity or a cause

How to Discover Your Life's Purpose

Sounds wonderful, right? "So," you say, "how can I find *my* life's purpose?" Let's look at several ways to approach this important discovery.

A. Focus on your inner child.   Just for a moment, put aside the critical parent and practical adult within you, and let your inner child come out and play! We have learned that life's purpose should be fun and joyful. For some of you, it will take a major change in your thinking to believe that you can actually *enjoy* your work. But it is true! So unleash your imagination and have fun with the questions that are posed in the following pages.

B. Examine the 10 clues to life purpose.   It will be helpful for you to now get a pen and paper, and take about 10 minutes per clue, writing down what comes to mind when you ask yourself these questions. Just imagine you are in one of my workshops and that you now have the opportunity to apply this information directly to *your* life—and finally discover that missing link you have been seeking.

Before we begin, I must make a confession to you: I am a list person. I make "to do" lists, want lists, budget lists, birthday gift lists, and so on. I learned early on that the best way for me to organize my life and to accomplish what I wanted to do was to make lists, set goals, and check them off as I accomplished each step. (I even make New Year's resolutions—and occasionally keep them!) The wonderful consequence of this "fetish," if you will, is that I have accomplished more by this tender time in my life (I'm in my early 30s) than many people have by the middle stage of their career. I credit much of my success to my habit of keeping lists and a careful daily calendar.

As we go through the following 10 clues and the other exercises in this book, I'm going to invite you to make some lists of your own. If you have resisted list making in the past, please give this a try. It is a very powerful tool to quickly access your true goals and desires.

Throughout this book, however, I also want to emphasize the importance that *balance* plays in our lives. Our experiences in this lifetime are designed to balance certain aspects of ourselves that may have been exaggerated in our last journey through life.

What does this have to do with lists and work? Simply this: although I was indoctrinated with the technique and importance of list making as a child, I have now *balanced* that indoctrination by learning to be in the "now" moment and flow with the natural progression. Even though I have a daily "to do" list, each morning I affirm my openness to the natural flow of the day. That is, I am not enslaved by my list but am simply assured in the knowledge that I am doing what is most important for me in each moment.

Obviously, there is a place for both discipline and flow in each of our lives. If we resist the natural flow, we will experience the inevitable results: tension and stress. If we resist discipline, we may live in constant chaos. You know which end of the continuum you are presently leaning toward. Whether or not you have tended to be a list maker in the past, please consider doing so now. (You might even want to start a career discovery journal to track your insights and progress as we go through this book together.)

Clue No. 1: What do you love to do when you have spare time? Your spare-time activities are important because they show what you enjoy doing when no one else is making demands on you. It is truly *your* time. How do you like to spend it? To think of it another way: what would you love to spend your time doing, even if you didn't get paid for it? Is there an activity you enjoy so much that money is not a consideration?

If you are already skeptical about how this will connect with your ideal job, consider this true story: Two women were in a workshop geared toward designing the right career. The leader went around the circle to all of the participants, asking them what they most loved to do. These two ladies couldn't stop laughing long enough to answer the first time around.

When the women finally regained their composure, the leader asked them the question again. With some amount of sheepishness, they answered, "We like to watch soap operas, silly as that may sound. But we can't see any way that could tie into a career opportunity." Once they admitted to themselves and the group what they loved to do, however, they went on to become very successful—writing syndicated summaries of the daily soap operas and selling them throughout the country!

You may not be able to easily identify enjoyable activities if you are burned out on your present career or have pursued your career because it was the "right thing to do" or because your family prodded you into it. We will discuss in a later chapter how to overcome blocks, including the negative programming from the past that has colored your beliefs. For now, simply close the door temporarily on your previous unfulfilling experiences.

Clue No. 2: What parts of your present job or life activities do you thoroughly enjoy? Even if you are miserable in your current job or career field, think about this question. If you think back to why you took the job or chose the career area to begin with, there are probably some specific tasks or objectives that are (or were) enjoyable to you.

Write them down, even if you don't think you will apply them in your next career. It might be a small thing, such as the receptionist who hated dealing with all the people in her job, but thoroughly enjoyed the few moments each day that she got to type letters and sort the mail. She later learned that she was not a people person, but a data person who enjoyed organizing things. (More about that in chapter 4.) That clue led her into her new job as a word processor.

As you go through these exercises, forget all about what others may think of your answers. This process is for *you*, and you need not share it with anyone else. So if the answers seem silly, write them down anyway. Another pair of homemakers in the northwestern United States realized that, even though it sounded implausible, they loved to clean house. They were perceptive enough to recognize that this was a clue to a business opportunity, and they are now well known as the Clutter Ladies. They make their living helping people clean up their messes and to stay organized.

Clue No. 3: What do you naturally do well? There are some things that you have always performed with ease. Perhaps you are naturally athletic, or can learn foreign languages quickly, with little effort. You may be a born organizer, or have innate intuitive abilities. The areas in which you naturally excel are indicators of your life purpose—particularly if you also *enjoy* doing those things.

Clue No. 4: What have your 10 greatest successes been to date (in your eyes)? For this clue, put aside what "others" in your life might say about you. What things do *you* view as your greatest successes? It may be something as simple as a gesture that helped someone in need—or it may be a widely publicized improvement you made in your company's efficiency. Whatever it is, list these achievements, as well as what it was about the accomplishment or event that makes you label it a success. (For example, the person who made an improvement in company efficiency may label this a success because of the benefit to the company, the way it made him or her feel, the money it saved, the recognition received, or any number of other reasons.)

Clue No. 5: Is there a cause or value or quality that you feel passionate about? Many times, the essence of our life purpose is revealed through a cause that attracts our commitment at a deep level. For example, if you feel strongly about world peace, or the save-the-whales movement, or antinuclear issues, list that cause here. Then see if you can derive the underlying value beneath the cause.

Do you feel passionate about the save-the-whales movement because of a love for Mother Earth, or for the whales themselves, or a desire to preserve the animals for future generations? What is it about this issue that attracts you to it?

Clue No. 6: What are the 10 most important lessons you have learned in your life? It is said that we teach that which we most need to learn. What do you feel are the most valuable or important things you have learned through your life experiences so far? (They need not be work related.) One lesson that was on my list included a simple realization in my days as a secretary of the importance of approaching challenges at work (for example, how to handle an issue for my boss) as though they were my own personal obstacles. This gave me a sense of pride and self-confidence in my own judgment that allowed me to experience increased peace of mind in my work. No doubt you have had experiences that were pivotal in your life. Sharing or using what you have learned through these experiences will often fulfill you at a deep level—and thereby carry out your life's purpose.

Clue No. 7: Think back over your life. Are there some issues or perceived problems that have occurred over and over again? This clue is related to the previous one. Out of these repeated issues may come your greatest lessons. But some of them are most likely continuing to occur. That is, you have yet to learn how to break the pattern. Do you keep choosing mates that put you down? Or jobs that are beyond your skill level? If there was a theme for your life's experiences, how would you describe it? Some examples might be "gaining an accurate assessment of myself," "learning to forgive," or "being a peacemaker."

These recurring issues or problems often represent the key qualities you are here to develop in this lifetime. You may have a tendency to intellectualize them, or to believe they are due to a particular childhood experience. The truth is, however, that even if the issues arise from a childhood experience, you chose that experience (more about that in chapter 12). So don't discard an issue

just because you have rationalized that it is due to an experience—
the whole process is part of your life purpose.

Clue No. 8: What do you daydream about? Your fantasies
have their basis in your subconscious mind. This is the largest part
of your mind, but not as easily accessed as your conscious mind. You
might liken it to an iceberg, in which only 10 percent of the total
mass (the conscious portion) is above the water and visible. It can
be easily reached. The submerged, or subconscious portion,
however, can only be accessed by more creative, specialized means.

It is in your subconscious mind that your beliefs reside, along
with your deepest desires for success and fulfillment. If there are
images or issues about which you repeatedly daydream (or dream of
at night), they are often aspects of your life purpose. Write down
the "uncensored"version of these. They are frequently your most
playful, meaningful moments—and their importance cannot be
underestimated.

**Clue No. 9: Imagine you are writing your epitaph. What would
you like to be remembered for? What would your life be incomplete
without?** This exercise is a good way to quickly access the essence
of your life and goals. Write down the first things that come to your
mind—before your other chattering voices (sometimes referred to as
the "committee") override your initial impulse. Another way to approach this one: imagine you only had 6 months to live. What would
you do differently than you are doing now? You may be startled by
the things that come to mind on this one. And once you realize what
is most important for you, the next question is: what is holding you
back from making those things real for you? (We'll discuss some
specific ideas for doing just that in chapter 4.)

**Clue No. 10: What would you do if you knew you could not
fail?** Our final clue is a fun, but very effective, game you can play
with yourself. If you have struggled to respond to the previous clues,
this one encourages you to look beyond any perceived limitations.
Perhaps you have been saying, "I'd really like to do _____,

but I know I could never succeed." Forget the last part of that sentence for now, and think about what you would do with your life if you could not fail. (We'll deal with the fear of failure in chapter 6.)

Now that you have examined these 10 clues, you have some scattered threads of the essence of your life's purpose. We will continue to work with these threads as we proceed through the remainder of the book, refining them and weaving them into a beautiful tapestry —the tapestry of your life!

C. Narrow down your responses to the 10 clues to glean the 10 most important aspects of your life's purpose. Does one quality or activity occur several times? Upon examining them, do you find that some of the meaningful aspects of your current job are similar to those activities that you choose to do in your spare time? If so, congratulations! You are close to fulfilling your life's purpose. We will examine how you can maximize those activities, either in your current job or in another context, as we continue through the book.

On the other hand, do you notice that none of the things you want to be remembered for are present in your current job? That is, do you feel that you must put on another "you" at work and that you can only be the real "you" outside the workplace? That, too, is a clue. Don't condemn yourself if that is the case. Just notice it and know that you are making important discoveries!

Now, on a blank sheet of paper, list the ten activities or qualities from your answers to these questions that are most important to you. Number them in their order of importance. These should be the things that you feel you absolutely must accomplish for your life to be complete.

D. Let the process of creative insight begin. Now that you have explored what is most important to you at an intellectual level, we move to the creative level. We will begin now to access your subconscious mind and your spiritual Self, to complement the work we have done at an intellectual level. Both the intellectual and the creative process require discipline and a commitment to your own growth and unfoldment. However, while the intellectual process can be accomplished by self-discipline, the creative process cannot be forced. It requires time to develop. So be patient with yourself here. Know that as you acknowledge the process of creation that is occurring in your life, your life purpose will be revealed to you—even if it takes weeks or months to become clear to you consciously.

Creation can be likened to the growth of a seed into a plant. First, the seed is planted. It then requires a time of germination, during which all appears dark and inactive, but in reality, much is occurring inside the seed. Eventually, when the time is right, the seed begins to sprout, and you see a tiny shoot come up through the ground. Soon, it bursts forth in full form for all to behold its splendor.

Your life's purpose is revealed to you in the same way. First, you plant the seed of your intellectual analysis (and your desire to know your purpose) in your subconscious mind. A period of germination occurs next. You may wish to hurry this process along so you can know it *now*, but patience is necessary while germination takes place. One day, you may have a flash of inspiration—just a glimpse of the picture that is your life's purpose—or a gradual awareness of it. This is the tiny shoot coming up through the ground. From there, the full-grown plant will develop—and you will understand your life's purpose and be able to begin consciously fulfilling it.

E. Learn to listen to your inner voice.   We learned in chapter 1 that we are now in the New Age, where information is the valuable commodity. Creativity is a critical skill for us in this New Age. Learning to listen to our inner voice is crucial to developing the valuable skill of creativity, and in turn, to discovering our life's purpose.

Many of us have not learned to listen to our inner voice. We grew up in families who taught us the Old World philosophy. We were told to follow the rules and do what was expected—not what we wanted—and to suppress our feelings. What we weren't taught, however, was how to listen to our inner voice, how to discover the insights our intuition could open for us, and how dangerous it can be to live our lives solely for other people.

Many of us only learn to listen to our inner voice when our suppressed anger and resentment take a physical toll on us. Cancer, heart attacks, and other physical conditions often result from our inability or refusal to be true to ourselves. You don't need to wait until that happens to you before you change! Begin to learn *now* how to honor your inner voice, and let it lead you into fulfillment.

Our inner voice speaks to us constantly. To hear it, we must cultivate the ability to listen to it. Like any skill, it simply takes practice to develop.

Many times, we quickly dismiss the urgings of our inner voice in favor of the chattering voices of our "committee." These are the voices that tell us what we "should" do, what is "right," how we don't deserve whatever it is we want, how we could never do the thing we love, etc., etc. The committee meets most frequently when an important decision must be made, or in the middle of the night when you wake up worried about something that has happened (or might happen!).

Five basic principles will assist you in learning to listen to your inner voice.

Principle 1: Follow Your Inner Voice in Decision making. To begin to recognize your inner voice, do something different the next time you make a decision. It need not be a major decision—perhaps it is simply what to wear to work tomorrow. Be willing to follow the very first thought that occurs to you. If you feel like wearing bright red, but the conservative member of your committee insists that tan would be much more "proper," wear red anyway! You will feel better, which will cause you to look more alive and friendly, and you will attract better experiences throughout your day.

The same process can be used with bigger decisions, too. One of my biggest challenges for many years was making decisions. I had been taught that to follow "God's will" meant doing something *other than* what I really wanted to do. This meant that every time I had a Major Decision to make, there were at least two voices to listen to (and choose between): my own inner urging and the "Right Thing To Do." I also found I attracted lots of advice from others, which was different from either of the first two voices—and mass confusion resulted.

Now I know that God's will for me is simply the Divine Urge within me to fully express my Self. I follow that initial urge and trust that it leads to the highest and best for me. And I don't pay much attention to the committee anymore. Major Decisions are much easier to make now—and each one leads naturally into the next one as I progress on my path.

Principle 2: Distinguish Your Inner Voice From Your "Committee." When you are first learning to listen to and follow your inner voice, you may confuse it with those of committee members. How do you tell whether it is truly your inner voice? First, your true inner voice will never guide you to do anything that is harmful to yourself or another person. It will always lead you to the highest result for all involved. If it seems to be leading you to a harmful activity, listen again—your inner voice will not guide you in that way. Second, you may notice that it is initially quieter than the other voices of your committee. This is why it is often referred to as the "still, small voice." Finally, as you begin to follow it, you will notice that your life becomes fuller, more fun, more joyful. This is a somewhat intangible result of following your inner guidance, but you will recognize it as it begins to happen for you.

Principle 3: Take Time to Listen. Treat your inner voice as though it were a new friend. Make a commitment to spend time listening to it regularly. It is helpful to "check in" periodically throughout the day. This means simply to stop what you are doing, close your eyes, take a few deep breaths, and notice how you are feeling. Do you feel tense? Joyful? Fully present or off center? Then listen, just for a moment, to see if your inner voice has an urging or idea for you to consider. Is there a simple way you could change your activities or your attitude to transform your tension into joy? To spend your time more meaningfully? Just five minutes of checking in two or three times each day will refine your ability to listen to your inner voice and will also increase the quality of your life remarkably.

Principle 4: Learn to Meditate. As you become more and more comfortable with your inner voice, you will want to spend more time focusing on it. I encourage you to learn a meditation technique that feels right to you and to practice it regularly. There are many benefits to meditation, including a greater ability to focus your mind and achieve a state of enhanced peace throughout your body, and it also gives you the tools to deal with stress and adversity as certain situations arise.

One technique I find helpful is simply to relax completely, using a progressive relaxation technique as taught in *The Relaxation Response* by Dr. Herbert Benson, or to use the beginning steps in the Symbol Meditation at the end of this chapter. Then, staying very quiet and focused, simply imagine a wise being (your Higher Self or a wise person you admire) coming to you. Listen to their advice or teachings for you. If you cannot easily imagine a specific person or image, simply stay quiet and listen for the words or messages that come to you in that moment. Ten minutes or up to an hour of this practice, done each day, will reap tremendous benefits for you. You will find that your level of overall satisfaction is enhanced greatly as you follow your inner guidance. Even if it does not make rational sense to you to follow its urgings, you will often find that it opens doors that will astound you. All that is required is to trust it and learn to listen to its wisdom.

Principle 5: Use the Symbol Meditation. To assist you in following your inner voice as a way of discovering your life purpose, I recommend the Symbol Meditation at the end of this chapter. We each have a preferred mode of interacting with the world. Some of us are primarily visual (seeing), some auditory (hearing), and some kinesthetic (feeling). Recent research has shown that we can effect change most quickly and completely in our lives when we combine as many of these modes as possible. Therefore, if you are simultaneously *listening to* your inner voice, *seeing* the symbol you have created through the Symbol Meditation, and *feeling* the wonderful experience of living your life's purpose, you will find yourself fulfilling it and progressing rapidly before you know it.

The next question we must answer, after discovering what we are here to do, is: Is it time for me to make a career change? That is the subject of the next chapter.

Action Steps from 9 to 5

1. Write out your responses to the 10 Clues to Life Purpose listed in this chapter, and begin to use the five principles for listening to your inner voice.

2. **Symbol Meditation.** Do the following meditation as often as you like. Notice how the images you see change, or stay the same, each time you do the meditation. You may wish to tape-record it for yourself, or have a friend read it to you. (This meditation is also available on tape in expanded form through the author. See details at end of book.)

Sit in a chair with a straight back, or on the floor with your spine erect. If you are on a chair, your legs should be uncrossed, feet flat on the floor. Your arms should be lying loosely in your lap in a receptive position. It sometimes helps to place your palms up.

Now close your eyes and take a deep, slow breath. Count to 4 as you inhale, hold just for a moment, and then release to the count of 2. Now again, slowly, breathe in, hold, and release.

Now relax your body completely. Begin with your feet, and move up through your legs, thighs, stomach, chest, arms, hands, shoulders, neck, head, and face. Take a few minutes to do this. Think of a peaceful, relaxing place. Bring that feeling into your body now.

When you are relaxed and breathing slowly, imagine a beautiful meadow. Everything is green and bright, the sun is shining, and there are beautiful flowers everywhere. You hear the sound of a brook babbling joyfully nearby. You have never felt so peaceful.

You are sitting in this meadow, enjoying the tranquility and beauty of it. You then notice a wise being coming toward you. You recognize it as your Higher Self, even if you have not seen it before. The being comes over to you and sits down near you. You realize that it is making itself available to you to provide whatever information you need for your growth and development.

You then ask this being to give you a symbol of your life's purpose, a symbol that represents your purpose in all of its aspects. Your Higher Self gives you this symbol now. Notice what it is. Do not judge or question it; simply accept it. Decide to remember this symbol. Hold it in your hands and examine it. Does it have color? Is it large or small? Does it remind you of an object in the physical world? How does it make you feel?

Thank your Higher Self for this symbol. Now take the symbol and place it inside the center of your chest. This is your energy center of love, the highest love in the Universe. Allow your symbol to energize you, to radiate light throughout every cell of your body. Feel it penetrate your being, allowing you to embody its essence. Allow yourself to experience what it is like to take the essence of this symbol, your essential life's purpose, into every aspect of your life. Your work, your relationships, your body, your possessions—all reflect your life's purpose as if in a prism.

You look across the meadow and see that your Higher Self is beckoning you to a bridge. The bridge is surrounded by other high beings, all very joyful and happy. There is a mood of celebration. You walk slowly toward the bridge, feeling the presence of your symbol within you. You realize that the beings are celebrating you and your newfound awareness of your life's purpose.

Your Higher Self explains that the purpose of the bridge is to provide a connection between your life's purpose and the physical world in which you live. If you are now ready to begin to fulfill your life's purpose, as embodied in the symbol, walk across the bridge. Your Higher Self meets you at the center of the bridge and accompanies you to the other side, where the other beings are celebrating and supporting you. You and the other beings rejoice together that you have discovered your purpose, and that you are now allowing it to manifest in physical form. Everything that is necessary for the unfoldment of your life's purpose will now come to you, easily, in perfect time, exactly when you need it.

You pause now to savor the moment. You congratulate yourself on this moment of awakening, and on your dedication to your growth. You know that whenever you wish to remind yourself of your purpose and of the support you have for the fulfillment of that purpose, or when you have questions about how to proceed on your path, you can simply return in your mind's eye to this bridge, this special place of celebration.

Then, when you are ready, you become aware of your physical body once more. You return to the present moment, and gently open your eyes.

PART TWO

Conscious Career Choice and Change

3

Knowing When It's Time
To Change

*Change happens not by trying to make yourself change, but by
becoming conscious of what's not working . . . Remember, the
darkest hour is just before the dawn—change often occurs just
when you've given up, or when you least expect it.*

—Shakti Gawain
Living in the Light

IT TAKES COURAGE to face what is not working in our lives. Perhaps we are sick, unhappy, unproductive, lethargic, or in dire
financial straits. But we have not yet realized that these experiences
are the result of not recognizing and fulfilling our life's purpose. We
fail to notice that these unpleasant experiences are becoming more
and more frequent in our daily life —and that a change is necessary
to revive our joy of living.

I am not suggesting that changing jobs or careers is the only way
to discover and fulfill our life purpose. We may simply need to
change our attitude and approach to our existing job. In either event,
discovering our life purpose initiates a process of examining our life.
We perform "lifestyle surgery" by asking ourselves: "How does this
activity (or job or relationship, etc.,) assist me in fulfilling my life
purpose?" Or, put another way: "Is God enjoying itself as me
today?"

Through this process, we may discover one of two things. We
may simply come to understand why we enjoy the work we do and
how we can increase our level of satisfaction even further. On the
other hand, we may realize that we have taken our job for the wrong
reasons. Perhaps we failed to do the necessary self-assessment before

33

taking our job, and thus made a choice of convenience, in an "unconscious" way. Or we may simply notice that our job does not allow us to express our creativity, our values, or our full potential. If so, our job may not seem to contribute at all to the fulfillment of our purpose. What do we do then?

If you have chosen a spiritual path for your life (and I know many of you have), you have three basic choices at this point:

1. Do nothing. That is, stay in your current job. This may mean you are, at least for now, saying no to your inner voice. If that is your choice, at least be honest enough to admit to yourself what you are doing. When you are ready for one of the next two steps, you can then move forward.

2. Change the system. A second option is to apply your ingenuity to find ways to change the present system. For example, introduce others at work to the concept of life purpose, and assist others in finding their purpose and applying it at work. Your environment will then become a more nourishing place for you to pursue your own life's purpose.

3. Change jobs or careers, or start your own business. This choice simply calls for you to find a new opportunity in which you *can* fulfill your life's purpose—where you can attain your potential, express your values, do your job well, and feel in every way comfortable and at home.

Author Aldous Huxley once pointed out that there are certain ways of making a living that do so much harm, at all levels, that "even if they could be practiced in a nonattached spirit (which is generally impossible), they would still have to be eschewed by anyone dedicated to the task of liberating, not only himself, but others." If you are in this kind of a job, and are also on a spiritual path, option number 3 may be your only reasonable choice.

The beginning point for discovering the need for change is to increase our self-awareness. We do this through realizing that we do have a life purpose, discovering what it is, and recognizing that we are not fulfilling it as we want to. Only then are we ready to begin designing a lifestyle that *does* fulfil our purpose.

In this chapter, we will examine the inner and outer signals that suggest a need for change of job or career to fulfil our life purpose. Then in the following chapters, we will design an ideal job for ourselves and set concrete goals for creating and experiencing that ideal job or career.

The Ostrich Syndrome

Rather than facing the need for change, many of us prefer to stick our heads in the sand. Like the ostrich, we want to avoid looking at our needs and challenges directly. Sticking our head in the sand alters our perception. We can then tell ourselves that there really is no problem—until our inner pain and emptiness can no longer be ignored. This is known as the Ostrich Syndrome.

Anna illustrates the Ostrich Syndrome. Since she finished college with a degree in accounting, she has worked at the same accounting firm. Every year brings the same routine: the long hours during the first four months of the year preparing tax returns, and routine filings for the firm's individual and business clients throughout the remainder of the year. Though she has been given regular pay raises over her 10 years with the firm, she has turned down promotions and rarely solicits new clients. She became bored with the job long ago, but she no longer lets herself think about that. She focuses on the daily routine and tries to do her job as well as she can. However, she has been ignoring the fact that her migraine headaches have been occurring almost weekly and that she is missing more and more work for sick time.

Anna has refused to acknowledge her unhappiness. As we will learn in a subsequent chapter, her migraine headaches are a signal that she is resisting the natural flow of her life. Their increasing frequency indicates that her resistance is also increasing. She needs to become willing to look more thoughtfully at her life and admit that change is needed.

Are you stuck in the Ostrich Syndrome? To find out, answer the following questions:

1. Do you take advantage of opportunities to test your potential?

2. Do you enjoy taking chances from time to time, seeking out new and different experiences?

3. Do you try to meet new people, make new friends, and bring new relationships into your life?

4. Do you give conscious attention to your career and personal growth on a regular basis?

5. Do you take on new responsibilities at work when you have the chance to (even if you have to create the opportunity)?

6. Do you appreciate feedback on your work?

7. Do you take care of yourself physically by eating right, exercising, getting enough sleep, etc.?

If you answered no to more than half of these questions, you may be using the Ostrich Syndrome approach to your life. You may wish to use the Action Steps at the end of this chapter to move beyond the Ostrich Syndrome and develop the courage to make positive changes in your life.

Compulsive Behavior

Compulsive behavior can also be an indicator that change is needed in our lives. A "compulsion," according to the dictionary, is an irresistible impulse to perform an irrational act. Do you find yourself:

- eating when you are not hungry?

- biting your nails "unconsciously"?

- stuck in a "habit" of having three or four drinks after work, when having just one on occasion used to be your pattern?

- smoking more than you want to?

- going on shopping sprees when you are under pressure, even when you know you can't afford them?

- working too many hours doing "busywork"—after your required work is done?

- doing anything else that you know is not in your best interest, but is used as an escape or "nervous habit"?

If so, consider the possibility that you may be exhibiting compulsive behavior—and that there is a message for you in that behavior.

There are as many addictions and compulsions as there are people who have them. You probably know what yours are. A discussion of specific techniques for overcoming these types of behavior is beyond the scope of this book. However, they are mentioned here to encourage you to look as objectively as you can at your habits. If you are engaging in compulsive or addictive behavior regularly, it may be a means you are using (consciously or not) to mask or cope with an unpleasant job or other situation. It may also be a way to avoid looking squarely at the emptiness in your life—perhaps because you have not yet discovered your life purpose or right career.

For example, Steve, an industrial engineer, had risen through the ranks of the engineering firm where he had worked for the past eight years. He was now in a department manager position but felt frustrated despite his progress during his time with the company. The only other promotions open to him were the CEO and Vice President ranks—both of which were filled by men in their 50s who were committed to staying with the company until they retired. He hadn't recognized this "closed door" consciously, however. Instead, he began stopping at a bar on his way home from work nearly each night to unwind from his work day.

Fortunately, Steve's wife helped him see that these drinking episodes were becoming more and more frequent and were beginning to affect his health—and in turn, his work performance. He realized that his drinking was simply an effort to mask his need for change.

He needed to face the fact that he had two choices: stay in his present job indefinitely and try to enjoy it, or begin looking for opportunities elsewhere. Once he was willing to face his choices and begin acting on them, he no longer felt the compulsion to drink at the end of his work day in a desperate attempt to cope.

If you have any type of compulsive behavior that is interfering with your work or your life, I encourage you to look at it. Could it be telling you that a change of job is in order? Or is there another message in that pattern? Confronting the issues beneath the behavior is the way to true freedom, for we defuse the power from our issues by facing them.

Workaholism

Workaholism—the very word connotes compulsion. Derived from the same root as "alcoholism," it was coined in the past two decades to describe the person who attempts to find meaning in life from work. Work becomes the person's entire identity. This is not a person who simply works as an accountant; he or she *is* an accountant.

Workaholics must be distinguished from those who work long hours simply because they love what they do. Workaholics work constantly to escape from personal dissatisfaction, to avoid examining the issues in their lives, or to gain approval from others. Yet no matter how much they work, it is never enough to meet their deep inner needs. No job alone will ever be able to do that.

If you find yourself working endless hours (especially if you are not being required to) but are feeling more and more unhappy, you may be suffering from workaholism. Again, don't beat yourself up. Just recognize that fact (with the help of a therapist or counselor, if necessary). Take some time to reflect on the issues in your life. Then, work through the remaining exercises in this book. Once you have reached the place where you are willing to take an honest look at your life, you have made a giant first step toward choosing greater fulfillment.

The Staying Trap

Another way we avoid dealing with the real issues beneath outer behavior is by rationalizing our actions. In the context of work, this can take the form of the Staying Trap. That is, we may stay in a job long after it has ceased to serve us because of a justification (which usually turns out to be irrational or false) for not leaving the job. This eliminates the need to seriously consider a change—at least for a while.

Are you stuck in the Staying Trap? See if you identify with any of the following Staying Trap statements:

- **"If I quit, it would mean I'd failed."** Some of us have been taught that "winners never quit, and quitters never win." Let me suggest that this cliche is simply a remnant of the Old World thinking we examined in chapter 1. We no longer have to endure an unfulfilling job situation for the sake of being loyal to the company. Dare to choose a job that satisfies you—even if it means giving up a situation you have been in for years. It is the ultimate denial of our selfhood for us to refuse to consider leaving a job that we have long since outgrown. Furthermore, by giving up one thing, acting on our inner guidance, we will always move into something greater and better.

    Think of it this way: If you do not make the choices that will allow you to grow so that you can achieve your goals, isn't that a bigger failure than "quitting" an unfulfilling job, and giving yourself the opportunity to move into something greater?

- **"I can't change careers after investing all this money and time in getting my degree and learning my profession."** This statement is addressed to those of you who have spent many years in a career area, or have obtained a degree or certificate to allow you to practice your chosen profession (for example, medicine, law, accounting, computer programming, management, or whatever). Now that you have struggled long and hard and "paid your dues," finally getting the job you were aiming for—what happens if you don't enjoy it? Or if it doesn't satisfy you? Or if after a few years you have had enough and simply want to do something else?

This Staying Trap statement has been an important one in my life, as I have moved from practicing law to writing, consulting, and presenting seminars full time. My inner dialogue went something like this:

"Here you spent four years in college and three years in law school—at a cost of nearly $20,000—and have worked in the legal field for twelve years. And you want to give that up? Isn't that wasting all the time and money and energy you have invested?"

I ultimately realized that nothing we do is ever wasted. Each experience and job readies us for the next. There is a rhythm and pattern to our lives, as we can readily see in looking back over the past. We just can't see the pattern as easily when we are in the midst of it.

I knew that I was happier doing seminars, writing, and consulting than I was practicing law. I began to dread doing my legal work—but looked forward with anticipation when I had a seminar to present. It was as if I *had* to make the change— regardless of my past investment in training and time. Perhaps you do, too.

The other important thing to remember here is that your life purpose is an essence or quality—not a job description. You may have thought it was leading you down a particular career path, but in fact you can fulfill the essence of your purpose more effectively through another avenue. In my case, the essence of my purpose is to facilitate the awakening process in the workplace, through integrating spiritual values and work. I thought I could do that most effectively through practicing law. It now appears that the same essence will be best fulfilled (for now, at least) through writing books, making tapes, and conducting seminars. I must simply trust my Higher Self to guide me into this phase of my growth.

In short, don't let the fact that you have trained for a particular career stop you from having what you desire at the present time. Have the courage to follow your inner guidance and to be all that you can be.

• **"What would everyone think?"** Along with the two Staying Trap statements we have just discussed, we are also often afraid of how we will explain our decision to quit to the "others" in our life. We feel compelled to have some rational explanation for our acts. My question for you is this: Why not let it be perfectly all right to do something just because you want to? No other reason. After all, whose life is it, anyway?

There is an interesting principle at work here. The Universe reflects back to us exactly what we believe—and exaggerates our doubts and fears until we are rid of them. Therefore, until you become absolutely clear in your own mind about your decision to quit, you will tend to attract people into your life who will reinforce your doubts:

"Well, you know quitters never win. You don't want to be a *failure*, do you?"

"How can you leave such a prestigious profession [or job] after so many years? You'll never find a better job than that!" etc., etc. . . .

Can you imagine what would have happened if some of the great people in history had let this statement stop them:

"Come on, Mr. Ford—a V-8 engine? We've been trying for over a year now, and it simply can't be done! If you keep on with this silly idea, the company will go bankrupt! People are starting to talk!"

"Run for office again, Abe? You have to be kidding! You've already lost eight elections and had a nervous breakdown to boot. You'll never be able to convince people to elect you President of the United States!"

You get the idea. Get clear on your intention, and move forward with confidence—doing something simply because you want to. If you let what other people think keep you from making choices to enhance your life, you will never know how great a success you can be.

• **"I'm sure there's nothing better out there—so I'll just stay here where I'm secure."** This is a variation of the Ostrich Syndrome. This person is afraid to even investigate to see if other possibilities exist. They feel "secure" (another term for being in a rut?) in their present job, and will stay there no matter what. It is just too scary for them to consider moving on to something different— "especially at my age" (or whatever the excuse is for that person). Many government workers find themselves in this trap, as does anyone who has vested pension benefits, who has a job requiring little creative thinking, or who feels unduly comfortable in their present situation.

The question to ask yourself now, though, is: Which is more important—being secure or being fulfilled? If the only reason you are staying in your job is to retain your security, you may be paying a very high price by ignoring your need for self-fulfillment. If security is your choice, just be certain you realize it—and the consequences it brings. You may be forfeiting your true Selfhood by refusing to consider other options and by staying where you feel safe. You may become numb to your true feelings and never experience the total joy of living a fulfilled life.

But, you ask, what if I take a new job and it doesn't work out? What would I do then? Find another new job! Your choice is not irrevocable—it can be changed! There is great freedom in knowing that our choices can be altered, again and again if necessary. Nothing is as permanent as it seems. So why not jump in and participate in the flow of life?

• **"I don't want to be selfish."** We may think that to do the thing we want, such as quitting a job, is a selfish act. But who said selfish means wrong or bad? Selfish means "arising from concern with one's own welfare," according to the dictionary. If we are not concerned with our welfare, how likely is it that someone else will be?

We must make the choices in our lives that will allow us to grow. Otherwise, we stifle our creativity, become frustrated, and often channel that frustration toward our family, friends, and business associates. Soon we find ourselves being irritable, frustrated, and generally "out of sorts" because we do not enjoy our work. And we are afraid it will be "selfish" to quit? The people around us will be eternally grateful to have a reprieve from our unhappiness! The "selfish" act of quitting a job that no longer serves us will ultimately benefit everyone concerned— the company you had worked for, the new company to whom you bring your enthusiasm, your family, friends, and others in your life.

If you make the decision to change jobs based on the desire to more effectively fulfill your life purpose, the effect is even greater: You will be able to serve others more effectively (and be more "self-less"in your new job, fulfilling your purpose), than in the job you formerly had. Have the courage to recognize that *your* needs are paramount, and that you have the ultimate responsibility to see that they are fulfilled. You deserve to work at a job you love!

- **"I'm too busy to spend time thinking about how it could be better."** This is a variation on the compulsive behaviors we identified above. This worker keeps busy with endless work and leisure activities, never allowing time for reflection or consideration on how the situation could be improved. All activities are used as an excuse to avoid taking a serious look at reality—and life purpose gets put on hold indefinitely.

You have heard the saying, "If you want something done, ask a busy person." Why? No matter how busy the busiest of us are, we can always find time to do that which is important to us. Filling our lives with activity can be a joyous way to live—when we have examined our purpose and overall goals and are using our activities to create the life we want.

If you have been saying yes to every request for your time and money, are involved in five different charities, numerous church and school activities, and spend 10 to 12 hours each day at work as well—please take a few moments to evaluate where all of this activity is taking you. You might list on a sheet of paper all of the activities in your life and the demands of each. Are there built-in conflicts?— for example, being on a church board and supporting a local political candidate with views different than church dogma; being a mother and a college instructor where your students' and children's needs may compete for your attention. If so, you will experience stress until you bring your commitments more into line with each other.

Ask yourself: Are all of these activities contributing to my personal growth and fulfillment of my life purpose? If not, which ones can you eliminate to make your life more joyful? Would a job or career change help to bring your activities into alignment?

If you have small children at home and are the primary caretaking parent, that responsibility and commitment must be factored in as well. Perhaps for the few years that your children are small, it will be necessary to work part time, have an office at home, or work in a less demanding position in your chosen field, or to make other accommodations in view of your family commitment. You can still enjoy your work—but please be realistic about what hours you can work and what work responsibilities you can assume and still give your family (and yourself!) the time and attention they need.

Simply taking time to examine your activities and balance them with each other and with your purpose will clarify your life direction (and may uncover some of the reasons you aren't progressing as quickly as you wish toward your goals).

* **"The company couldn't survive without me."** Whether you own the company or simply sweep the floors at night, it is important to recognize this myth. You are *not* indispensable! I know, we like to feed our own egos and believe that we are—but somehow businesses continue, despite the exodus of some of their key managers and leaders, every day. Ford survived without Iacocca. When we go on vacation, the important issues are somehow handled. Even if you own your own business, there is a natural point of growth in which you have to make an important decision: Do I continue to do the work myself, or do I become an effective manager of others who actually do the work?

One famous entrepreneur recently said that after eight years in his company, he realized that the board no longer needed him in the company to keep it going—even though his identity was a large part

of what made his product famous in the first place! This may simply
have been an excellent example of effective management. But in any
event, he left. Some viewed his decision as a big risk, but he felt it
was the best way for him to express his commitment to himself at this
time in his life.

No matter how much responsibility you have, how many employees you supervise, or how much proprietary information or expertise you possess, please do not do yourself the disservice of staying
at a particular company because "they need me." You deserve the
best—and this may include moving to another work setting, in some
cases, if that is what your Higher Self is guiding you to do.

The myth of indispensability has come home to many employees
abruptly in the event of a merger, downsizing, or some other radical structural shift. Suddenly you are given two weeks' notice of
termination—after 14 years of employment. How could the company
do this? How can they get along without me? Believe me—they will
find a way. Don't let this Staying Trap statement keep you from taking the steps you need to take for your growth.

The Staying Trap is just a mental game we play with ourselves
to keep from facing needed changes in our lives. What we must do
is recognize the erroneous logic we are using and be willing to look
at our excuses head on. Are you ready to stop fleeing from your dissatisfaction and move forward with your life? If so, getting out of
the Staying Trap may be the first step.

Burnout

Now let's look at a completely different phenomenon that may also
foreshadow the need for change.

John had been a computer programmer in a small company for
three years. At first, he thoroughly enjoyed his job. It was creative,
fun, and paid him better than any job he had had before. However,
he started to find himself resenting his job. His job responsibilities
had doubled in the past three months, with no corresponding increase in resources, time, or compensation to assist him in fulfilling

those responsibilities. He felt physically tired all the time, with no energy to do even his routine duties. His attitude toward his job, as well as his wife (who stays home with their two small children), as well as the other people in his life, was quite negative. He felt trapped in a hopeless situation, since his requests for more money or an assistant had fallen on deaf ears. Yet he felt obligated to generate an income to support his wife and family.

John was suffering from burnout. His job no longer met his needs, and yet he couldn't see a way out. The pressures of "making a living" and meeting the demands of his superiors at work left little time or opportunity for John to explore other options- and yet his work performance and general outlook on life were deteriorating more with each passing day.

Burnout is formally defined as a state of physical, emotional, and mental exhaustion caused by long-term involvement in situations that are emotionally demanding, according to a recent book on the subject entitled *Career Burnout: Causes & Cures*, by Ayala Pines and Elliot Aronson.

Burnout nearly always includes three components: physical exhaustion, emotional exhaustion, and mental exhaustion. Symptoms of burnout include:

- physical depletion (low energy, fatigue, weakness);
- feelings of helplessness, hopelessness and entrapment;
- disillusionment;
- development of a negative self-concept; and
- development of negative attitudes toward work, people, and life itself.

Many of the people who become my clients are in the throes of burnout. They finally reach the point of recognizing that something must change, and they come to me for guidance through the necessary process of career transition. John, who we met above, fits the typical profile of the burned-out worker.

Causes of Burnout

What causes people to burn out?

Paradoxically, the people who are most likely to burn out, according to Pines and Aronson, are those who enter their career highly motivated and idealistic, who expect to obtain from their work a sense of meaning in their lives. When they burn out, they feel a sense of failure even more keenly than others, for they believe they have failed in finding the solution to their "existential dilemma"— the meaning of life.

The root cause of burnout appears to be our need to believe that our lives are meaningful, and that what we do is useful and important. People who choose the helping professions (minister, counselor, doctor, psychologist, nurse) are especially vulnerable, as are those working in a government or other bureaucratic setting. Burnout results in a feeling that no matter what we do, we cannot have a real impact on the world.

External events may trigger burnout, such as the doubling of John's work responsibilities without a corresponding increase in resources. It can also be provoked by a "midlife crisis"—the feeling that our contribution may be far smaller than we had initially planned, or that we have not accomplished what we had expected to by this time in our life.

Role conflict also contributes to burnout, especially in women. A woman's time at work is clouded by concerns about her family, and vice versa. Sex-role stereotyping adds another factor that can complicate even the smallest of decisions. Women must learn to separate their family and work roles as much as possible, and to allow themselves transition or "decompression"time between the two.

Certain aspects of our approach to life can also make us more susceptible to burnout, regardless of occupation. For example, exhibiting "Type A" personality traits can promote burnout. These traits include such characteristics as competition, speed, high energy, doing several things at one time, and active hostility and aggressive behavior toward people and situations. Tempering these traits with the "Type B" traits will help to balance the individual. "Type

B''people are less ambitious and competitive, and more relaxed. They are able to focus on one activity at a time and approach the world with more appreciation for its natural flow.

A strictly rational approach to life may also dispose one toward burnout. Psychologist Carl Jung and the Myers-Briggs Personality Assessment tool based on his work call this a "thinking," as opposed to a "feeling," approach. "Thinking" types develop strong powers of analysis, skepticism, and an ability to weigh events objectively in relation to logical outcomes. "Feeling" types, on the other hand, focus on developing sensitivity to people's feelings and needs, have a need to affiliate with others, are quite warm when it comes to interpersonal relationships, and desire harmony.

Whether you tend toward thinking or feeling will have an impact on how burnout affects you. For example, burned-out thinking types tend to become more concerned with others and to have a lower achievement orientation. Burned-out feeling types, by contrast, tend to become hostile and lack concern toward others, but their achievement orientation is not affected. That is, during burnout, thinking and feeling types become more like each other.

A third factor that seems to influence whether or not people will burn out, according to Pines and Aronson, is their degree of "hardiness." That is, are they involved in and curious about their environment? Do they feel they can influence their world? And do they love challenge and view change as natural and necessary for growth? These factors will both prevent burnout and assist in healing it once it occurs.

Finally, one's motivation for success and attitudes about success once it is achieved seem to affect one's tendency to burn out. If, for example, we judge our success by always comparing it to what others have done, we will experience ongoing disappointment. There is always someone who has more, does it better, etc. No level of success will suffice if we insist on constantly setting a new standard for ourselves without stopping to congratulate ourselves for what we have already accomplished. Then, successful events become associated not with happiness, but with disappointment. If we live constantly in the future instead of the present, each success will only last for a split second and will immediately be overtaken by a sense of let-down: "Is this all there is?"

Some important spiritual factors may also play a part in burnout. If you are working from a sense of obligation, rather than from love and devotion, for example, you will be more likely to burn out. If you lack a sense of life purpose and direction, you will perform your daily activities without any intrinsic meaning or objective. This can also contribute to burnout. Third, low self-esteem can result in your (unconsciously) punishing yourself through working at a job you don't enjoy, or through choosing a job that you know is not suited to you, is beyond your skill level, or is not consistent with your long-term goals. Any of these factors can result in your being more likely than others to burn out.

If you resent getting up in the morning, let alone going to work, and feel trapped in your present situation, you may be suffering from burnout. The question then becomes: How do you deal with it?

Using Burnout as a Vehicle for Change

One of the best ways to prevent or lessen the impact of burnout is to be aware of its danger, be prepared for it, and take active responsibility for doing something about it. Whether that means balancing the roles and responsibilities in your life, as we discussed earlier, or simply taking some time off to reevaluate your life, remember that *you* must be responsible for dealing with your own career satisfaction. Blaming outer circumstances simply delays the inevitable. Change must begin by acknowledging your personal responsibility for the situation—and then choosing the best of your available options and moving forward.

The question might then be asked: "If burnout results from long-term involvement in emotionally demanding situations, why don't people simply escape from the situation before it begins to take such a toll on them?" Part of the answer lies, no doubt, in the rationalizations of the Staying Trap and the Ostrich Syndrome. We rationalize and bury our head in the sand until it is too late and until we are so depleted that our situation seems hopeless.

If that is where you are right now, don't despair. You *can* work through burnout and come out healthy on the other side. I have done it! Prior to starting my business, I was so frustrated and negative in my previous job that it seemed there was no way out—and yet what emerged was the best situation I have created to date.

Burnout may be the greatest challenge you have faced in your life. It can either lead to tragedy or to a quantum leap in your growth, depending on how you approach it.

Typical approaches to burnout, according to Pines and Aronson, are:

- leaving your profession or career entirely;
- finding another job within your career area;
- moving up the career ladder to gain distance from the adverse environment;
- becoming "dead wood," that is, staying in a job for its security and maintaining an apathetic attitude; or
- using burnout as a stimulus for becoming aware of problems, for expanding skills and abilities, and for growth.

When facing your own burnout, the following steps will lead you into the direction of positive change:

1. If possible, take some time off. Whether it is a day, a week, or a month, or longer, taking some time for refreshing and reevaluating your situation can help you view it from a new perspective. Use vacation time or other paid time, if necessary, to build some space between your routine of frustrating activity and your inner needs. You may find that taking some time for yourself will recharge you sufficiently that you can then approach your job with new energy. If you are truly burned out, however, your energy will likely not return after a short time off. More far-reaching changes are necessary. But the time off will allow you to begin the self-evaluation process (using the remainder of this book as a guide, as well as a counselor, if neces-sary) to change your situation.

2. Expand your awareness of the situation. Simply recognizing that you may be suffering from burnout is the beginning. The next step is to differentiate the actual demands upon you, and what you can and cannot control, from the demands you place upon yourself. For example, if you know your family needs to have dinner each night, that is an actual demand. If you demand of yourself that you cook a gourmet meal each night, that is an internal demand that may be unrealistic considering the other responsibilities you have. Perhaps one or two nights your spouse could cook, or you could go out to eat. Recognizing that part of your "unchangeable responsibilities" are actually self-imposed can help you change them.

3. Don't blame yourself. I encourage you to relinquish the idea that your burnout is all your fault, that it is something you have cre-ated and therefore must suffer through. Yes, it is true that you have made certain choices in your life that have resulted in some unhappi-ness that is now taking the form of burnout. But since you have cre-ated the situation, you can also un-create it. That is, you can change!

This is a danger of learning any universal truth: Some of us have a tendency to use the new truth to beat up on ourselves. ("Oh, if I'd only known this when my kids were small—they would have had a much happier childhood," or "Well, this illness just proves that I don't like myself. I guess I'll never change.") Truth is only benefi-cial if we use it to empower ourselves, rather than to tear ourselves down.

4. Take responsible action to change your situation. One of the reasons you are suffering from burnout is that you have attracted an environment at work that does not support you. At this point, I recommend that you have a brainstorming session with yourself. Do some of the exercises in this book, find out what your ideal job sit-uation is like, and begin to set goals and take steps to create it. Learn your positive personality traits, the qualities and environment that motivates and empowers you, and some skills for enjoying your life to a greater extent. Then begin to change, one day at a time. You have the power to create what you want in your life—and now is the time to begin!

Reasons Not to Change

In some instances, a change of job or career is not advisable. Why? Because changing one's outer circumstances will not change the inner root cause of the dissatisfaction.

For example, let's assume you have changed jobs several times in the past few years. Even though the companies are in diverse areas or are very different from each other in size or other ways, your experience in each situation has been the same. Perhaps you always end up in the department with the overbearing supervisor. Or you are always singled out for disciplinary action, even if others have committed similar infractions.

If you notice a theme or common pattern such as these in each of your jobs, most likely there is an underlying issue that must be resolved within you. No amount of job or career changes, no matter how drastic, will resolve that issue. The person with the overbearing bosses, for example, may need to learn to value herself more and learn to speak out for what she knows is right. Once she recognizes the true cause behind the situation and develops her ability to be assertive, she will no longer need to attract the overbearing bosses.

The key point here is that you should not change jobs *solely* to get away from an uncomfortable interpersonal situation, particularly if it is similar or identical to situations you have attracted in previous jobs. Instead, discover and deal with the underlying issue first. Ask yourself this question: What do I expect to gain, or how do I expect my experience to change, by getting a new job? That is, what is the *essence* of your desire for a new job?

Once you have discovered the essence behind your desire, see if there is some way—even if it is a small one—that you can begin to bring that essence into your life now. For example, if you think a new job will bring you more money, perhaps there is a way to create more money from another source—or at least to be open to receiving it from another source. If you think a new job will give you more stimulation, perhaps there is a way you can bring challenge to your present job by taking on a new task or responsibility. After doing this, if you do decide to change jobs, you will be doing so for the right reasons—and furthering your life purpose in the process.

Whether or not a change of jobs or careers is in order for you, it is now time to gain a clear image of your ideal job and career so that you can begin to translate your life purpose into action. For that, we turn to the next chapter.

Action Steps from 9 to 5

1. Now that you have explored the indicators of change, and some of the traps that prevent it, take an honest look at your situation. Are you using the Ostrich Syndrome, compulsive behavior, or one of the rationalizations of the Staying Trap to try to hide your need for change? Have the courage to lift the blinds and let in the light of the Truth now.

2. If number 1 seems overwhelming, but part of you does want to break through to the truth, use this affirmation as often as you think of it during the next few days and weeks: *I am willing to look clearly at my life and work and to make the changes that will help me grow.* Just stating, sincerely, your willingness to see the truth and to change will open the necessary doors for you to move forward.

3. If you are stuck in one of the rationalizations of the Staying Trap, ask yourself this question: "What is the worst that could happen if I quit my job (or changed careers)?" Look honestly at the answer to that question, and if you can handle that, then consider the consequences of other options. You will probably find that once you look at the worst possible scenario, it isn't as bad as you feared.

4

Designing Your Ideal Job
or Career

*". . . when you work you fulfill a part of earth's furthest dream,
assigned to you when that dream was born,*

And in keeping yourself with labour you are in truth loving life,

*And to love life through labour is to be intimate with life's inmost
secret."*

—Kahlil Gibran,
The Prophet

THERE IS A DREAM waiting to be born through you. Are you ready to let it emerge? If you are, you are about to experience that "inmost secret" to which Kahlil Gibran referred: the bliss of working with love.

Whether or not you feel you need a career change at this time, I invite you to embrace the concept of *designing* your job or career. Designing your career—as compared to falling into it by accident—is akin to the difference an interior designer can make in a home. Rather than being filled with furniture of mismatched styles and colors, the professionally designed home has a sense of flow, of style, and color coordination, and of crafted beauty.

When you design your career, it too has a sense of organization and purpose, as well as craftsmanship. Rather than taking the first opportunity that presents itself, you begin by doing some ground-work to gain a clear understanding of what you really want. You then craft a career that will satisfy those desires. Only then can you truly fulfill your life purpose.

If you do not desire a career change, the concept of career design will enable you to bring added dimensions to your present situation that will in turn increase your level of fulfillment at work. In fact, I recommend to most of my clients that they seriously explore this avenue before deciding to make a career change. In some cases, simply being willing to look at their career from this perspective has allowed them to experience more fulfillment than they imagined possible by making subtle (or not so subtle!) changes in their present situation.

That was exactly my initial strategy when I became dissatisfied at the law firm where I worked prior to starting my own business. Once a large case that had occupied nearly all of my time for six months was settled, I began exploring how I could craft an opportunity within that structure to bring me more satisfaction. I knew that one area of law that fascinated me was personnel and employment. Yet I had not had the opportunity to practice in that area to any large extent. I approached the partners in the firm to see whether they would allow me to explore creating an employment law practice within that firm. They allowed me to proceed, and I did. However, that opportunity ultimately seemed blocked as well, and the even greater possibility of opening my own practice then made itself available.

I believe that it was important for me to have brought my creativity to bear on my then-existing situation, "recreating"that job so that it did satisfy me, prior to changing to another situation. In fact, I believe that improving my attitude toward that job made it possible for the new opportunity to reveal itself to me. You may find that to be true for yourself as well.

It is said that one of the best ways to find a new job is to learn to love the one you have. If nothing else, you leave as a happier person! And the Law of Attraction (which we will discuss in chapter 12) brings an even more loving opportunity to you, attracting like to like. The concept of career design can help you love your present job, whether you plan to stay there or not. So where do we begin?

The Preliminary Sketch

The first step is to describe, as clearly as you can, what your ideal job or career is like. Imagine that you have a genie or a magic lamp that will grant you your ideal job upon demand. Can you describe that job in a way that is clear enough for someone else to share your vision? You can think about this process as one of making a preliminary sketch (much as an artist or other designer would do) of your new career and/or job.

You already know more than you realize about your ideal career or job. When I ask you to "imagine your ideal job," what first comes to mind? Jot down those initial impressions, using these questions to guide you:

1. Where are you?
2. What line of business are you working in?
3. Is the atmosphere busy or relaxed?
4. Are you working with other people, or alone?
5. How do you feel?

If you are unhappy in your career, you probably have some definite ideas about the characteristics your new career will include. ("Well, it certainly won't include a boss like Jim!" or "I never want to do data entry again!") Or, maybe there are things that you have always wanted in a job but never had.

You may only be sensing glimpses of this job or career, but try your best to capture those first impressions. You might also try this exercise after you do the Symbol Meditation in chapter 2, or first thing in the morning when you awaken. Your subconscious mind is most accessible at those times.

The important thing is to *start where you are, with what you know.* The answer to your quest for career satisfaction does not lie in a career counselor's office, an employment agency, or even in this book. The answer lies within you—but perhaps the counselor, employment agency, or even this book may be able to facilitate your discovery of that answer that already exists at the center of your being.

Just starting from that perspective will cause both your conscious and subconscious mind to be more open to the impressions that come, rather than waiting for someone or something outside of yourself to give you the answer.

Filling in the Gaps

To fill in the rest of the "picture" of your ideal job design, we will look at seven critical factors:

1. Your life's purpose
2. The values that are important to you
3. What motivates you to work and to achieve success
4. Your work skills
5. Your past experience
6. The career area and job description of your ideal job
7. Your ideal working environment

Your Life's Purpose

We explored your life's purpose in depth in chapter 2. I hope that you have responded to the 10 Clues to Life Purpose and have been using the five principles for listening to your inner voice, including the Symbol Meditation. If so, you probably have at least some idea of your life's purpose by now. If not, continue to use those techniques until you do gain insight into your purpose. And keep making your lists (or writing in your journal) as we go through these factors!

Your Critical Career Values

The second critical factor in job design is your values, as they relate to work. Fulfillment in work comes when the life and work values that are important to you are met through your work. At the same time, the company for which you work ought to share at least the most important of those values. Otherwise you will experience constant turmoil and conflict, as well as a feeling that you "can't be yourself" at work.

Values are simply things about work that, to you, are intrinsically valuable or desirable. They can be accessed most easily by asking yourself the question: "What do I want out of my work?" or "Why do I work?" Begin by asking yourself these questions now, and write down your responses. If you get stuck, look at the previous value and ask what is important to you about that. For example, if I said that one thing I wanted out of work was the opportunity to be creative, I might ask myself: "What is it about creativity that is important to me?" If my answer was: "I need to express myself," then I have stated another value.

You may have discovered some of your important values in responding to life purpose clue number 9—writing your epitaph. If you can truly put yourself (mentally) in the situation where you are approaching the end of your life, your important values will be right at the surface—and may very well jolt you into action!

Some values commonly expressed are listed below. You may wish to rank each of the listed values as (1) not important, (2) moderately important, or (3) very important to you in your choice of career.

Values at Work

_____ Enjoyment (having fun at what you do)

_____ Helping other people (in a direct way)

_____ Friendships (developing close relationships with co-workers)

_____ Helping society (contributing to the betterment of the world)

_____ Freedom (flexible schedule, independence)

_____ Recognition (being recognized for your work in a tangible way)

_____ Creativity (having the opportunity to express your ideas and yourself in your work; innovation)

_____ Location (being able to live where you choose)

_____ Competition (matching your abilities with others')

_____ Power and authority (being in a managerial or leadership position; being responsible for supervising others; having decisionmaking authority)

_____ Achievement (accomplishing desired objective; mastery)

_____ Compensation (receiving equivalent in value or effect for services rendered)

_____ Variety (a mix of tasks to perform and people to deal with during each day)

_____ Security (feeling of stability, no worry; certainty)

_____ Prestige (being seen as successful; obtaining recognition and status)

_____ Aesthetics (beauty of work environment; contributing to beauty of the world)

_____ Morality and ethics (working according to a code or set of rules; enhancing world ethics)

_____ Intellectual stimulation (working in an environment that encourages and stimulates thinking)

_____ Public contact (working with customers or clients, as opposed to working alone or working with objects only)

_____ Pace (busy versus relaxed working atmosphere)

_____ Risk (monetary or other risks—for example, new product development or start-up enterprise)

Now, think about your current job. How many of the values you have marked "3" for "very important" are being fulfilled through that job? None? That gives you a very important insight as to why you feel dissatisfied with that job.

As you go through the remaining exercises in this chapter, keep these values in mind. Remember, if your important work values are not met through your new job or career, it simply will not fulfill you or carry out your life purpose.

What Motivates You

Recognizing your values will give you some clues as to what will motivate you in your new or existing job: If your values are being met, you will be satisfied and motivated to continue to perform well. However, those who have studied motivation have discovered that some factors are more important than others in whether or not you stay motivated.

Psychologist Frederick Herzberg did extensive work in the area of motivation earlier in this century. How? He asked people a simple question: What do you want from your job?

What would you expect the typical answer to be—more money, better employment policies, more benefits, job security?

Surprisingly, those factors were not mentioned. Rather, most people's answers contained factors related to the *tasks* they perform in their jobs (such as responsibility, achievement, recognition, advancement, possibility of growth, etc.). When these factors were present, the workers were satisfied. Herzberg called these "motivating factors."

Considerations such as salary, policies and procedures, physical working conditions, benefits, and job security were not on the list of motivators, but were labeled "hygiene factors." This was because although the absence of those things made people unhappy, giving them those things did not make them satisfied with their work. They wanted more of the motivating factors in order to feel fulfilled.

You may also recall that in chapter 1 we discussed Daniel Yankelovich's research concerning the changing priorities of people as far as what they want from their work. He found that the top ten qualities people want in their work today to be:

1. **Working with people who treat you with respect;**

2. **Interesting work;**

3. **Recognition for good work;**

4. **Chance to develop skills;**

5. **Working for people who listen if you have ideas about how to do things better;**

6. **A chance to think for yourself rather than just carry out instructions;**
7. **Seeing the end results of your work;**
8. **Working for efficient managers;**
9. **A job that is not too easy; and**
10. **Feeling well informed about what is going on.**

High pay, job security, and good benefits were not even in the top 10 (although they were in the top 15) factors! People want work to be fun and satisfying in itself. They are no longer willing to work eight or more hours each day at a job they don't enjoy so that they can then find time to have fun somewhere else. In addition, more and more people seek to experience self-actualization, to use Abraham Maslow's term. That is, they seek satisfaction and the opportunity to experience their full potential, both at work and throughout their lives. Are you one of these people?

You may wonder how all of this relates to your designing your ideal job. Quite simply, it helps you to (1) be more realistic in what to expect from a job, and (2) gain some insight into what truly motivates you to do your best (as opposed to factors that merely make you less unhappy). If, for example, you are unhappy in your present job because of the turnover among the employees and the low pay, it will help you to realize that simply getting into another company with better pay and more job security will *not* necessarily result in fulfillment. Why? Because both of those factors are hygiene factors. Therefore, although their absence causes unhappiness, their presence does not necessarily result in happiness.

I liken this phenomenon to some of the aspects of cleaning house. If you don't dust the furniture for a month, people may notice the buildup. But if you dust faithfully every week for a year, no one is likely to notice the absence of dust. There is a kind of "neutral" zone that just maintains the status quo, but doesn't necessarily increase the quality of your life.

Certainly, if you are unhappy because your present job lacks some of the hygiene factors, your new job could include them. But you might also go beyond those factors in designing your ideal job. What kinds of growth do you want to experience in your job? What kind of a path of advancement? What about responsibility—do you want a lot, very little, or a graduated amount?

If you build the motivating factors into your job, you will not only be happier initially in your new situation, but will also experience ongoing challenge and personal expansion. Therein lies a key to career satisfaction.

If you feel you need more information on what motivates you to do your best, you may find it helpful to go to a professional psychologist or career consultant and have a personality assessment tool administered. The information from such tools can serve as yet another useful piece of data to use for designing your ideal job.

One final note on motivation: take just a moment and ask yourself how it *feels* to be successful and fulfilled. Write down as many descriptive adjectives as you can think of. Get a clear picture of success (by your own definition) in your mind. As you go through the remaining exercises in this chapter, as well as your actual job search or job change, keep that feeling in mind. When you do something or see an opportunity that awakens that feeling within you, you are on the path of your life purpose.

Your Work Skills

Your skills and abilities also play a role in your ideal career. On a piece of paper or in your journal, make a list of what you consider your work skills and abilities. List at least 20. You might use three of the clues to life purpose to assist you: the second clue, the aspects of your current job that you did well; the third clue, your "natural abilities;" and the fourth, your 10 greatest successes to date.

If you have a skill that you have thus far only used in a hobby or leisure activity, list that as well. Don't limit your skills to the narrow job area you think you will be entering—at least not yet!

We will use these skills you have listed as one factor in our career design process. However, it is important that you not get caught up in tunnel vision in this process. Many career counselors place far too much emphasis on one's skills and not enough on passion and purpose. I believe that can be a critical error. So I encourage you to keep expanding your options as we go along. Imagine yourself as a multifaceted crystal or diamond; when you have appreciated one side of it, turn it over and look at the opposite side to see what insights lay hidden there. When you think you have reached a conclusion, keep challenging yourself to ask "but what if . . . ?" "couldn't I also do . . . ?" and similar questions, until you arrive at an option that not only suits your personality needs, but also fulfills your life purpose *and* is something you feel excited about!

Your Past Experience

Chances are, you have had some experience in the world of work and are now seeking some kind of change (rather than entering the work world for the first time). No matter what your situation, you have had some experiences in your life that you have enjoyed and that will be of benefit to you in the next step in your career path. List those experiences now. You might want to group them by overall skill area (for example, communication, organization, financial management, etc.). Avoid a chronological, resume-style list. If you want to say "10 years in the radio field," that is fine, but don't list each station where you worked.

Then put a star or asterisk next to the areas of your experience that you enjoyed most—that gave you the feeling of success you want to recreate and expand in your ideal job.

The point here is to remind yourself about ways your experience may feed into your next job or career, or how that career may use your past experience in a new way. Remember, though, that your most important key to creating your ideal job is your "Enjoyment Factor"—the things you love to do; those that make you feel happy, successful and fulfilled; they are activities that you would do even if you didn't get paid for them.

Seeing the Possibilities

You may have always been told that you would be a "great secretary" or "sensitive artist" or—you know what your "label" has been. I encourage you to set those labels aside for a moment and set forth on an adventure.

Now it is time to do some homework. (Did you think you were done with that?) With your responses to life purpose clue 1 (your spare-time activities), 2 (aspects of your current job that you enjoy), and 3 (your natural abilities), as well as the five previous factors, in hand, it is time to do some research. Your local library has a wide selection of resources to assist you in designing your new career. Begin by spending some time browsing through the *Standard Industrial Classification (SIC) Manual*, published by the U.S. Bureau of Budget. This will give you all of the job classifications in most of the major career fields.

The purpose of this research is to expand your horizons. As you browse through, jot down the SIC number and description of the job classifications that *sound like fun to you*, that you would enjoy doing, and feel you could do well (even if you might need additional training or education to do so). Please don't choose a code *only* because it "fits my training" or "is in the line of work I'm comfortable in." Be playful and childlike. Ignore all of the adult conditions such as money, location, education, experience, licenses, etc. *Don't rule something out because you don't think you can make enough money doing it.* (We'll talk more in a later chapter about why.)

This exercise will be particularly valuable if you discover one or more career or job areas that you had never before considered for yourself, but about which you feel very excited. Come up with at least 20 job classifications that sound like fun to you.

You may list as many as 50 or 60 classifications. After you are finished with this first list, narrow your choices down to your top 15 favorites. To do this, keep in mind *first*, the choices that sound like the most fun, and *second*, your leisure activities, favorite job tasks, and natural skills. In this part of the exercise, you may take into account such things as education, location, and other "practical" considerations to some extent—but don't limit yourself too much.

If you want to continue this research in more detail, your librarian can guide you to other directories such as *Dun and Bradstreet, Standard and Poors, Thomas Registry, Moody's,* and local and state directories, as well as individual industry reference book. The U.S. Department of Labor's *Dictionary of Occupational Titles* is also helpful in generating ideas to expand your horizons.

At this point you probably have a list of 15 career areas and/or job descriptions that sound like fun to you, and are at least within the realm of possibility for you to create for yourself. Now, let's return to your list of values from earlier in the chapter. Can you narrow your list of job types further by comparing your important values with each of your 15 choices? If you can see at the outset that your important values cannot be fulfilled in one of your chosen careers or jobs, then eliminate it from your list since it will not result in the satisfaction you are seeking. (Note, however, that you may not be able to determine whether your values will be met until you have a particular company in mind.)

Be careful that you don't eliminate options before you are fully informed. If some of the items on your list are areas you have not considered before, you may want to do some networking (see next section) or additional research on that career area before deciding that you cannot fulfill your value(s) in that job.

For example, Sue had a work history in the field of journalism. She had become tired of the pressure of constant deadlines. The more she resisted the deadlines, the more the quality of her work declined. She knew she needed a change. She recognized that one of her important values was freedom. In going through the research process described above, she chose as one of her desired career areas the field of telemarketing. She had never explored that field before, and at first blush may have considered eliminating it from her list because it may not have met her need for freedom—she believed she would still have external demands in the form of quotas or required numbers of calls.

In fact, in doing further research and networking with telemarketers, she discovered that the degree of freedom she would have would depend entirely on the structure of the company in which she worked. Without that additional research, she would not have continued to explore this field—working for a nonprofit organization that is part of a cause she feels passionate about. Also, the job meets her other needs for contact with people and for making the world a better place.

Your Ideal Work Environment

Now that you are gaining a clearer focus on the right career field for you at this stage in your development, let's refine the picture even further, and examine the aspects of your environment and how they enhance or detract from your career satisfaction.

Part of your work environment is the geographical location in which you work. Have you always dreamed of working in another state or country, but never took the step of moving there? Perhaps this is a perfect time to explore that option realistically. Are there companies with jobs in the area you are seeking in that location? Will your family and other responsibilities allow you to make that move at this time?

A second aspect of your work environment is the pace of the business or office. Do you enjoy an environment that is bustling and busy, or do you prefer a peaceful, slower pace? Once you know your preference, you will want to ask appropriate questions about the environment when you interview in the companies of your choice.

The degree of support in the work environment is also important. As we noted in chapter 3, one way to avoid burnout is to surround ourselves with a supportive environment—one in which we have a sense of significance, autonomy, challenge, and support, and in which there are relatively few unmodifiable work stresses. To determine the degree of support in a company you have not yet worked in, you may wish to either observe the workers interacting with each other while you are there, or ask others in the industry or community what kind of reputation the company has in that regard.

In addition to this relatively intangible aspect of your environment, you also need to evaluate whether you work best alone, with one or two co-owners, or in a large company setting. To help you evaluate your optimal work setting, consider the following profiles of the solo worker, the partner, and the team personality.

SOLO WORKER PROFILE

The solo worker:

- is independent;
- prefers working alone, likes privacy;
- is highly creative and contemplative;
- has a few carefully chosen friends;
- resists authority;
- is motivated by opportunity to create and to get credit for creation;
- likes to take risks; and
- fears losing control most of all.

PARTNER PROFILE

The partner:

- enjoys (and needs) give-and-take feedback when making decisions and when engaging in conversation;
- is most creative in the context of a close relationship;
- has a few long-term friends;
- needs equal amounts of time alone and with others;
- is an excellent listener;
- feels that power comes from shared resources;
- shares risk-taking with his/her partner;
- fears rejection by his/her partner above all else.

TEAM PERSONALITY PROFILE

The team personality:

- enjoys the esprit de corps of a large organization, including the process of gaining a consensus;

- wants to be alone about 20 percent of the time;
- is motivated by competition;
- forms many friendships easily
- is comfortable with authority figures;
- is most creative in the context of praise from team members and from a leader;
- enjoys belonging to clubs;
- shares risks with team members and a leader;
- fears loneliness most of all.

You may find you have aspects of two of these profiles, or maybe even all three—but you probably have more qualities of one group than any of the others. Recognize that as your preferred working environment, and be sure to build those qualities into your design for your ideal job.

If you are a team personality type, also consider how large a company you wish to work for. Though the team dynamic is present in the 10-person company as well as the 1,000-person company, your day-to-day experience in those two companies will be quite different. Which would you prefer?

Next, consider whether you prefer to work primarily with people, with data, or with things. Think about your hobbies and past jobs—what activities have given you the most joy: those involving interaction with people, working with data or information, or working on things with your hands? Your preference in this area will influence the types of jobs you choose and also the types of jobs that will result in the greatest satisfaction for you.

Finally, if one of your important work values is aesthetics (the beauty in your environment), be sure to factor that in as well. Working in some government jobs, or for nonprofit corporations, will probably not satisfy you, since budgetary constraints will not permit original artwork, designer office furnishings, and other aesthetically pleasing features.

The environment in which you work can affect your outlook on your job and, ultimately, your effectiveness in it (even if at a subconscious level). It is important that you choose an environment that will assist you in experiencing fulfillment, not frustration and stress.

The Path of Entrepreneurship

One of the hallmarks of the 1990s is the explosion of entrepreneurial ventures (that is, people owning their own businesses). Women are particularly active in this trend and now start their own businesses four to five times as often as men. It is projected that by the year 2000, women will own fully half of the businesses in the United States. Entrepreneurship may be the next step on your career path if you fit the profile of the entrepreneur *and* are prepared to make the commitment that will be required of you.

Successful entrepreneurs share six characteristics. First, they are achievement oriented. They have a high need for success and desire concrete measures of their progress.

Second, entrepreneurs are independent. They like to work on their own and actually seek out opportunities to take personal responsibility for solving problems.

Self-direction is a third characteristic of entrepreneurs. They have self-discipline and enjoy being their own boss.

Entrepreneurs are also passionate about their work. They have a strong, almost overwhelming, drive to make their dreams come true. They have a high energy level and can work long hours when necessary. Work is fulfilling in itself for these people.

Fifth, entrepreneurs are persistent. They will do whatever it takes to accomplish their goals, continuing their efforts until the desired end is reached. They have the ability to believe in their ideas and dreams when no one else does, and to bounce back from discouragement and setbacks along the way.

Finally, successful entrepreneurs are willing to take moderate, calculated risks to achieve their goals.

If you share these traits, and have an idea, and some business expertise or experience, owning your own business may be an option for you to explore.

Integrating Work and Your Life's Purpose

Now that you have examined the key factors for your ideal job, how do you integrate them with each other—and, particularly, with your life's purpose?

There are two basic approaches to take: the path of the intellect, and the path of the heart. They can work to complement each other, or you may wish to choose one over the other.

The path of the intellect involves a simple logical analysis of the factors you have examined. You articulate your life purpose, values, motivating factors, skills, and experience, and compare that with your selection of ideal job descriptions and ideal work environment. You mentally analyze how you can accomplish your life purpose through each of your chosen job descriptions, and you pursue the one or two that will most directly accomplish your purpose. This technique may well lead you toward your goal, but it is best augmented with careful contemplation, meditation, and by listening to your intuition as to which path to pursue among those your intellect has chosen.

The path of the heart takes a different approach. It will briefly consider the information we have just covered and will then rely primarily on your intuition and inner guidance to determine your next step. As you learn to listen to your inner voice and let it lead you into the right action, you will find yourself pursuing your life's purpose in the perfect direction for you. You may also need the structure and knowledge you have gained in the preceding exercises to give your intuition some form, but you will be fulfilling your life's purpose as you follow that inner guidance.

Shakti Gawain, in her book, *Living in the Light*, refers to this process as the integration of spirit and form. She makes a statement that embodies my personal commitment perfectly: "Those of us who choose to be spiritual seekers and transformers must now move *into* the world *with the same degree of commitment* to our spiritual selves as we would have if we renounced the world. This path is much more difficult!'' The point is that many spiritual disciplines require renouncing the material world and spending one's time in an ashram, monastery, or retreat center to maximize one's spiritual growth. I believe there is a place for such times apart, but I know that more and more of us are called to a path that requires integrating the spiritual and the material—and as Shakti says, this path is much harder!

Shakti suggests two simple (but not necessarily easy!) steps to integrate spirit and form. First, simply recognize and feel both the consciousness of your spirit and the consciousness of your form (mind, personality, and ego). We often say, ''I said to myself,'' or other similar language that sounds like there are two people inside of us. This process of recognition is nothing more than that. Second, she suggests that we love and accept both aspects of ourselves. Each has a vital part to play in our lives, and in our growth—so we may as well recognize them and allow them to simply be.

In addition, it is critical to be patient with ourselves, to allow for the time lag between the urging of our spirit and the tendency of our form toward the safe, secure patterns. Manifestation takes some time on the earth plane, and the sooner we can make peace with the process, the sooner we will experience peace and a natural flow in our lives.

The process of using our daily activities as tools for awakening is referred to in the eastern religions as Karma Yoga. This is the path many of us have chosen. A technique frequently used by those on this path to awaken is that of the Witness. We will discuss this technique more in a later chapter, but I mention it now so you can begin to integrate your life's purpose (a spiritual concept at its essence) with your daily work. The Witness technique is simply to bring a third component into every action. It is as if you are watching yourself do everything you do. The Witness does not judge or condemn; it simply observes your actions and reactions and comments on them. ''Oh, she is getting angry now,'' or ''Oh, she thought she had handled that one, but there it is again.'' Just like meditation, it sounds simple and unstructured (and it is), but it is an effective tool for developing awareness and for bringing a higher perspective into everything you do.

The method you use to integrate your life's purpose and your job will depend on your perspective on life. If you are most comfortable with a purely intellectual approach now, please use that—and save the meditation and path of the heart for later. If you are a spiritual seeker and enjoy the path of the heart, use that path with a sprinkling of intellectual analysis.

The important thing is to begin. There is a path to fulfillment that is right for you—but you must diligently seek it and apply what you know in order to experience the result you desire.

Once you have chosen your path and begin to design the perfect job and career through which to fulfill your life's purpose, you need to set a clear route toward success. That is the subject of the next chapter.

Action Steps from 9 to 5

To clarify your visual image of your new career or job, make a collage of all its features. Look through catalogs, magazines, and old photographs. Cut out anything that resonates with your Inner Self as a part of your new job, or a quality you desire to experience in your work. Paste these on a piece of poster board, together with appropriate handwritten or calligraphed messages, captions, etc., in a creative format that expresses you.

When you are finished, put the collage away for a few days. Then get it out and look at it. Do any new messages appear now about your new job that you hadn't realized before?

5

Setting Your Course
for Success

"To get somewhere, you must know where you're going."

—Denis Waitley

CONGRATULATIONS. YOU HAVE come a long way since we began. You now know more clearly what your life's purpose is, and whether or not it is time to make a job or career change. You have begun to design a job that is perfect for you—one that you will not only do well, but enjoy doing. But that is not enough. Until you translate your newfound awareness into action, your life will not change—and you will not be fulfilled. So let's begin taking some concrete steps to make your ideal job/career and your life's purpose a reality for you.

Perhaps you are hoping you can skip this chapter and move on to something more exciting (and less demanding) than goal-setting. If so, please read on anyway—you are among the majority of people if you dislike setting goals! In a survey of the 1953 graduating class of Yale University, only *3 percent* of the graduates had written goals and a plan for achieving them. When the same graduates were again interviewed 20 years later, in 1973, the results were startling. The 3 percent with specific written goals were worth more financially than the other 97 percent combined! Not only that, but these 3 percent also demonstrated higher levels of happiness and joy, as measured by the researchers, than did the other 97 percent.

All of us want to experience greater wealth, happiness, and joy, right? The problem is that many of us make those qualities the goals in themselves—an approach that is destined to fail. Money, happiness, and joy—as well as the other good things in life—were natural by-products to the 3 percent interviewed who obtained them. They came as the result of clear, well-designed goal-setting and planning, *not* because those graduates pursued money and happiness as direct goals.

Wealth, happiness, and joy will naturally follow you, too, when you are fulfilling your life's purpose through your work. (More about that in a later chapter.) For now, though, let's understand the importance of setting goals for yourself, the qualities of achievable aims, and how to summon all of your inner and outer resources to attain the goals that are important to you. Even if you have resisted setting goals in the past, now is the time to break away from the majority of people who fail to accomplish what they want in their lives. Join this forward-thinking minority—and let's move ahead together.

The Role of Goals in Success

Have you ever wondered *why* goals are so important to achieving success? The answer is stated quite succinctly in the quotation at the beginning of this chapter: "To get somewhere, you must know where you're going." The largest part of "you" is your subconscious mind. It is the largest and most influential part of your mind. Goals serve as a road map, if you will, for your subconscious mind.

We talked earlier about how your subconscious mind is like the 90 percent of an iceberg that is submerged beneath the water, invisible to the eye. Yet it is by far the majority of the mass of the iceberg. The 10 percent that is visible cannot move anywhere without the permission and cooperation of the 90 percent that is submerged.

You may think that your actions are governed by your conscious mind; that is, the thoughts that you are aware of each day. In fact, the reverse is true. Your subconscious mind, the "submerged"part of your mind, contains all of your beliefs, your values, your deepest desires, and the sum total of your experiences. If you consciously state that you want to do one thing, but your subconscious has a different objective, your subconscious will win the battle—and you will not achieve your consciously stated goal. Perhaps it seems unfair, but the subconscious *always wins* when there is conflict between your conscious and subconscious goals.

So what goes into this subconscious part of your mind? You are bombarded with various kinds of stimuli every day. You think thousands of thoughts within your mind, about yourself, other people, and your experiences. You also receive ever- increasing amounts of input from your environment that enter your mind at both conscious and subconscious levels. Madison Avenue has developed innumerable techniques to capture our attention, even for a moment, to influence us to purchase a product. Subliminal technologies (in which sounds or words inaudible or invisible to the conscious mind are embedded in another conscious image or sound) originated in the advertising world. Advertisers know how your mind works! (Thankfully, these same technologies are now being harnessed in self-help audiotapes and videotapes to be used to our benefit!)

Your task, in the face of the countless thoughts that go through your mind, and the endless images and sounds in your environment, is to decide what you will attend to and what you will not. *You* have the final decision as to what you allow to enter—and to stay in— your subconscious mind.

What's important to realize is this: if you don't take an active role in regulating what goes into your subconscious mind, it will absorb whatever is in your environment. It will not remain empty! If you have ever tried to start a meditation, you know how your mind constantly moves from thought to thought, idea to idea. If distractions are all that is available, it will focus on those. It is difficult at first to discipline it to the point where it is quiet and gently focused on one idea or image at a time.

We have said that your beliefs and deepest desires reside in your subconscious mind. You may be wondering, "Does that mean that every passing thought, censored or not, becomes part of my belief system?" The answer, of course, is no. What does become part of your beliefs are the things you focus on *repeatedly*. So if you always see the negative side of a situation, or continually tell yourself that you will never succeed—those ideas will become your beliefs. They will shade your perception of your world.

What has once become a belief can be changed by using the

same method that created the belief to begin with. Setting goals and reinforcing them, through the methods we will discuss in this chapter, is the way to shape your beliefs to support you in achieving your goals. You will learn how to focus on the thoughts that will lead you to your heart's desires, rather than to a destiny of self-sabotage and frustration. And then something amazing will happen: you will begin to encounter people, ideas, opportunities, and resources to assist you in accomplishing what you want at every turn. Why? Because you have set goals to implement your life's purpose and are sending repeated messages to your subconscious to help you achieve them. Your subconscious then dutifully draws to you all that is needed to fulfil the goal you have set for yourself.

Sounds wonderful, right? So why don't more people accomplish what they want? Some of the reasons many people become frustrated in the goal-setting process is because their goals are too general, unrealistic, not measurable, or they rely on someone else's actions for their achievement. If you design your goals so that they are achievable, rather than frustrating to you, you will begin to experience success. And with that success will come the wealth, happiness, and joy you desire.

Your Goal-Setting Style

Often when I discuss the process of goal-setting in my workshops (many of which are done in New Thought churches), I encounter resistance from some of the participants. "I've already done goal-setting hundreds of times," people will say. "I'm burned out on the process. Part of why I like New Thought is that it helps me learn to honor my intuitive side, my right brain—and goal-setting seems to be a left-brain process."

I empathize with these people. My goal here is not to multiply your past frustrations by getting you to fall short of your goals! In fact, I am drawn to New Thought for the same reasons these people have stated. I grew up in an environment that rewarded my over-achievements and in which my intellect was my most prized possession. I could reason and intellectualize any issue. The problem was, I was taught to ignore my true inner feelings, to disregard my intuition, and to do what was "right" according to external standards. Soon I became disillusioned with this approach to life and began exploring other options. New Thought and eastern religious traditions filled the void in my upbringing and in my consciousness.

So where does goal-setting fit into this framework? I have discovered that there are two kinds of people in the world. Some of us grew up as I did, with a left-brain emphasis, lots of structure in our lives, relying on our intellect to guide us. We are the overachievers, the Type A personalities. We feel compelled to fill our time with activity. What we need is to balance that intellectual skill by learning to honor our intuition and right brain.

The rest of us grew up in an environment where we were encouraged to explore our artistic or musical abilities, had little structure or external demands, and learned to listen to our intuition. We cared little about school and tend in adulthood to be the Type B's, the laid-back type of person. We find it easy to let time go by without doing anything. What we need is an intellectual, left-brain balance to lend needed structure to our lives and assist us in moving forward. (My husband is of this latter type, and we balance each other quite well!)

If you are a Type A, you may wish to use more passive, intuitive techniques of goal-setting and learn more about the power of your emotions in getting what you want. Type B's, on the other hand, will want to develop more structure in their lives. Therefore, the standard goal-setting methods just described will work well for them.

The key here is to *balance* your masculine and feminine energies—to be fluent in the path of the intellect and the path of the heart. The masculine part of you is the part that wants to take action, to be in control, to think. The feminine part, on the other hand, represents your intuition, emotions, and inner urgings. When the feminine intuition and male action are blended, a wonderful creative process occurs, and you feel more centered than ever before.

As you consider the goal-setting ideas in this chapter, and the tools for goal achievement in the next, I encourage you to choose the techniques and tools that feel right for you. Use those that will balance your masculine and feminine, Type A or Type B, and move you onward in your growth. You can trust your inner urgings to guide you into the truth for you. And you can always change your mind! Use these tools to work and to play—to create the career and life you want for yourself.

The Qualities of Achievable Goals

For your goals to be achievable, they must possess four qualities. This is true whether you are designing goals for your job or career or for any other area of your life. However, we will be discussing them primarily in the context of work here.

1. Achievable goals are specific. You must be able to describe, in precise terms, the result you are seeking to achieve. Let's say, for instance, that your goal is "to be more efficient." Is that specific enough that you can clearly describe what it looks like when it is achieved? No. What I mean by "being more efficient" may be doing more things in an hour than I currently do. You may define efficiency as having things run more smoothly in your life. Thus, we could each set the same stated goal, but be seeking two entirely different results!

Instead, let's restate the goal to be "to make no more than two typographical errors per day in my job"; or "to increase my production from five units per hour to ten units per hour by January 31;" or "to only handle each piece of paper that crosses my desk only once." These are *specific*, right? You can easily visualize the result desired.

Now, your subconscious mind has that critical map it needs to assist you in achieving your desired goals.

To ensure that your goals are specific, be sure they answer the following questions:

A. **What** will you do?

B. **When** will you do it?

C. Have I **quantified** as much as possible? (for example, two typos, three miles, 50 percent of my time, etc.)

2. Achievable goals are realistic. What if, in setting a specific goal, you set it way beyond your ability to achieve? For example, let's say your goal is to successfully complete a 26-mile marathon next month. That's specific—but if you haven't jogged a mile in your life, it is not a realistic goal for you. Therefore, your chances of achieving it are almost nil—and you are setting yourself up for frustration and failure again.

The problem with setting unrealistic goals is that you reinforce your negative beliefs that you cannot achieve the things you desire. Then when you have an opportunity to achieve a realistic goal, you sabotage yourself and give up before you start. Why? Simply because you have conditioned yourself to fail through your prior experiences.

One important principle must be remembered here: *there is no such thing as failure.* Failure is simply our interpretation of an event that has occurred. Let's imagine you are a secretary, and every letter you type has been returned to you with at least one typographical error in it. You decide to improve yourself and set a goal that you will type at least six letters with perfection tomorrow. If you type five of them perfectly but make an error on the sixth, have you failed? You have if you simply compare your goal to your actual performance—but what if, instead, we compare your performance yesterday with your performance today? You have improved 500 percent! Hardly a failure!

The same principle applies with larger goals. If your goal is to find a new job in a company in a new industry, and during the first month of your search you don't get a single interview, have you failed? What if what you *did* do was research the industry, find out what companies in your area work in that industry, and network with people working in the industry to gain an understanding of the important concepts, people, and structures in that industry? In my opinion, you have succeeded: you are taking the critical steps to achieve your goal.

How do you know if your goal is realistic? It ought to be "just out of reach, but not out of sight." That is, it might stretch you a bit but not be impossible. If we return to our marathoner at the beginning of this section, a more realistic goal might be to run in a three-mile race next month, and aim for completing a marathon six to nine months from the time that the running program is begun on a daily basis. This will motivate our runner to consistently increase his or her distance and speed, but in a gradual way so that he or she will achieve the goal in a reasonable time. A side benefit is that each time he or she runs one more mile, or runs the same distance one minute faster, a small success is achieved. The runner can reward herself or himself and build upon the little successes to achieve the ultimate desired goal.

Whatever your goal for your job or career, be certain it is realistic. It ought to be something you cannot presently do with complete success. (After all, if you were doing it, you wouldn't need to set a goal, right?) At the same time, it ought to be something you feel you can do within a reasonably short period of time (for example, one week, one month, two months). If you have a larger or more long-range goal, break it down into subgoals (in other words, smaller pieces) to keep you motivated. Be willing to stretch yourself and become an increasingly greater person, ever closer to attaining your heart's desire.

3. Achievable goals are measurable. If your goal meets the first criterion (that is, it is specific), then it will most likely also be measurable. That is, you have a way to tell when you have achieved the goal. Our secretary who wanted to reduce the number of typographical errors she made to two per day can measure the accomplishment of her goal by counting the typos in her work. Our would-be marathoner can measure the miles that are run and the time that it takes. If your goal is to spend at least 50 percent of each day counseling people one-on-one, you can simply keep track of your time and tell whether or not you have achieved your goal.

Whatever you have as your stated career goal, be sure to build in some measuring devices. These are important because they give you opportunities to celebrate your successes along the way to your long-term goal. Each time you reinforce the fact that you are succeeding, you cause your experience of success to multiply. Then you can set larger goals and achieve larger successes, in an ever-expanding circle.

"But," you say, "what if I set measuring devices and don't achieve what I want? Then I'll just be disappointed." Perhaps. But if, like the typist who wanted to type six letters perfectly and fell short by one, you are progressing in the direction of your goal, you congratulate yourself for your progress and go for it again the next day. Perhaps the next day she met her goal of six letters, so she set a new goal of ten perfect letters. The following two days she typed eight perfect letters but couldn't quite get to ten. Then, she made it!

Imagine, instead, that she simply said to herself that she wanted to "type better" or "type more accurately." Is that the kind of goal that makes you feel like moving forward? No—it is too vague and general, and wouldn't give her subconscious a specific goalpost toward which to strive. As it was, she "failed" her initial goal the first day, but soon she achieved that one, and by the end of another week had increased her accuracy by 1000 percent—all because she had a specific, realistic, and measurable goal that motivated her to move forward.

To be measurable, your goal should answer the question: **how will I know** when I have achieved my goal?

4. Achievable goals rely only on your own personal responsibility for their achievement.   The final quality of achievable goals is personal responsibility. If you depend on someone else's actions in order for your goals to be achieved, you risk frustration and "failure" not because you couldn't do what you set out to, but because someone else didn't come through. For instance, let's say your goal is to become the supervisor of your department by January 31. This goal depends on your existing supervisor leaving the department for some reason, upon your superiors giving you a favorable performance review, and upon someone recommending you for the position—and someone else approving that decision. There are obviously too many variables outside of your control for this goal to be achievable for you.

But let's look instead at the *essence* of your goal. Do you want more money? More responsibility? To move out of a line job and into a staff position? More flexibility in your schedule? In other words, what is it about being a supervisor that is appealing to you?

Once you have become clear about the essence of your goal, you can substitute a statement that embodies this essence for your previously stated goal. It must still be specific, realistic, and measurable —but this time you will be more likely to achieve it because it depends only on your actions for its achievement (plus the resourcefulness of the Universe, which you will attract if your goals are carefully formulated). Examples of how the would-be supervisor's goal might be restated include: "I will be making $500 per month more than I am now by January 31," or "I will be working as a supervisor of others, with increased responsibility for performance evaluation, department productivity, and effective employee management." These new goal statements do not limit our worker to a job within the department he or she is now in, or even in the same company. Yet they effectively state the true aspiration and meet the criteria we have been discussing.

There is a very important reason to state your goals in this way. The Universe is the ultimate networker. It has more resources available to you than you know, and greater opportunities than you can conceive. If you state your goals in an open-ended fashion as I have suggested, you leave the door open for an even greater form of the goal to come to you.

I had a powerful experience like this a couple of years ago. I had been in a job as an associate lawyer in which I was very unhappy. After applying my creativity to attempt to transform the job to achieve the things that were important for my fulfillment, it became apparent that I could not do so within that firm. I discovered that I am the type of person who needs to have a direct relationship between the effort I expend and the compensation I receive. So being paid a salary as my sole compensation was not for me!

I began looking for other jobs in the legal field in all different contexts, seeking an opportunity to express myself creatively and be rewarded for the extra effort and "value added" that I brought to a prospective employer. I avidly searched for the right position, but the right opportunity seemed to elude me. Then I began using two powerful tools. First, each day I wrote out a description of my ideal job (including the intangible things I wanted such as compensation directly related to my effort, creative expression, and flexible schedule). I also began using an affirmation on a daily (or more frequent) basis: "I am willing to do whatever is necessary to have the thing I want." I maintained an attitude of openness to the highest form of my heart's desire, and very soon, I was contacted by a national company who was seeking part-time counsel within their offices. This contact allowed me to start my own business with a minimum of risk, and I could finally experience the direct relationship between my effort and my compensation. If it worked, I got the credit—and if I didn't, I had an opportunity to change my approach until it did work.

The important message in this story, however, is that I didn't consciously know that starting my own business was the way to achieve my goals of creative expression, relationship of income to effort, and flexibility. But the Universe did. And as I became more open to the highest expression of my goal, it found me. And yours will find you, too, if you set achievable goals and remain open concerning the form in which they come to you.

In the next chapter, we will learn how to achieve these goals which we have now set for ourselves.

Action Steps from 9 to 5

1. Look back at your ideal career and your life's purpose. Using the criteria discussed in this chapter, design one or two goals to assist you in creating your ideal career and fulfilling your life purpose. Remember, they must be specific, realistic, measurable, and depend on *you* for their achievement. They ought to be made for a fairly short timeline (for example, within the next 60 days). Write each goal on a sheet of paper.

2. **Masculine/Feminine Meditation.** This meditation is to assist you in the process of balancing your masculine and feminine energies. To begin, use the body relaxation technique in the first 3 paragraphs of the Symbol Meditation on page 28.

When you are relaxed, bring to mind a symbol or image that represents your masculine energy. Notice what it is. It may resemble someone you know, or it may be abstract. Ask the symbol if it has any message for you at this time. If you have any questions, ask them now. Simply receive the message and answers to any questions you have, without judgment but with curiosity and openness, as though seeing something for the first time. Notice how you feel about this symbol.

Once you feel the communication is finished, release the image and come back to your centered, relaxed state.

Then, bring to mind a symbol of your feminine energy. Again, it may be abstract or realistic. Repeat the process you did with your masculine energy, receiving any message and the answers to any questions simply and without judgment. Notice how you feel about your feminine energy. Is it more familiar to you than your masculine self, or less so?

After your communication with your feminine energy is finished, release that image and come back to your centered, relaxed state.

Now, ask both your masculine and feminine energies to come to you simultaneously. Notice whether they are compatible or not, in relationship with each other or separately. Ask them if they have anything to say to each other or to you. Simply be open to this communication, whether it is in words, images, feelings, or another form. Ask them any further questions you may have.

When this communion is complete, take a deep breath and release the images of your energies from your mind. Know that you can come back and commune with these symbols or images whenever you wish.

6

Achieving Your Goals

"The way to work is to begin right where we are and, through constantly applying ourselves to the Truth, we gradually increase in wisdom and understanding, for in this way alone will good results be obtained."

—Ernest Holmes

IN THIS CHAPTER, we will explore ways to achieve the goals you have set. Of the techniques that are discussed, I encourage you to choose those that will help you balance your particular personality disposition. If you are a Type A person, burned out on goal-setting, you might focus on the processes that use a "softer" approach, emphasizing the subconscious mind. These would include visualization, following your inner guidance, the power of emotion, loving yourself, subconscious role modeling, and similar techniques. Meditation on a regular basis will also assist you in calming your mind and help you to move forward from your inner center rather than focusing on external demands.

If you are a Type B who already recognizes your inner voice, I encourage you to take some time designing specific, realistic, measurable goals for which you alone are responsible. Write them out, and refer to them on a regular basis. Turn your focus, in the goal-achievement techniques listed below, to making the commitment, setting priorities, doing affirmations on a regular basis, and masterminding so that you have support for your stated goals when your desire for "time out" threatens to sabotage you. In other words, focus on developing the conscious tools that will enable you to use your subconscious and your inner voice even more effectively, and that will move you in a positive, forward direction in your life.

So no matter what type of person you are now, there is a style for setting and achieving your career goals that will empower you and balance the areas within you that have been overemphasized in the past. Choose the techniques that you are drawn to at first, and expand your repertoire as you build your success.

10 Principles for Achieving Your Goals

1. Making the Commitment.   Each great accomplishment begins with a commitment to its achievement. Your first step in getting what you want out of your work and your life is making a clear statement of what that is. The second step, which is just as important, is to make as strong a commitment as you can muster to achieving that goal. See it as completed. Promise yourself that you will do *whatever is necessary* to have what you want. Then, as Thoreau says, advance confidently in the direction of your dreams to live the life you have imagined. Move forward with your commitment as the power behind your activity, taking one step at a time. The natural result of your activity will be the achievement of your goal.

2. Setting Priorities.   Many people have become skilled (or even burned out) at setting goals. Yet they still have not achieved what they want. Why? Something else always seems to get in their way, to be "more important" than the achievement of their goal. Does that sound familiar?

To overcome this all-too-common situation, you must set priorities for yourself. Quite simply, you must decide: "Am I going to achieve this goal or am I not?" If you've done the previous step, you have committed yourself to accomplish it—so you must now restate that commitment every single day by setting priorities that help you achieve your goal.

Here are two simple ways that I find quite effective. First, do the things that will take you toward your goal *first thing in the morning*, before other issues, phone calls, emergencies, and the like have an opportunity to distract you. For example, if your goal is to find a job in a new industry, use the first hour or two of the day (even if it is before you go to work at another job!) to research the industry, have breakfast with someone who knows about the industry, etc.

Many of us are at our best first thing in the morning. For these people, you will be giving your best time of the day to what is most important to you—instead of what's left over after a full day of working. Even if you aren't one of these people, cultivate this skill. You will find that it enhances your energy for the rest of the activities in your day, and best of all, you will feel a sense of progress toward what you may have been putting off for a long time. Your subconscious very quickly gets the idea that you mean business—and it will come to your aid in powerful ways to help you achieve your goal!

Incidentally, that is precisely the way this book is being written. Most of us have said to ourselves at one time or another that we want to write a book—but we never find the time to do it. I have all kinds of perfectly legitimate excuses for not finding the time—running two businesses, for one, as well as my clients' needs, fulfilling my responsibilities in my church and various professional organizations, and spending time with my husband. But writing this book is important to me. It has been percolating inside me for nearly 10 years. So I have blocked out time every morning work in the quiet of my home office, writing consistently for three to four hours each day until it is finished. I then spend the balance of the day at my downtown office, seeing clients and tending to my other responsibilities. I see progress each day, and you are holding in your hand the evidence that this approach does work. There is always a way to do what you truly want to do. But it depends on you! So make time for what's most important to you. The rest will take care of itself.

3. Listening to Your Inner Voice.   This technique is especially important for those of you who are Type A's, as I am. Once you have set your course for success by stating a goal, making a commitment, and setting daily priorities, your Inner Self will guide you to the actions that will help you most effectively move toward your goal. But you must be able to hear it. What does that require? It's actually quite simple. You must learn to be quiet, to calm your mind, and to be receptive to the impressions that are there. Like anything new, it requires practice. The five principles we discussed in chapter 2 will help you learn this vital skill.

The best way I know to begin to learn this skill is to learn to meditate. First thing upon awakening, spend a few minutes or more meditating. There are many techniques, which you can learn by attending classes, joining a meditation group, or reading a book such as *How to Meditate*, by Lawrence LeShan. Meditating will enable you to experience the feeling of a calm, quiet mind. You may then wish to simply sit, in an open and receptive manner, and let your Higher Self speak to you.

The voice of your Higher Self will often be the softest of the voices in your mind (until you become accustomed to it). It will never instruct you to do anything that will harm another person, but will always lead you in your highest, most spiritual path.

Once you learn to listen to your Higher Self in the context of meditation, I recommend that you set aside five minutes several times during your work day to "check in." That is, simply go within and see if there is an activity you want to do or something you want to change, or a better way to spend your time, so that you can move in the highest direction for you.

We will talk in a later chapter about how to use this valuable tool in making decisions. For now, simply learn to recognize this inner voice of yours, and heed its advice—no matter how irrational or crazy it may seem sometimes. It will always lead you to the best and highest path.

4. Using Affirmations. We have learned that the subconscious mind acts on the thoughts it receives, and that you have the ultimate decision as to which thoughts will be allowed into your subconscious. One of the ways you "program" your subconscious mind to assist you in fulfilling your goals and purpose is through affirmations. Affirmations are, quite simply, positive statements made in the present tense that you repeat to yourself to produce a desired result.

The Universe (God) already knows what you want and rushes

to bring it to you. ("Before they call, I will answer." Isaiah 65:24).
You need not beg from God or even state your desire more than
once. So why use affirmations? Because you are working on
yourself—repeating the affirmation until it becomes a part of you at
a subconscious level. You can only demonstrate in your life what you
have already accepted in your mind and being. Once you embody
your goal, then what you desire is yours.

Here are some examples of affirmations in the area of
job/career:

- "I now have the perfect job for me. It includes (describe
  its features)."
- "My income now exceeds my needs."
- "I now attract an abundance of satisfied customers to my
  business."

You get the idea. And you can design one (or more!) to fit your
situation, by using a few simple steps:

**A. Using the goal you have set, design a simple affirmation
(one to three sentences), in the present tense, which states the goal
as if you already have it.** Don't use "I will" or "I might" or "I
should"—but instead, "I am," "I have," etc. The reason for this
is that your subconscious mind cannot tell the difference between
what is real and what is imagined. Once you create an image in your
mind's eye, through repeating an idea over and over, your subconscious begins to believe it has actually happened—and creates
that result for you! (This is also why those who look for the worst
in every situation, expect disaster at every turn, and worry constantly
will experience what they fear: their subconscious sets out to prove
them right!)

**B. Repeat your affirmation as many times and in as many ways
as you can.** Our subconscious is sometimes slow to be retrained. It
wants to hold on to its old ideas. So you must launch a campaign to
make sure that the new idea takes hold. Write your affirmation on

3-x-5 cards and place them at conspicuous places throughout your house, in your car, in your wallet, and on your desk or workspace at work. Write it out several times when you awaken and before you go to sleep at night (so your subconscious works on it while you sleep). Record it on a tape recorder and play the tape before you go to sleep. One technique that my husband and I enjoy using is to write our favorite affirmation with an erasable felt pen on the bathroom mirror, where we see it several times each day. Wherever you are likely to see the affirmation throughout the day, place a reminder of it for yourself.

If you are working to eliminate a particularly stubborn belief or pattern, you will want to do all of these things, as often as possible, until you begin to see your new belief or pattern beginning to take form. Less entrenched beliefs and patterns will require less effort to change. The key is to involve your voice, your eyes, and your ears in the process, so that you change at all three levels. This kind of a "mass attack" on your subconscious will result in relatively rapid change.

If, when you repeat your affirmation, you find that so-called "negative" beliefs, or the opposites of what you want to accomplish, keep coming to mind, try the following technique. Divide a sheet of paper (or a page in your journal) into two columns. At the top, write your affirmation across the center of the page. Then, in the left column, write the "negative" thoughts that come up, leaving some space between them. Do this for five to ten minutes. Then, next to each of the items you have written in the left column, turn each one into a positive statement and write that statement on the right. For example:

Affirmation: I am now working in the job of my dreams.

Negative Thoughts	**Positive Affirmations**
I don't have a college degree.	I have all the skills and experience I need to perform the job of my dreams.

(Of course, I am assuming that you know what this dream job is as you are making your affirmation.) This technique will help you overcome your doubts and fears so you can move more effectively toward your goal.

C. Be specific enough, but not too specific.   When doing affirmations, it is important to find that critical balance between being too specific ("I now have a blue 1990 Chevrolet Caprice") and not being specific enough ("I now have a new car that I like"). My favorite analogy is ordering from a mail order catalog. You wouldn't send an order in to Sears and say, "send me something I would like," would you? It is the same with the Universe. You need to make your affirmation specific enough so that you attract the thing you want, but you don't want to limit the ways the Universe can bring it to you.

Let's take the example I used above: "My income now exceeds my needs." This affirmation establishes the balance of specificity. Alternatives might be: "I now make a salary of $25,000 per year." This is too specific because: (a) you might also attract expenses of $25,000 or more per year, therefore not getting the benefit of the additional money, and (b) you have limited the channels for your increased income to your salary only. What if you got an inheritance, grant, or gift? Or if someone forgave a debt or lowered your payments on an ongoing bill? Or you received merchandise or services instead of money, thus increasing your abundance in yet another way?

The affirmation "my income now exceeds my needs" lets your income increase, but without corresponding increase in expense, and it does not limit the sources from which abundance can come.

How do you strike this balance? One easy and very effective way is to say, *"This or something better* now comes to me, and the highest good of all concerned is served." This leaves your affirmation "open at the top" so that something even better than what you have imagined can come to you, without harming anyone else. If the Universe wanted to bring you a new Mercedes, and all you asked for was a new Volkswagen, you have limited what you can receive. And notice it is not because the Universe wouldn't give it to you—but because your thinking was too small. If you go to the well with a thimble, all you will come back with is a thimble full of water. If, however, you bring a large tub, or a hose, you will receive more. What size vessel are you willing to bring to the well of life?

5. The Power of Visualization.   Visualization is yet another technique that has a powerful impact on your subconscious in enlisting its help in achieving your goals. Visualization is simply creating a picture in your mind's eye of a situation you want to experience. You have already experienced a form of visualization if you have done the Symbol Meditation in chapter 2, or imagined your ideal job in the exercises in chapter 4. Used when you are in a receptive, meditative state, and on a repeated basis, visualization can transform your life into the kind of life you have imagined.

Visualization can be used to either create a new situation in your life (for example, a new career or job) or to change your past by imagining it with a different ending or result. All that is necessary is following these six simple steps to effective visualization:

A. Set your goal.   You have already done that earlier in this chapter.

B. Get into a meditative state, with your mind clear.   Your subconscious is most receptive when it is in a calm, meditative state, sometimes called an alpha state. Use one of the relaxation techniques you have learned when you began to meditate, such as focused breathing, a general body relaxation (such as the first part of the Symbol Meditation in chapter 2), a mantra, or similar method to relax your body and calm your mind. (Note, however, that visualization and meditation are NOT the same—visualization is an active process involving the creation of pictures in your mind; meditation is a passive process of quiet focus or being receptive to your Higher Self).

Once you are relaxed, imagine a TV or movie screen in your mind. Erase from it any images that were there, and be sure you see a clear, white screen before moving to the next step.

C. Create a clear picture of the situation you want to create or change. Now, pretend you are making a movie in your mind of what you wish to experience (or a past event you want to change). If you want a new job, take all of the parts of that job that you accessed in the previous chapter, and see yourself in a job with those aspects. What is the career area in which you are working? What geographical location? What does the office, store, or plant look—and feel—like? How do you spend each part of your day? How much money do you deal with? How much do you take home? What kind—and how many—people do you deal with? What specific activities are you participating in?

You get the idea. Make the picture as vivid as you can, seeing yourself actually doing the job that up to now has been just a dream.

D. Reinforce that picture with sounds, smells, tastes, and positive feelings. Now, before you leave the picture, add other sensory "cues" or aspects to it. Do you hear any particular sounds? Smell any smells? Taste any specific tastes? How do you feel? Build in as much positive, pleasurable feeling to your picture as you can. Experience the feeling of fulfillment, success, happiness, joy, and all the other positive feelings you associate with your ideal job.

This will involve *all* of your senses in your visualization and will multiply its impact on your subconscious.

E. Release your visualization to the Universe for action giving thanks that you already have what you have visualized. Once you have fully experienced this picture in your mind, with all of your senses, then let it go. You might imagine your screen being put into a balloon and rising off into the distance, or you might just see it fade away until you again feel aware of your body. This is important because of the principle that we must let go and participate in the flow of circulation (both of money and of ideas) in order to let in the natural flow. If we insist on holding on to how our job (or money or relationship or whatever) will come to us, it simply delays the manifestation of it. So let it go—and watch eagerly as it comes back to you in tangible form!

F. Repeat your visualization at least twice each day until you are experiencing what you have visualized. Finally, as with any type of reconditioning, your visualization must be repeated. Do the entire process at least once each day for 21 days or until you receive what you are seeking (whichever comes first). When you think of it during the day, even in casual moments, simply take a glimpse of the picture in your mind's eye and affirm that it is yours. Use your visualization and affirmations together for maximum results. And be sure you are using them for positive purposes, with no intent to harm anyone else. Let the highest good of all concerned be served by your use of your powerful mental tools. You will thereby not only be creating your own highest good, but raising the overall consciousness of all of us in the process.

6. The Energy of Emotion. Most of us have heard of positive thinking, and perhaps are even familiar with affirmations and visualization. And we also know of cases in which these techniques appear to work, and others in which they don't. Why don't they work all the time?

There are several possible reasons. One important one, however, is that the person using the technique has failed to involve his/her emotions in the mental work. You *must* bring your emotions to bear on the achievement of your goals if you are to attain them. If you only work with your mind, or only believe something in your mind and your heart believes the opposite, you will not achieve the results you desire.

How can you do this? One way is to associate a great deal of pleasure and excitement with your desired situation. As you do your affirmations and visualizations, focus on the feelings you are experiencing. If you don't feel excited, think of something that is exciting to you and transfer that same feeling into your voice, body gestures, and emotional state about your new job or whatever you are seeking. Tony Robbins' techniques for attaining personal power, which have helped many people achieve their goals, are based on this principle: Our subconscious will seek that which it associates with pleasure, and will flee from that which it associates with pain. Your task, therefore, is to be sure that you associate as much pleasure and other positive emotions as you can muster with your desired situation. Your subconscious will then work with you (instead of against you) to help you achieve it.

7. Role Modeling. We don't hear much about heroes today. But one of the ways you can accelerate your growth, especially if you are seeking a career change or other major shift in your experience, is by finding a "hero," or role model, to follow.

Begin by thinking of someone who has achieved what you are seeking to achieve. If you don't know anyone who has succeeded in the field you wish to enter, do some research, ask those in the industry, and find out who an appropriate role model would be. Then study that person: How did they get where they are today? What specific steps did they take? Did they have to develop certain qualities to achieve their success? What important lessons did they learn along the way?

Once you have chosen one or more role models to assist you with your career change, spend some time with the person(s) if possible. Find out what their typical day is like. Go through a day with them if you can. In other words, get as much insight into their world as you can.

Then take the next step: imagine yourself in their position. Not that you want to take their job, or assume their place in the industry—your place will be unique because you are unique. But this process will help your subconscious mind experience what it is like to be successful in that position and field so it can begin to effectively create similar success for you.

If this is difficult for you, try the following visualization technique. Imagine that the person is standing in front of you. They turn around and you notice that they have a zipper down their back. You unzip the zipper and step into their body. You then go through a day as them. Notice what it feels like, how they/you act, what they/you do, etc. This is a powerful way to clearly visualize the world through their eyes (and ears, etc.).

Finally, set your goals and subgoals to follow the precise steps that they have taken to achieve their success. In other words, use what has already been shown to work for them. You don't have to reinvent the wheel—or the computer! You may discover along the way that your path has some different twists and turns, and that your success is created in your own way. However, using the "tried and true" method is an excellent starting place to point you toward your own success. You can later modify that approach, if necessary and appropriate, to create your own brand of success. But begin by religiously following the steps your role model has taken, and you can create the same results they have.

8. Surround Yourself with Supportive People.   Few of us can accomplish our goals in a vacuum. We need people around us who will support and encourage us, whether it is a time to celebrate our progress or a time of challenge when we feel like abandoning the quest.

Master Mind Groups are one way to obtain this needed support. Based on the writings of Napoleon Hill, these groups can be as small as 2 people or as large as 20. They should not be so large that those participating cannot have their desired opportunity to share, however. These groups meet at regular intervals (often weekly, though that is decided by the group) to allow participants to share their goals and their progress toward those goals, to encourage each other, and to access the Master Mind consciousness that is present when two or more people gather with a common intention. This consciousness makes ideas and insight available through the combined energy that is often not accessible by an individual working alone.

Whether you choose to join or start a Master Mind Group or not, it is important to surround yourself with people who support you and who share your positive outlook on life. Otherwise, when you get discouraged you will find it easy to listen to the negative people in your life and give up on your goal before you achieve it. (We will talk more in a later chapter about how to deal with the "others" in your life if they don't support you—or even sabotage you—as you move forward to fulfill your life purpose.)

9. Persistence and Perseverance.   To achieve your goals, you will need to develop the qualities of persistence and perseverance. Why? Because until you become skilled at setting and achieving goals and changing your old programming, you will most likely not achieve your goal on the first attempt. You will need to keep your focus set on your goal, do repeated affirmations, visualizations, role modeling, and draw on the support of the positive people you have surrounded yourself with. You *will* achieve your goal—but you may also have opportunities to lose heart as you face challenges, disappointments, delays, and other perceived setbacks along the way.

Persistence has been the hallmark of nearly everyone who has achieved a level of success in their lives. For example, did you know that for every commercial role actors land, they have been turned down for 29 others? And even the best basketball players only make about 50 percent of their shots. The "overnight successes" in the music and entertainment industry often occur only after years of training and low-paying engagements. Persevering in the face of disappointment and even "evidence" that you can't or won't ever achieve your goals will pay off. You can achieve anything that your mind can conceive, if you put your emotions and beliefs behind it and persevere!

10. Loving Yourself and Reinforcing Your Progress.   Our final tool in achieving our goals is to recognize yourself for even small amounts of progress. If you are seeking a new job, and you get an interview scheduled, congratulations! You are moving in the right direction. If you are seeking to increase your income and you find a dollar on the street, congratulations! Your increased prosperity is beginning.

Remember to be patient with yourself. Change, especially if it is major change, does not occur overnight. Our mind and spirit can quickly imagine a new situation, but its manifestation in the physical plane takes time. We will explore some techniques to speed the process through using the Six Principles of Magnetizing in a later chapter. For now, be sure to recognize and celebrate yourself for each step you take toward your goal. As Socrates said when asked how to get to Mt. Olympus, "Make sure every step you take is in that direction."

Think about some special things you can do for yourself to celebrate your successes. They need not be expensive or extravagant —they might include such simple things as a bubble bath, a walk in the park, or buying yourself a new piece of jewelry or an ice cream cone. Take the time to celebrate the small things. This will reinforce them and enable them to multiply until, before you know it, you are celebrating the achievement of your goal . . . and you have moved to an even higher level of growth, armed with all the tools you need to succeed!

As you progress on the path toward your goal, you will encounter some challenges. They are not insurmountable, but they must be dealt with to accomplish the end you desire. Overcoming those perceived "problems" is covered in the next three chapters.

Action Steps from 9 to 5

Choose one or two of the goal-achievement techniques to use for the accomplishment of each of your goals. (For example, you might want to use affirmations and a daily visualization to create a new job.) Begin using them now! The techniques you choose could match your goal-setting style (so if you are a Type A, they could involve your intuition and right-brain skills, and vice versa for Type B's). Use these techniques as long as you feel you are progressing toward your goal, but use each one *at least* 21 days in a row before changing techniques. (This is sufficient time for your mind to get used to the new pattern and form a new one.)

Be sure to keep using one of these techniques until the date you have set for achieving your goal. If you have not reached your goal by that time, set a new goal and begin again. YOU CAN DO IT!

And don't forget to congratulate yourself for each step you take that is in the direction of your goal, no matter how small it seems. This will build a belief in your subconscious that you *can* succeed, and will propel you toward the achievement of your heart's desire.

PART THREE

Fear and Other Problems

7

Overcoming Fear

"True success is overcoming the fear of being unsuccessful."

—Paul Sweeney

SUSAN FELT PARALYZED. At any moment, the door would open and the company president would ask her to come in for her interview. Could she do it? Her hands were clammy, her mouth was dry, and she wondered what she would say first. She had waited for this moment for so long—and had invested years getting her M.B.A. and learning how to manage her department well. But vice president of operations? She had to sell herself well. And she was determined to overcome her fear of increased responsibility, managing the company instead of just one department, and dealing with the other male managers' remarks about her being a woman.

Have you ever been in a situation like Susan's—afraid to move ahead, but determined to do so anyway? If you have, do you remember how powerful you felt after completing the act you previously feared? That is the gift you can give yourself as you prepare to move forward to bring your life purpose into form in your career. You *can* move through the fears that have plagued you.

But perhaps there is a fear that you just can't seem to face. You wouldn't even get to the interview stage where Susan was. In fact, you wouldn't apply for the job at all. The feeling of fear is just too uncomfortable to experience (again). So you stay in your comfortable, familiar situation, going through your daily routine and avoiding any thoughts of change.

I find that fear is one of the key barriers that keeps people from moving forward in their lives and work. As wonderful as fulfillment at work sounds, they seem unable to move toward fulfillment because of various kinds of fear.

We will examine those fears in this chapter, as well as how to overcome them. Then, in the next chapter, we will look at other blocks, such as resistance, excuses, procrastination, and old programming, and how to move past them as well.

What is Fear?

Fear began in the human experience as a logical response to situations that held potential danger or threat. In the days of the cave men, fear of large animals and other "things that go bump in the night" was quite logical—in fact, those who didn't take intelligent action on the basis of those fears did not survive!

Today, there are still situations that warrant fear: fear of pain from a hot burner on the stove, or fear of pain or death when we are driving down the road and see a car or truck heading directly at us (in our lane). I call these Rational Fears.

But let's face it: aren't most of the fears we experience unwarranted and irrational? Take, for example, the woman who refuses to speak before a group as an adult because of an embarrassing experience in the fourth grade when she got up in front of the class to give an oral report and was unable to speak. Or the man who had always wanted to be an artist but is afraid to pursue classes in art or display his work because he once had a childhood drawing ridiculed by his classmates.

How long will we continue to let our childhood experiences prevent us from having a full, complete adulthood? Not only did these experiences happen many years ago, but our perception of them is nearly always distorted. Have you ever gotten together with your brothers and sisters and started discussing family vacations in your childhood? If so, no doubt you noticed how each of the siblings in the family remembers the vacation entirely differently, one focusing on the great fishing trip with Grandpa, and the other on the wonderful desserts that Grandma cooked.

Our perceptions and our thoughts make up our experiences, whether or not they are accurate. So if we change our perception, our experience changes, too. Fear is simply a learned, or conditioned, response to a situation. What has been learned can be unlearned.

I remember my first conscious experience of fear. It happened on the first day of school, when I was 6 years old, not wanting my mother to leave me there alone. It was a terrifying feeling! But I got through it, and school became my first love. Similar fears occurred each time I did something new for the first time: my first piano recital, my first report at school, the first day of junior high school, the first day of college, the first day of my first "real" (full-time) job. And I am here to tell about them!

Now I approach new situations with slightly less trepidation. But I know that I must go through them in order to grow. By applying the techniques we will discuss in this chapter, I have learned to move through fear, rather than letting it immobilize me. But before we discuss those techniques, let's examine what this thing we call fear really is.

"Fear is the opposite of love." There is a Bible passage which states that "perfect love casts out fear." That passage simply declares the universal principle that, just as light and dark cannot inhabit the same space, fear and love cannot reside together. Sanaya Roman states it in a different way when she says that "fear is a place that has not yet discovered love." Love and fear are opposites of each other. Does this give you one clue to overcoming fear? We will examine that clue in a moment.

"Fear is a false perception." A popular acronym calls fear "False Evidence Appearing Real." Fear is just an appearance but is not the truth of the situation. We must look beyond this appearance and our emotions, and instead see the truth about ourselves and the situation.

"Fear is a feeling that we 'can't handle it.' " No matter what the "it" is in this sentence, every fear boils down to a feeling of not being able to cope. If we are afraid of failure, we are actually afraid that if we fail we won't know what to do (that is, we can't handle it). If we fear rejection, we are afraid that we won't be able to cope if another person fails to accept us. To pierce through this misperception, it often helps to analyze the situation that we are reacting to with fear. The first Action Step at the end of this chapter will help you with that process.

"Fear is a cry for love and healing."   Since we know that fear and love are opposites, it stands to reason that any area in which we are experiencing fear is simply a cry for love. We want love to enter in and heal that belief or past experience so we can move forward with confidence. Instead of avoiding situations that evoke fear, we can use our fear as a message that a particular area is ready to be healed. Our fear then becomes a benchmark of our growth. That is, it shows that an area that had challenged us in the past is now ready to be raised to a higher level. Viewed in this way, fear can serve as the impetus for our growth, rather than as a barrier to it.

"Fear is our growing edge."   If you want to find your life's purpose or passion, look for what scares you the most, and excites you the most—simultaneously. Fear is not only an impetus for growth, but the bridge to it as well. You must go through it to experience the power of overcoming it. You can think of your fear as the star that lights your path and guides your way into your highest potential. Until you have the courage to move through it (rather than around it), you will not experience the higher awareness and fulfillment that lies on the other side.

Myths About Fear

Like many of the uncomfortable emotions we experience along our path, fear is one of those emotions that we wish would go away. I'm here to tell you that it won't. Let's look at some of the myths surrounding fear so that we can intelligently and realistically face it.

Myth No. 1: "Fear goes away as we mature."   If you are not experiencing fear in your life from time to time, you probably are not growing. I'm sorry to disappoint you if you think that mature people no longer experience fear. Fear is a natural part of life. It is our growing edge! So it follows that as long as we continue to grow and expand ourselves, we will experience fear from time to time. We may as well learn to love and appreciate it for what it is!

I have learned that trying to "get rid of" in our lives, or to "get out of the way" so we can do the next thing, is not usually an appropriate response to a situation. The people and situations we attract into our lives are perfectly designed to facilitate our growth in the areas we need it. Once we stop trying to "get rid of" this work task, or this job, or this mate, and begin to view the task, job, or mate as a gift to us from Life, sent to teach us something important—we are then free.

The same is true of our fears. Once we recognize them as the gifts they are, sent to free us from the restriction we have experienced in a particular area of our lives—then we can gladly walk through the fear into the next level of growth.

Myth No. 2: "Fear is a sign that we ought to stop moving in a particular direction." On the contrary: if you are feeling fearful about taking the next step, you are probably about to take a quantum leap in your growth. If you will move through the fear (instead of around it), you will find power and increased fulfillment on the other side of the experience. You will be guided as to which direction to go, but if your Higher Self is guiding you, it will not usually use fear as the guide. Rather, it will sound a resonant chord deep within you that you ought to change your direction. In short: your inner voice will not sound like fear, but will sound like love gently guiding you onto the right path. You will soon learn to tell the difference.

Myth No. 3: "Fear can always be explained." You will encounter situations where you feel fear but cannot explain it intellectually. It may be in a situation unlike anything you have previously experienced (so you can't blame your childhood). Or it may be exactly like many others you have experienced, but despite your analyzing it, it will not go away.

If your fear is based on a childhood experience, or from something you have heard or read but never experienced for yourself, it often has no basis in fact. It is simply an irrational response to a situation, which no amount of intellectualizing can overcome—until we hear the message behind the fear.

My best example of this is that to this day, whenever a nurse or doctor comes near me with a needle, I create a tremendous reaction of fear—clammy hands, cold skin, heart racing, lightheadedness, etc. I know precisely what childhood event triggered that response. And I know that shots don't really hurt that much, and that my biggest pain is the anticipation of the shot, rather than the shot itself. Yet I still generate this irrational response. The message? Fear does not always make intellectual sense. And it cannot be dealt with on an entirely intellectual level. For this reason, both the suggestions in this chapter and the Action Steps at the end of it for overcoming fear begin with an intellectual analysis process, but they don't stop there. They also encourage you to use techniques to change the *underlying belief* that is causing your fear, for often true transformation can only occur at a subconscious level.

I encourage you to simply accept that the feeling of fear is there and deal with it from that perspective. Whether or not your conscious mind is able to access the "reason" for it, you can still eliminate it. So don't always insist on intellectual analysis as the only answer!

The Fears That Bind Us

Now that we know some of the characteristics and origins of fear, and what fear is *not*, let's consider some of the specific types of fear that plague us along our career path—and how to overcome them. See how many of them you have experienced, or are currently facing in your job or career path.

Fear of the Unknown. All of us have some degree of apprehension about new situations. Whether it is the first day of school or the first day of a new job, our first date or our first baby, new situations are just that: new (that is, unfamiliar).

We have two alternatives in new situations: face them directly, or stay stuck in the old, familiar, secure patterns. If we choose to stay stuck, we will eventually become bored, and life will lose its zest and excitement. To continue to grow, we must face new situations and walk boldly into them. If we choose to think of them as adventures, rather than the Unknown, we can approach them with the excitement of a child. Our universe will expand and broaden, and at the same time we will expand and broaden as people.

Fear of Risking or Making a Mistake. Being afraid to risk holds many people back from doing what they want to do. Though sometimes this fear is sometimes perceived to be just another way to characterize the fear of the unknown, it is different. Fear of risk is fear of the act of moving ahead, rather than fear of the situation itself.

The way the game of life works is that we must step out—"risk," if you will—to move forward. There is no success without risk. And with risk comes the chance of getting some result other than what we have labeled success. If that happens, we simply try another approach until we get the result we want. The important thing is to take one step into the feared action. That one step will make the next step seem less risky, and soon you will achieve your goal.

Sometimes, what others see as risk does not seem that way to us. When I was preparing to start my own law practice two years ago, many people asked me: "Doesn't it feel like a big risk to go out on your own?" I had to answer that it didn't. In fact, I hadn't even thought about my new venture in terms of risk until others began to question me about it. Why? Because I was simply following my purpose, doing what I wanted to do—indeed, what I felt I *must* do. There was really no other choice for me. And I had confidence that all of the details would be taken care of, as they always have before.

Particularly in work decisions, it is important to take *calculated* risks, rather than long shots, to succeed. In a recent study of women entrepreneurs, most of them had worked in their field for an average of 12 years before starting their own businesses. They had become familiar with how businesses in their field operated, and had evaluated the risks of their particular business idea before opening their own store or plant. In short, it is a myth that entrepreneurs are the type who "play the odds." They take calculated risks (if they are successful) and know how they will deal with each potential outcome *before* it happens. The same principle applies in your career choice, and in overcoming your fears.

The situations in our life that pose risk are our current opportunities for growth. As we make risk our friend, rather than a stumbling block, we see our greatest Self come forth. Within each risk is the seed of your next great success. So move into it with joy and confidence!

Fear of Failure. Fear of failure is rampant in our society. We are trained from childhood to succeed, to excel, and to avoid "failure" at any cost. And we soon set our own definitions of failure and success, which we try daily to achieve.

What is failure, really? Isn't it in the eye of the beholder? In chapter 6, we examined the situation where a typist set a goal for reducing the number of errors in her work. She didn't quite achieve it the first week, but she did much better than she had in the past. Has she failed? Only if she defines it that way. Even if you step out and do something you have never done before and fall far short of the desired result, you have succeeded just because you have done it. And the result will follow shortly.

Anyone who succeeds (no matter what definition of success we use) must become close friends with "failure" as well. Did you know that Babe Ruth not only had the all-time record for home runs, but also the all-time record for strike-outs? Abraham Lincoln had a string of defeats and "failures" before becoming one of the most noteworthy Presidents we have had. There are countless similar examples. The point is, those who have achieved the greatest success, in the eyes of the masses, often have a companion record of the greatest number of "failures" that got them there.

I challenge you to set up your own definitions of success and failure so that it is easy for you to succeed and hard to fail. Perhaps your definition of success is equivalent to every day that you wake up in a warm, safe environment. That is an easy one to achieve and helps you enjoy the process of attaining your goals. But if your definition of success is a certain income level, a certain physical fitness level, two kids, a loving spouse, a $500,000 house, a certain kind of job, being loved by everyone, etc., etc.—it is hard for you to succeed! There is nothing wrong with having goals to obtain those things, but don't make them an intrinsic requirement before you can call yourself a success.

Likewise, don't define failure as falling even slightly short of the mark on a project, saying a critical remark to a friend, or any other relatively minor thing. If those are "failures" to you, you may spend hours beating yourself up over a minor event when you could be moving closer to your goals instead. If you make it easy to succeed and hard to fail, you will keep yourself motivated and will much more quickly experience the life you desire.

Fear of Success.   You may be surprised to see "fear of success" on this list. After all, don't we all want success? If we didn't, why would we work so hard to get it?

In reality, many of us do fear success. We fear the demands it may bring from others to continue to excel and achieve. As it is, we can go along, day after day, doing "as well as can be expected," and no one expects any more from us.

We fear that we may alienate our less successful friends if we achieve the level of success we want. And we fear success because it is new. Perhaps we have not succeeded in our career before. We don't know the rules of the game. Will we be able to cope? To "do it" well?

It is said that there are two causes of unhappiness: not getting what you want, and getting it. Have you ever wanted something so badly that you could taste it, but once you got it, you were disappointed because it wasn't as good or efficient or fun as you thought it would be? Many people have the same experience with success. If they have involved their whole identity on what they do, rather than who they are, no amount of success will satisfy them at a deep level. They achieve one goal—for example, they get the promotion they have been longing for—and they still feel empty. They then become afraid of even trying to move up the next step of the corporate ladder, for fear that that, too, will not be enough.

In fact, it won't. This Empty Success Syndrome can only be overcome by developing a healthy self-image, apart from your work. We must each recognize that we are valuable just because we are, not because of what we do. We do not have to earn our place on the planet—we already have it. So when will we begin to recognize it and enjoy it? Once we face our self-image and self-esteem issues, we can then move up the corporate ladder and appreciate our success, rather than fear it. The reason? It no longer defines our identity, but simply gives us a new role or set of rules by which to play the game of life. And we enjoy it all.

Fear of Poverty.   In our career, as well as in life, many of us fear poverty. The financial "experts" tell us that most of us are 60 to 90 days from bankruptcy. But those "experts" are not taking into account the law of provision of the Universe.

The fear of poverty is often based in a concept of God that withholds from us—"God helps those that help themselves." In fact, that passage appears nowhere in the Bible. What *does* appear is the powerful truth that just as God feeds the birds of the air and clothes the lilies of the field, God cares for the physical needs of each one of us.

Perhaps you were raised believing in a judgmental, withholding type of God. Do you realize that you can change your experience of that God by simply changing your perception? That is, although God is constant and unchanging, our perception of God does change. By changing our concept of God, and recognizing the supporting, providing nature of God, we will take a large step toward eliminating our fear of poverty.

Once we realize that the Universe supports us in all that we do, and that no matter what happens in our life we will be cared for, any former fear of poverty can be released. We no longer need to work 20-hour days in a desperate effort to overcome the relative poverty that we experienced as children. We can relax in the knowledge that we are always provided for, no matter what happens to the stock market or the economy or the business for which we work.

Fear of Ridicule. Is there anyone who hasn't experienced embarrassment and the ridicule of one's classmates when doing something foolish as a child? We often avoid taking a risk or stepping out into new territory for fear we will stumble and fall, or do something foolish for which others will ridicule us. Overcoming this fear requires, first and foremost, the development of a self-concept that values experimenting more than it heeds the occasional ridicule of others. Thomas Edison, the Wright Brothers, and many other people we now regard as famous faced ridicule from nearly everyone around them as they pursued their "crazy" inventions. If they had allowed that ridicule to stop them, we may not be reading by electric light and flying from coast to coast by airplane today.

We must learn to value ourselves enough to follow our own path, whether others agree or praise us for it or not. If you have made a decision to change jobs, you may have already dealt with this fear as you left. You reached a point where you realized you must follow your heart, your purpose, your inner guidance—regardless of what anyone else may say or think. Developing that ability to move forward on your own highest path leads to increased personal integrity. The wonderful side effect that also occurs is that you give others the courage to change as well, by setting an example. And the planet begins to be transformed, in a gradual but sure progression.

Fear of Growing Up. A final fear that many of us harbor, often unconsciously, is the fear of adult responsibility. We may have grown up in a strict environment or a lax one, but at some point developed a dislike for "responsibility." We like being catered to, having our own way, and not having to discipline ourselves.

Are you resisting the idea of moving forward in your career because the next step would require you to "grow up"? If so, think about your alternative. Being a child isn't so great after all. It leaves you limited to depending on others and deprives you of the wonderful freedom of carving your own destiny. You will never achieve your life goals (if you have set such goals) because you have never taken the time to develop a plan for their achievement and follow it through.

Isn't it about time you grew into the adult body you have been living in for the past several years? Adulthood is truly the most liberated state of humanness. "Responsibility" is nothing more than "response-ability"—the ability to respond appropriately and intelligently to the situations in your life. That's not so scary, is it? You will discover uncharted territories of personal power and freedom once you make the commitment to grow up, assume the control of your life, and move forward. So I encourage you to make the commitment, follow the suggestions in this book, and let your career grow into a source of fulfillment rather than drudgery.

What Can I Do About It?

Now that you understand what fear is and the types of fear that may plague you along your career path, how can you overcome it? I have given you some specific suggestions above as we discussed each type of fear. Following are some general ideas that can be used to move through any type of fear as it comes up in your life.

1. Analyze the situation.   This technique is particularly helpful with ongoing fears that seem somewhat irrational. It is an intellectual approach that dares to face your fear head-on and dissect it. It requires that you ask yourself these questions:

A. What is the worst that could happen? Could you handle these results?   If your worst fears came true, what would be the result? If that happened, what would you do? Would you be able to cope? Give yourself as many options as you can generate, brainstorm style.

After you have dealt with the worst scenario, go to the second worst. Could you deal with this situation if it happened? What would you do? Move through all possible results, hypothetically, and design some plans of action if these things occurred.

Now, consider the likelihood of the worst case actually happening. It really isn't very probable, is it? What about the second worst? Of the possible results, if the most likely happened, you *would* be able to cope, wouldn't you?

This process tends to defuse the fear. It is no longer an unknown: you know exactly what to expect and what you would do in the face of various possible outcomes.

B. What will I lose out on if I *don't* do this? How would I feel? Second, consider the price you are paying for your fear. If you don't move through the fear and do what you are afraid of, what will the result be?

Be fairly objective in the first part of this step. List specific things you will lose. For example, a fear of moving to a new town to accept a transfer (which is also a promotion within your company) may cause you to lose:

- added income;
- freedom;
- the adventure of getting acquainted with a new geographical area;
- the potential of new friends and colleagues;
- kids' continuity in their schools;
- added prestige;
- added responsibility and power within the company; and, perhaps most importantly,
- the ability to move up even further within the company (since not moving may be perceived as a lack of initiative and drive to succeed).

Then, consider how you will *feel* if you don't do this feared activity: powerless? stuck? helpless? This step will help you see, in tangible terms, the price you are paying for your fear. Is the price great enough to motivate you to move through it?

Remember, as you do this, that *there is no failure*. In dealing with fears of risk taking, making mistakes, and failure, we must realize that there is no such thing as failure. There are only experiences, events, and our interpretation of those experiences and events. It doesn't matter if someone else labels your experience a "failure" or not. Perhaps it was actually your greatest success, in your eyes, because you had the courage to do something you had never done before—and did it (even if you didn't win a world record)!

If you use the technique of analyzing the possible outcomes from an event, as well as how you will approach each one if/when it happens, then you cannot fail. If you don't get the result you were after, then change your approach or try another method until you *do* get the results you want. It is only by moving, however—by trying something—that you will learn the approach that works for you. Then, you have achieved success (regardless of what anyone else thinks).

C. What are the benefits to me if I do this? Our third step asks you to look at the other side of the scale: if you take the plunge and move forward through your fear, what will you gain? For example, our employee considering the transfer might gain the opposite of the losses he would suffer if he didn't accept the transfer:

- promotability
- freedom
- more money
- new friends, colleagues
- a new geographical environment
- added prestige
- growth for the entire family

Then you must weigh both sides of the scale, asking yourself how much you want those benefits? More than you want to avoid the consequences of not doing it? Which side of the scale weighs heavier? Am I willing to move ahead, despite my fear, to obtain the benefits it will bring to me?

2. Recognize that you DO control your thoughts and emotions, and you can change them. As powerful as fear may seem at times, it is just another of the emotions in your repertoire. You choose, at some level, to experience it. Your subconscious thinks it is serving you by creating this emotion within you. Can you determine what the message is that your subconscious seeks to give you through this fear reaction? Perhaps some sign of perceived danger has triggered the response. If you are not aware consciously of danger, it may be that you have reacted the same way so many times that your fear has now become a pattern. Whatever the origin, fear is a chosen, self-created response to a situation. It can be changed.

One woman had been taught by her mother to cut the end off the Christmas ham before cooking it. She continued to do so faithfully, each Christmas, until one year she asked her mother why that was necessary. Her mother didn't know. She said *her* mother had taught her that and she had just passed it along. When she later questioned her mother about the reason, her mother answered, "When I was cooking Christmas dinner, my pan was too small to hold a whole ham, so I always cut off the end so it would fit the pan!" Of course, the roasting pans used by her daughter and granddaughter were large enough to hold the whole ham—but they had been *conditioned* to go through this ritual, thereby wasting a perfectly good portion of the ham.

Your fears can become as conditioned as cutting off the end of the ham. Perhaps every time you see a needle, or an elevator, or a tall building, or a small space—or a new situation—you develop the symptoms of fear: racing heart, clammy hands, cold skin, and general panic. Next time you find yourself in the situation that evokes fear for you, try this: see if you can choose another response to the situation. You might use something outrageous, such as laughing uproariously, or shouting excitedly. This will interrupt your normal response—and may begin to develop a new pattern as well.

To prepare yourself to face the situation that formerly caused you fear, you may also wish to use the technique of visualization. In your mind's eye, visualize the situation, but with the outcome you desire. Let's say, for example, you are afraid of giving presentations at meetings in your job. So you visualize yourself standing before a department in your organization. Usually, you feel shaky, clammy, and nervous; you stumble over your words, speak softly, and can't wait to be finished.

This time, though, you imagine yourself feeling very confident. You might even stand the way you would if you felt confident. You see yourself giving the presentation in a lively manner, your ideas being well received, your voice easily carrying to the back of the room. And you are enjoying the process! What used to be a dreaded activity is now fun for you.

If you use a "mental movie" like this often, and particularly right before your next presentation, you will soon find that your presentations improve markedly and the old dread no longer occurs to you—you are too busy having fun!

3. "Just do it!"   I think this slogan, used by Nike in a recent advertising campaign, says it all. Whatever it is that you want to do, even if you face some fear about doing it, just do it (anyway). I know this is easier said than done, but it is the only way to grow and overcome your fears, once and for all. And I have had two excellent opportunities to do just that.

Example number 1:   When I had the opportunity presented to me to start my own business, in the midst of feeling very dissatisfied with my previous job, I had a decision to make. I could stay where I was, and continue to look for the "right" situation working for someone else—or I could take hold of this wonderful opportunity to own my own business, even though it was a little scary—I didn't know where the money would come from, didn't have any clients to take with me, etc. I did it—and I have never regretted it.

Example number 2:   I am right now in the throes of another opportunity to move through fear. My Higher Self has guided me very specifically, over the course of the past summer, to give up our home, my law practice, and the "security" of the place I have lived all of my life to go on the road with my husband doing seminars fulltime. When the idea first came to me, I felt great excitement and commitment. But then the fears came up. Am I ready yet? What if it doesn't work? Can we support ourselves this way? Maybe I should stay here for just a while longer . . . etc., etc. You know how the voices go. But we eventually decided to "just do it." It is an exciting leap of faith for us, but we are already seeing the pieces falling into place. And we believe that it will lead us into greater opportunities than we have ever experienced. You'll have to wait until my next book to hear how it went!

So whatever your fear is, I can tell you that there is power in looking straight at it, recognizing its presence, and going ahead anyway. And there are some tools you can use to motivate yourself to do the thing you fear, even if you haven't been able to face it before.

A. Divide it into manageable chunks. If you can't yet handle moving ahead with the whole activity, try dividing the feared act into smaller chunks. For example, if you fear changing careers, begin by doing some research into the field you wish to enter. Don't quit your job and interview with 20 different companies right away—just begin the process of exploration. Then, step by step, you can move into the processes of resume revision, interviewing, and ultimately moving into your new position. Many times the hardest part is the startingout process—but that gets the momentum building so that you then have the courage to move ahead with the next step, slowly but surely accomplishing what you want for yourself.

B. Summon the power of your Higher Self. If you are struggling to take even the first small step, it may be appropriate to simply recognize that as yourself—your little self—you are powerless. Yes, I believe we are each a manifestation of God. I am not suggesting false modesty here. However, the actions that we take— particularly in the demonstration of our life's purpose—will only have power as we bring God, or our Higher Self, into those activities. God always empowers us to do that which we are led and guided to do. We are never given a mission or a vision without the means—both internal and external—to accomplish it. So call upon the Higher Power that resides within you to assist you in moving forward. It will strengthen you to do that which of your own strength you could not do.

C. Be willing to choose growth over security. Finally, make a commitment to yourself (based on your analysis of the situation) that you are willing to make choices that accelerate your growth. State that willingness to yourself: "I am willing to do whatever is necessary for my growth." That willingness sends a powerful message to the Universe, and the Universe will respond by moving you into new areas, at a pace that is just right for you.

Security may seem a "safer" and better choice now. In the long run, however, the feeling of helplessness—as well as fear of perpetuating that state—is much stronger than your fear of growth. Choose to be the best that you can be, even if it means experiencing some temporarily unpleasant emotions.

D. Let your fear die from lack of attention. We know that our subconscious mind goes to work to create what we consistently focus on in our mind. Therefore, if you focus on the worst-case scenario (that is, what would/could happen if your fear was true), guess what you will create?

Instead of focusing on your fear, use one or more of these techniques to eliminate or diminish it. Then, if it comes up again, simply refuse to pay attention to it. I'm sure you have had people in your life along the way who you wished would go away, but every time you turned around, there they were. If you continued to ignore them every time you saw them, eventually they did go away, right? The same is true with your fear. If every time your fear presents itself, you will simply ignore it and immediately replace that picture with one of your desired outcomes (or with one of love), it will soon get tired of bothering you and go somewhere else!

4. Learn to love your fear. This last technique calls upon your feminine energy to deal with fears, even if they fail to respond to intellectual or analytical approaches. Since love and fear are opposites, learning to love your fear will necessarily cause it to disappear.

A. Realize that the Universe only brings good to you. Fear often arises from a belief that God wishes to punish you, or that there are forces for both good and evil in the Universe. In truth, there is only good, and the misuse of good. As the Bible puts it, "It is the Father's good pleasure to give you the keys to the kingdom." The Universe longs to pour out blessings upon you. You will only experience what you fear most when you focus your attention on it. You thereby cause it to materialize through the natural, spiritual law of attraction (more about that in chapter 10). So the first step to loving your fear is to develop a trust in the Universe, a deep belief that it is a good place to be and that only good will come to you.

B. Send light to your fear. One way to easily visualize love is by imagining it as light. Light is one of the most powerful forces in the Universe. Sending light to your fear is a way to visibly dissolve it through the force of love.

Sanaya Roman, in her book *Spiritual Growth*, tells the story of a woman who was afraid of elevators and heights. Though she tried to analyze the fear and "talk herself out of being afraid," nothing seemed to work. Then she tried the approach of loving her fear. She got on an elevator, feeling the panic, but sending love to her fearful feelings. She noticed that as she rose upward in the elevator, the feelings of panic began to subside. When she got to the top, she felt a rush of elation and expansiveness. I would guess that she never again experienced the panic in the same way again, and that each time she did this exercise, the feelings became less and less.

By analyzing our fears, recognizing that we do control our thoughts and emotions, moving into our fear by "just doing it,"and loving our fears, we will soon learn to use our fears as tools for growth. Situations will arise that used to evoke great fear, and we will experience the sense of power as we walk through the situation and can remain centered and fearless.

In addition to fear, we also often sabotage our progress by procrastinating, resisting our good, and making excuses. In the next chapter, we will learn how to use those experiences, too, as keys to creating fulfillment in our life and work.

Action Steps from 9 to 5

1. Is there one fear that is currently preventing you from moving forward in your career path? What is it? Write that fear at the top of a sheet of paper. Then, divide the paper into three columns. In the first column, write down all of the possible negative results that could occur if this fear were true. (For example, if you fear failure, some of the results might be embarrassment, loss of your job, etc.) In the second column, write down the counterbalancing benefits that you would receive from moving forward anyway, despite your fear—for example, you might succeed! Finally, in the third column, write down how you will feel if you don't do what you fear (that is, disappointed in yourself, stuck, etc.).

    Now that you have evaluated your fear and its possible consequences, what choice will you make: to move forward, or to stay stuck in your current familiar situation? The choice is up to you!

2. **Meditation for Healing Fear.**   If, despite analyzing your fear, you still seem unable to move forward, the following meditation will help.

    To begin, use the body relaxation technique in the Symbol Meditation in chapter 2. When you are relaxed, bring the emotion of your fear into your awareness. You may see a visual image come to mind. If so, notice what it is and ask it if it has a message for you. What is it here to share with you? If you wish, ask it any questions you may have.

    Now return to feeling awareness of the fear. Don't think about the situation that is causing the fear, but just the emotion itself. Do you notice that the fear is focused in a particular part of your body?

What part? Consciously send light to that body part and ask your Higher Self to heal that fear.

If your fear had a color, what would it be? Does that color have a message or meaning for you? What about its sound? Its smell or taste? What is it?

Now, allow yourself to fully feel and experience your fear, including its color, sound, smell, or taste. Then imagine its energy entering your body, running its course with full intensity, and now dissolving. You might imagine bubbles or a vapor rising from your body, carrying the fear away.

Now, to take the place of the fear, call to yourself as much love as you can imagine. Each fear has a positive emotion as its opposite. If another positive emotion comes to mind that will help replace this fear, call it to yourself, too. Bring these emotions in through your crown (the top of your head), and let them permeate your being. Pause for a moment and savor these feelings.

Finally, bring to mind the situation that used to cause you fear, and inject these positive feelings into that situation. Strongly associate the situation with love and whatever other positive emotions you called to yourself. From now on, when you think of that situation, you will feel loving, joyful, and peaceful, rather than fearful and afraid. Let your former fear die from lack of attention. Refuse to place your valuable energy on the fear. Instead, focus on love and the positive emotions in back of your fear.

Now, become aware of your body once more, taking the wonderfully positive feelings with you into the place where you are sitting right now. Thank your Higher Self for the healing that has taken place. You now move forward with joy and courage, taking the steps that you know will lead to your highest good.

8

Delaying Your Good

"If you must begin, then go all the way,
because if you begin and quit,
the unfinished business you have left behind
begins to haunt you all the time."

—Trungpa Rinpoche

TOO MANY OF US read self-help books, listen to the advice of friends or family, and know we "should" make changes for the better in our life—but we never seem to quite "get around to it." Until you move past the "should" to the "will" state of mind, you will not achieve your career goals or fulfill your life's purpose.

But how do you get through your resistance, stop procrastinating, eliminate your excuses, and move ahead? That is what we will examine in this chapter.

Resistance

Two Ways of Staying Stuck

There is a law of physics that says: "For every action, there is an equal and opposite reaction." Nowhere will you find that principle more apparent than when you decide to make a change in your life. Have you ever decided: "This is the day I will start a diet, and finally lose the weight I need to lose," and then encountered the coffeecake at work that someone just happened to bring, family members who want you to have "just one bite" of their favorite dish, an invitation to lunch at your favorite Italian restaurant, and other challenges, one after the other, all day?

Each time we make a decision to change a behavior or an attitude, we must be prepared for this law of physics to have its natural effect. Sometimes we attract other people into our lives to challenge or tempt us away from our new objective, and other times we find resistance within ourselves.

What do we mean by resistance? It can simply be defined as any force that enters in—either from internal thoughts or external situations or people—that exerts force in opposition to your chosen goal or action. Whatever its source, resistance gives us an opportunity to reinforce our commitment to our goal. So, if you choose, you can view it as a gift, rather than an opponent.

There are two types of resistance. The first, internal resistance, has its source within us. It is that intangible force that causes us to hold back, to refrain from doing what we know is in our best interest. If you find it hard to get up in the morning, or if you keep distracting yourself by doing meaningless errands or lingering at the coffeepot when you know you ought to be working on the report that is due tomorrow, then you are resisting.

External resistance, on the other hand, comes from the other people in our lives. This is the reaction you get from your spouse, family, or co-workers when you decide to improve yourself. They may try to drag you back into their comfort zone (which was formerly yours, too). They may accuse you of being selfish. Or they may sabotage your efforts, as did the husband who kept buying his overweight wife ice cream and rich desserts even though he knew she was trying desperately to stick to a weight-reducing diet.

The tragic result of resistance in our lives is that it deters us from achieving what we really want in life. In other words, it either postpones or eliminates altogether any hope we have of experiencing fulfillment. It is yet another way to run away from adult responsibility. When we succumb to it (for example, by listening to our friends' criticism instead of following through on our idea or goal), we have allowed resistance to become stronger than our will and determination to succeed. At best, it causes us to be late with projects or to give less than our best to our work. At worst, it causes that which is not working in our life to stubbornly remain. No one who is committed to achieving fulfillment in their work can afford the high cost of resigning him/herself to resistance.

Overcoming Internal Resistance

So here you are. You know you need to begin the research for the report you are scheduled to present to a key client next week. You have had the assignment for two weeks already, knowing this meeting was coming. But you can't seem to get started. What do you do?

1. Detached Observation through the Witness. First, of course, you must notice that you are resisting. You can use the Witness technique, which we first encountered in chapter 4, to do this. As you will recall, this technique encourages you to develop a neutral third person in every situation, which simply observes you acting and reacting but does not judge you. As you observe yourself and your pattern of resistance, you see it from a new, detached perspective. Very shortly, you will begin to see that the resistance is not serving you, and that there is a path through it.

Each experience we have in our life has a message for us, either obvious or hidden. Resistance is no exception. It often masks hidden issues that require special attention from us to discover. You might try asking yourself, "Why am I resisting this situation?" and see what answers your mind generates. Just asking the question will send your mind searching for the answer—and you may be surprised at what it finds!

One man noticed that whenever the time came to balance the books in his business at month's-end, he resisted doing that task. What was, at the start-up stage of his business, a source of joy for him was now drudgery. He began to observe himself from a detached perspective as the end of the month approached. He realized, through that process, that his resistance was not about the task itself. Rather, it was an attempt to avoid facing the fact that sales had been down. He felt very inadequate within himself because he could not determine the cause of the downturn in sales. So he resisted calculating his profit because it was painful for him to look squarely at what he viewed as a personal failure.

Through this process, he recognized the true problem— decreased sales—and began to take action to improve the situation. He knew that he had to take responsibility to increase sales if he was to keep his company in business. Once he did that, he was able to turn the company around so that it was once again profitable. As a result, he had a renewed joy in balancing the books in order to see his progress at the end of each month.

What about the case we referred to at the beginning of this section, where you seem unable to get started researching an important client presentation? Could it be that you have developed a dislike for this client, or disagree with the values served by its business, and therefore don't really want to make another sales presentation to them? Or perhaps you are secretly trying to "get back at" your boss, who values this client very highly but has been overcritical of your work lately. An easy thing to do would be to hold back your best work for this presentation, wouldn't it? Through using the Witness technique and your own powers of analysis, you can discover for yourself what the real reason behind your resistance is. Then you can deal with that underlying issue and overcome the problem.

2. Consulting Your Higher Self.   Your Higher Self knows exactly why you are resisting, even if you haven't yet discovered the reason. Often your resistance is the gateway to your next step of growth. That is, once you discover what the underlying issue *is*, you will realize that it is the area in which you next need to expand.

You can consult with your Higher Self (that is, the spiritual part of you) to obtain its insights into your resistance. One way to do this is to simply relax and get into a meditative state; then sit quietly and see what insights come to mind. Or, you may wish to visualize the situation you are resisting and remain open to the insights that come to you about it. Another way to consult your Higher Self is to imagine it as a wise being—visualize it in a temple of wisdom where all answers to life's questions are given, and simply approach this being in your mind's eye with your question or situation. It will speak to you, as you remain open, and reveal the issue you are to work on.

3. Taking One Small Step.   Once you have recognized the issue you have been using resistance to shield, you are ready for the next step: moving through it. Often if we will just take one small step toward our goal, the wheel of momentum begins turning, and we find it much easier to move to the next step. Knowing that your presentation deadline is fast approaching, you might read just one article on the subject of your presentation. Or you might summon the courage to discuss your boss's excessive criticism with him/her and enlist his/her help on the presentation to this client. Just one step is all that is necessary. The rest will then begin to follow naturally.

4. Supporting Yourself.   We often resist moving forward because we don't believe we deserve anything better. Therefore, another step in overcoming resistance is to begin to support ourselves. No, I'm not talking about financial support here. I'm referring to emotional support, the kind of support we give to our children as they learn and grow. How about being your own parent, and designing some nurturing into your life?

For example, instead of focusing on all the things you did wrong or badly today, why not take some time at the end of the day (or as often as you think of it) to list your accomplishments for that day? Maybe you gave a smile to someone that needed it. Or perhaps you received a compliment on your appearance or your work that day. Congratulate yourself!

Give yourself the treat of a few moments of fresh air, a walk in the park, a flower on your desk. Support yourself as you move forward, and not only will your resistance disappear, but you will find that others are supporting you, too.

Overcoming External Resistance.

What about the situations when resistance comes from other people, apparently outside of ourselves? How can we effectively deal with this external resistance so it does not deter us from achieving our goals and fulfilling our life's purpose?

1. The Mirror Effect.   Many times other people simply mirror back to us our own doubts or fears about our choice or decision. Although each of us appears to be a separate individual, we are in reality all connected at a deep level. We are all part of one Universe, one system. We each have the same experiences—with different characters in the script and different details—at various times of our lives. This enables us, for example, to empathize with others when they encounter a situation, whether tragedy or comedy, windfall or loss, happy or sad.

This connectedness has broad implications for our day-to-day experiences. If we are not yet sure about what we think we want to do, or have some fears about doing it, other people in our lives will sense our doubt or fear at some level and will reflect back to us that doubt or fear.

Stacy, for example, had just decided that she wanted to leave a job she had had for 10 years. She told her family about her decision, though she hadn't yet realized that she had some fear about giving up the security to which she had become accustomed. Several of her family members predictably said, "What about the progress you have made with ABC Co.? Aren't you afraid to leave that security?"

Now, Stacy could have gotten angry at these people for reacting the way they did. But that is not productive. That is like getting mad at the mirror because it reflects the few extra pounds around your midsection. Instead, she might view these reactions as important messages. Rather than immediately deciding she won't do what she intended to after all—that it would "rock the boat" too much in the face of these reactions—she could take a closer look. These reactions are simply a tool to reveal those doubts and fear to her that she was not previously aware of. They are issues to be considered and thought through before she takes action. They do not need to sound a death knell for her idea.

One way to minimize the magnitude of this kind of reaction when you decide to change is to first be very clear in your own mind about your decision. Think through your doubts and fears in advance—to the extent you are aware of them—before you relate your plans to others. Consider what the reactions of others in your life are likely to be, and how you will handle those reactions if they arise. Even if you still have doubts or fears, the feedback you now get from others will be mere questioning, rather than challenging, in tone.

When I decided to start my business in 1987 and make some

other major changes in my life at the same time (such as getting married), I didn't take the time to anticipate the reactions that my family and current employer might have to my decisions. I was excited about these changes, so I assumed that they would be, too. I encountered extreme resistance to my choices—and it was some time before the emotions cooled and the new changes were accepted!

I had a chance to see whether I had learned from that experience just this year, when I decided to follow my inner guidance, write this book, sell our house, and go on an extended seminar tour (with the possibility of permanently moving to another state in the process). Before I told anyone of my plans (other than my husband, of course), I thought back to the last incident, two years ago, and the reactions that had occurred. What would those same people, as well as the new people in my life who would be affected by this decision, think about my intended plans? How could I act more compassionately now than I had in the past? Once I thought through the likely reactions, as well as how I would deal with each one, I began sharing my plans with friends, family, and business colleagues, one by one. *Not one person had a negative, resistant reaction!* I felt I had learned an invaluable lesson, and this situation gave me a chance to demonstrate what I had learned.

You will find that as you follow your life's purpose, relying on the guidance of your Higher Self, you will encounter less and less resistance to your actions. Why? Because you will step forward more and more often in confidence and peace, sure about your direction. You will no longer need to attract doubt and fear into your experience.

2. The Downward Pull. Many times, even if you are clear about your direction and sure about your decision, others will react in an unsupportive way. They will attack you or ridicule you or otherwise try to dissuade you from following through with your intended action.

If you are facing this type of resistance, it is helpful to realize that these reactions may simply be their way of attempting to deal with their own attachments and fears. For example, your colleague may feel threatened by your decision to change jobs because she will then have to face her own dissatisfaction in working in that company. Or your spouse may feel threatened by your decision to go back to college to finish your degree because he is afraid he may lose your love, or won't be able to adapt to the necessary changes in your lifestyle that result from your decision.

These reactions, as well as that of the husband we met earlier who insisted on buying his wife fattening desserts when she was on a diet, are examples of attempts to control others to cope with our own fears. If, for example, this woman lost weight, she might become more attractive to other men, and this might threaten her husband. But can you also see that his self-esteem must be very low to believe she would leave him? Intrinsic in this behavior may be a belief that she is too good for him, or that he doesn't deserve her.

Each of these people feels comfortable with things as they are. The changes their spouse or colleague wishes to make will most likely interrupt the normal routine, and perhaps take them out of their comfort zone. This evokes—you guessed it—the fear that they can't handle it (which we examined in the last chapter). How do you, the person who wants to make a change, deal with this kind of resistance?

If you have recognized that these people are acting out of fear of their own loss or inability to cope, you can give or send them more love to dissolve their fear. Most likely you have anticipated their reactions. If so, you have thought through ways to handle them, such as explaining how your decision will benefit all of you in the long run, reiterating your commitment to the relationship and your simultaneous need to continue growing personally, or whatever you sense the person needs to be reassured of as you explain your plans.

At a subconscious level, you can do a powerful visualization exercise before telling them about your plans. Simply relax and get into a meditative state, and imagine the scene as you wish it to be. You tell him/her about your plans, and they support you 100 percent. Then, before leaving the scene in your mind, imagine a beam of light (representing love) radiating from your heart to theirs, filling them with love and acceptance of themselves and you. You will notice that, if you do this before you actually give voice to your plans, your spouse, colleague, mother, or whomever will not react as severely as they may have without it.

As you carry out your plans, keep sending these people extra love. Continue to reaffirm your commitment to your relationship with them, and let them know that you still love them. Reassure them that you value their support, and soon they will begin to support you as they see your growth.

You can use the entire situation as an opportunity to expand your compassion for the other person. You recognize their fear and let them know you respect their feelings, while at the same time being firm about your commitment to your purpose and about moving forward toward your goal. When you can begin to follow your highest path with love, but without attachment to the approval of others, you will find yourself expanding to entirely new levels of fulfillment and awareness.

I am assuming now that your relationship with this person (or people) is basically healthy, rather than codependent or addictive. If you have done all of the appropriate energy work and talked to them lovingly, but nevertheless they continue to lash out and attack you, consider distancing yourself from them, as is explained in the next section.

Another way to transform your perspective on resistance is to look at the resistance you attract as a gift. The people who resist your decision are just doing their job. They are *supposed* to do what they are doing. Why? To develop your ability to be compassionate and to clearly state your viewpoint, as well as to strengthen your commitment to your path. If you are truly committed to do what you have stated, the resistance from others will fortify your commitment to your goal.

My husband and I had an opportunity to experience this phenomenon when we first began dating. My parents tried every trick in the book to alienate us from each other, since their expectations of the type of man who was "right" for me was quite different from my own. The ultimate result was a strengthening of the commitment my husband and I had to each other, and we married several months later.

3. Consider Distancing If Necessary. If, despite all of your best efforts, you still find your friend or colleague or family member attacking you, consider distancing yourself from them for a period of time. That is, simply refuse to be around them for a while. This technique is particularly appropriate if you can recognize—or later discover—that there are unhealthy or abusive aspects to your relationship. It may take a few days, weeks, or even months before they can be with you without attacking. Or your desire for change may even lead to ending the relationship. Distancing will enable you to determine whether or not the relationship can continue after you have carried out your decision.

It may help to realize that the reason behind these vicious attacks is that these people are secretly upset with themselves for not improving in the area you are moving in. They think, "If I can't have it (whatever it is—new car, new job, thinner body), then she can't either, and I'm going to make sure she doesn't!" You must then make a very difficult choice between your own path of growth, and the easier (but far less satisfying) path of compliance with the expectations of others. Please don't sell yourself short—you deserve to be the best you can be, even if it means some distance between yourself and your loved ones for a while.

4. Keep Your Focus on Your Inner Guidance. The first thing I recommend that you do if you encounter resistance to your decision from other people is to go within. That is, check in with your Higher Self, and be sure that your stated intent is, in fact, the best way for you to go. If you have decided, for example, that you need to change jobs, and your best friend cautions you about giving up your prestige, salary, and responsibility, check in with your Higher Self to determine the basis for this feedback. Is your friend reflecting your uncertainty? Or is your friend acting out of her own self-interest and fear of loss of your love? Of equal importance, do you think you ought to continue with your plans to find a new job?

If at each stage you check in to determine the meaning of the resistance you are encountering, you will sense whether to continue that path of action or change your approach. Sometimes, the resistance comes to us simply to guide us to the best possible outcome, as with the couple who wished to open a small gourmet shop and the negotiations on the space they wanted fell through unexpectedly. They then checked in with their inner guidance and still felt they had to pursue their dream. Later, they were guided to a much better space, with much better potential for growth of their business, but in a part of town they may not have considered if the other negotiations had been concluded.

5. Learn to Center Yourself.   Another way to handle the resistance from others in your life is to learn a technique of "centering" yourself. That is, you can do an overall relaxation technique, recite a word or phrase, or think of an image while breathing slowly, that will bring you back to a balanced place where you feel peaceful. If you have been practicing meditation, as recommended in some of the previous chapters, you know what it feels like to be centered. Your meditation techniques, in shortened form, will serve this purpose.

Once you learn a technique that works for you, use it! If you get into a situation that sets you off balance (like a critical or condemning remark from a well-meaning—or not so well-meaning—friend), withdraw from the situation as soon as you can and center yourself. Soon, you will be able to come back to center without having to physically withdraw, by just going inside yourself in the midst of the conversation. That will take some practice, however, so at first I recommend physical withdrawal so that you can learn, very clearly, the feeling you are seeking to maintain.

If you are facing resistance as you begin to move toward your goals, I encourage you to keep your eye on your prize, to keep yourself motivated to take that next step, and to ignore the distractions as much as possible (while at the same time learning the lessons and hearing the messages that they have to bring). If you take a strong stance and are progressing toward your goals and fulfilling your purpose, you have already accomplished more than many people do in their entire lifetime.

What You Resist, Persists

There is another important reason why we must take the initiative to deal with resistance in ourselves: the phenomenon that what we resist, persists. My husband graphically illustrates this principle. He has a strong dislike for blueberry pie. Whenever he orders berry pie, even if the waitress tells him it is something other than blueberry, it is often blueberry anyway. Why? Because he has such a strong resistance for blueberry pie that he attracts it to him.

Let's take a work-related example. If what you state as your desire is a new job, but you are actually resisting (quite strongly!) the overbearing boss in your current job...the result? The energy you are putting into resisting your overbearing boss is *stronger* than the energy you are placing on your desire for a new job—and you simply create more of the old situation. You may find that the old situation actually gets worse, instead of seeing any progress on the creation of a new job.

Resistance is a powerful magnetic force, drawing to it *more* of whatever it is attached to. So if you are resisting a situation in which you feel victimized, you will tend to attract more victimizing situations, until you can release the resistance and transfer your energy to a more positive object or state.

If you say to a child, "Don't play in the street," what is the one thing the child is sure to do? It is as though he does not hear the word "don't," but just "play in the street." Likewise, if you say to the Universe, "Don't give me more work to do," the Universe may very well respond by giving you more work. It only hears: "Give me more work to do." That is why we must state our affirmations and prayer/treatments in positive statements, rather than focusing on what we don't want. "Don't" is a form of resistance that simply attracts more of its opposite.

Tony Robbins expresses this principle very accurately when he says that the two reasons we do anything are to avoid pain or experience pleasure. If the desire to avoid any pain in what we say we want is stronger than the desire to experience the pleasure of it, we will not create it. For example, if you associate more pain (such as fear of not being able to cope, fear of a new situation, self-doubt, etc.) with a new job than pleasure (challenge, more money, new friends, advancement, etc.), you will not attract that new job until you tip the scales in the other direction. That is, you must change your focus to the pleasure *and* eliminate the associated pain (using the techniques outlined in this book) to create what you want.

Overcoming resistance requires frequent self-examination, and our willingness to deal with the underlying beliefs that are causing you to resist. Then, you can use this principle of attraction in a more positive way (as we will explore in a later chapter).

Procrastination

Is It Really Procrastination—Or Inner Guidance?

Procrastination, or putting things off that could be done now, is another way we sometimes delay our good—postponing our fulfillment until some never-quite-reached future time. Though some procrastination includes internal resistance, it is more than that.

Answer these questions to see what kind (if any) type of procrastinator you are.

1. In school did you always put your term papers off until the night before?
2. Do you put off the completion of other important tasks until the very last minute?
3. Do you always have excuses as to why things aren't done exactly on time?

If so, you are probably a Habitual Procrastinator.

On the other hand:

1. Are you usually well prepared?
2. Do you usually do things in advance?

3. Are you usually on time, or sometimes even early, for appointments?

4. Occasionally, do you find yourself putting something off for no apparent reason?

If so, you can be referred to as an Occasional Procrastinator.

These two types of procrastinators' habits come from different root causes—and have different solutions.

Habitual Procrastination: Causes and Cures

Think back for a moment. Have you always been a procrastinator, or did you develop this habit at a particular point in your life? Often procrastinators discover that they developed the habit as a way to cope with a painful situation—usually one in which they failed to measure up to someone's expectations, or made a significant error in judgment.

Two fears commonly underlie procrastination: the fear of doing the task wrong or badly, and the fear of not meeting your own previous standard of performance. If you believe you have "failed" once, by not doing a project the way it was supposed to be done, you may stop yourself from even beginning another one for fear you will recreate that experience.

1. Moving Through Fear of Failure. We know by now that there is no such thing as failure—unless you label it so. Failure is just an interpretation of an event that has occurred. Yes, sometimes we may do a task in such a way that our supervisor or client is less than impressed with our efforts. But that does *not* mean, as we may tell ourselves, that we can "never do anything right," or that we are a "failure." It simply means we have an opportunity to learn something. (If nothing else, we can learn how *not* to do it next time!) And next time *will* be different. Give yourself permission to do a less-than-perfect job—and plunge in anyway!

2. The Curse of Perfectionism. But suppose the opposite is true: we have done an outstanding job on something, such as solving a particular problem, in the past, and now are expected to apply our skills to another problem. We may be afraid to begin a new project out of fear that we will not be able to generate as outstanding a result as last time. In other words, we face a fear that we can't equal or exceed our own past performance.

When we face this perfectionistic side of ourselves, we must remember that none of us does an outstanding job on every task. We all have "off" days. Our task is to continue to observe ourselves without judgment, to perform each task with complete focus and loving attention, and not let ourselves be limited or bound by our past. It may assist you to make a list of the benefits of insisting on everything being perfect, as well as the detriment, or cost to you, of such thinking. The standards you set for yourself could be guidelines, flexible enough to adapt to particular situations—not inflexible mandates that cause you to "freeze up" in each new circumstance.

3. Project Management 101. Project management—the organization and management of a project to keep everyone on task and ensure that deadlines are met—has recently become a discipline in itself. And I am about to give you a couple of simple project management tips that will help you overcome your procrastination.

First, when you have a large project to tackle, it will continue to overwhelm you until you break it into smaller pieces. Take a look at the whole project, and see where it can naturally be separated into phases or functions. For example, if you are expected to prepare a report on the current state of the art on your company's chief product, you may divide the project into these phases: research of the company's product history; research into competitors' products' history; research into recent scientific developments; consolidation of research into a rough draft; preparation of the final report; and presentation of the final report.

You can then outline each phase of the project, by listing the tasks related to each phase, and break each task down as far as necessary to give your project direction. Once you see the "blueprint" for your project ahead of you, you will be able to take each step in order without being overwhelmed by the magnitude of the entire task. Then, simply take the first step and progress from there!

4. Developing Discipline and Other Skills. Habitual procrastination may also originate from a lack of self-discipline or problem-solving skills, or low tolerance for concentration. If you suffer from a lack in one of these qualities, you *can* learn to change. Instead of declining to start because you know you can't finish, how about deciding to spend 10 minutes working on some aspect of the task you are putting off. Just 10 minutes each hour or each day, depending on the time frame you are working within, can make the difference between making progress and staying stuck. (You may also want to refer to the time management suggestions in chapter 12.)

5. Learn to Judge Time Accurately. Procrastinators often judge time inaccurately. They either set unrealistic deadlines for a task, or allow too much time and end up trying to do everything at the last minute. You may wish to keep track of how you spend your time each day by keeping a detailed log for a week or two. Once you realize how long certain activities actually take, you can plan your time so that you no longer need to procrastinate and cram at the last minute.

6. Using Your Natural Energy Cycle to Achieve. You will find that there is a time during the day when you feel more energetic and motivated than another time. Perhaps in the morning you are ready to tackle the world. If so, you might do your most challenging tasks then. If, on the other hand, you don't wake up to your highest energy until mid-morning or after lunch, plan your schedule accordingly.

7. Clearing Out the Distractions. Be sure your work environment is designed to be free of distractions, especially during the time when you plan to concentrate on the Big Project. Close the door, if you work in a an office, or go to a quiet place in the library or wherever your favorite place is to concentrate. Have your phone calls held or unplug the phone; hang out a "do not disturb" sign; or do whatever else will assist you in concentrating, and decrease the likelihood that you will be deterred by a distraction.

8. A Concentration Contest. If you seem to lose your concentration easily, start a contest for yourself. Today, spend 10 minutes on the project. Then tomorrow, make it 12 minutes. And increase the time you spend, slowly but consistently, just as someone in physical training might do to build a muscle. Your muscle of task completion will be developed in no time! And be sure to reward yourself after you have successfully focused for your allotted period of time. Go for a walk, have a refreshing cold drink, or just allow yourself a few moments to stare out the window. This will encourage you to continue making progress in the area that has challenged you.

9. Asking Appropriate Questions. Are you putting off doing the task because you don't know how to do it? We must all be willing to ask for help from time to time. We must also learn to take the initiative to find the information we need. The first step is to determine what you do and do not know, and then to decide the best source to obtain the information you need.

10. Are You Ready for a Change? Another cause of habitual procrastination, especially if it has just begun in the recent past, is deep dissatisfaction at work. If you find yourself procrastinating on nearly everything you are required to do at work, and dreading each day's activities, I recommend that you go back to chapter 3 of this book to determine whether a change of job or career is in order! Procrastinating because you don't enjoy the task to be done—whatever it is—on a frequent basis, is a strong indicator of the need for change.

Occasional Procrastination: Inner Guidance Disguised

Occasional procrastination by the person who is usually punctual often contains an important message that must be ferreted out. Julie was such a person. Although she was known as dependable and nearly always finished projects early, she noticed that she was putting off a planned meeting with a prospective supplier of components for the products her company manufactured. She had planned to call the supplier several times to schedule a meeting but never seemed to quite get around to it. Then one day, she received notification that the supplier had gone out of business and was being sued for selling dangerously defective parts to several other local manufacturers.

In this case, Julie's procrastination had a message for her. It was her inner guidance leading her to put off scheduling the meeting until all of the facts were known. And it probably saved her company a substantial sum of money as well.

Once you have begun to listen to your inner voice, you will occasionally find that although you have deadlines to meet on tasks or projects, you just can't seem to get started on them. Many times, it will turn out that the project was not needed after all, the customer changed his mind, or that you would otherwise have wasted your time and effort in carrying out the planned task. While it may look, from the outside, as if you are procrastinating, in fact, you are following the guidance of your inner voice in each activity and are operating at the higher level of energy, spirit, and cause, rather than solely at the physical level of effect.

How can you tell the difference between this type of procrastination and self-defeating behavior? Notice when you start to do the project whether you feel more like you are pushing against the current, or flowing with it. If, even after you have been working at the task for a while, you feel as though you are forcing yourself to do it, try leaving it alone for a while and switching to another activity. If you later feel an inner urge to return to it, then do so. If not, you may find that your Inner Self is trying to lead you in a higher direction. You will learn to distinguish between the two situations as you work with this principle consistently.

If you have been a procrastinator in the past, I encourage you to discover the joys of meeting deadlines, of being on time, and of having a sense of control and mastery in your life. Procrastination can only detract from your productivity and effectiveness at work—unless it is the occasional type that stems from the guidance of your Higher Self. As you explore the issues that lie beneath procrastination and learn to stop delaying your good, you will experience more and more satisfaction in your work—right now.

Excuses

Diane wanted to get out of the assembly job she had held for the past 12 years and do something that challenged her intellectually—perhaps in the field of accounting. However, she didn't have a college degree in accounting, and she had been told that no one could get a job in that field without one. So she continued working at the same routine, day after day, hoping that someday she would be able to do something else.

James was entering the job market for the first time, having recently completed high school. By applying his positive approach and speaking and reasoning abilities, he had won first place in the high school debating competition. His teachers encouraged him to pursue a career in the field of corporate training, conducting motivational sessions for employees. In fact, there was an opening at a local high-tech firm. But James decided that he was too young for such a job. Why would anyone pay attention to a 19-year-old telling them how to stay motivated and be more productive?

Diane and James have stifled themselves and their opportunity to experience fulfillment in their work by using excuses. Excuses are offered as justifications or explanations for not pursuing our own highest good, or for not discovering and following our life's purpose. Each of us has one dominant excuse that we use to justify our not moving ahead with our purpose (even if it is something as mundane as losing 20 pounds or waiting until we move somewhere else). That excuse must be faced and either eliminated or set aside before you can begin to fulfill your life's purpose.

Which of the following excuses have you allowed to hold you back?

"I'm too old." This one is usually followed by what you feel you are too old to do—change jobs, go back to school, learn something new, etc. It is said that you are only as old as you feel—and this excuse will make you feel older! If you have reached a point in your life where you no longer reach out to make new friends, no longer seek to learn new things, and resist any form of change in your life, watch out! Nothing will cause you to age more quickly than to stagnate in this way. And nothing will keep you young more effectively than a positive attitude and constant learning and growth.

As our societal values change, so does the distribution of people within the population. The median age in the population is expected to be close to 40 by the year 2000. The impact of this shift is already being seen throughout society. McDonald's and other progressive corporations have instituted special programs designed to recruit the older worker into the workplace. College students are no longer just the 18- to 22-year-olds, but include students of all ages. If there is something you have always wanted to do, now is the time! Don't decide you can't do it because you are too old.

"I'm too young." James allowed this excuse to keep him from applying for a job that could have been very fulfilling for him. Many first-time workers are afraid that their lack of experience will be a stumbling block to their getting the job they want. But it need not be. They also have a fresh outlook on life that is refreshing to many employers. And they almost always have some experience, even if it is unpaid volunteer work, that demonstrates their natural ability and commitment. They can use these factors to present themselves favorably to an employer.

The consumer, customer, and employer of the '90s is far more concerned with results than with age or appearance. The emphasis now is on quality, service, and excellence. If you can produce the results desired, can be a team player in the company, and have confidence in yourself and your ability to excel, you *can* achieve what you want. Steven Jobs refused to allow his youth to hold him back from achieving great success in the computer field. Tony Robbins has accomplished tremendous success at the ripe young age of 29, presenting his motivational seminars regularly to Ph.D's and corporate CEO's. Olympic athletes, actors, and countless others have overcome this excuse by choosing to pursue their own goals regardless of their age—and their accomplishments have been remarkable.

"I don't have any experience in that field." Are you committed to fulfilling your life's purpose? Are you truly willing to do *whatever* is necessary to have what you want (without harming anyone else)? If you are, there is a way to do what you want—whether you currently have any experience doing it or not. All of us started out with no experience. By building on each of the jobs and events in our lives, we have accumulated the experience we now have.

There are several steps to getting started if you want to get into a new career field without prior experience in that area. First, be sure you understand what is involved in the job you wish to have. What skills are necessary? What is a typical day like? Then examine your past job history to see what skills, education, and experience you have that can be translated to the new job. Chances are you already have some of the necessary skills from other jobs you have done. You can highlight these skills and other qualifications as you talk to people in their field seeking that right opportunity.

After you have done this research, begin to do some networking interviews with people in the field you wish to enter. Find out as much as you can about their company and the field in general. The added benefit to you of going through this process is that you will begin to be known by people in the field, and the people you talk to may well lead you into just the opportunity you are seeking.

If you cannot find a position with the precise job description you are seeking, look for a job that is one or two levels below it where you can at least develop some experience in your chosen field. If, for example, you want a job as a paralegal, and no jobs of this type appear to be available, perhaps you can begin as a file clerk, legal secretary, or messenger within a law firm to get some experience within the legal field that can lead to a paralegal position.

There *is* a way to make the change you desire. Beginning with that belief, and applying your ingenuity and the insight of your

Higher Self, you will attain your objective, with or without experience.

"I don't have a college degree in that field."   Many jobs in this information age appear to require a college degree. As a practical matter, however, many employers will accept equivalent experience or transferable skills in lieu of a college degree for certain jobs.

One woman found out how true this can be when she decided to leave the legal field and get into the field of television production. She had no experience in TV production, nor a degree, both of which appeared to be required. However, she was able to obtain on-the-job training behind the camera as payment for the legal services she provided to the station. One year later, she produced an award-winning television show—and without a college degree and the 10 years' experience that were, according to all of the "experts," an absolute requirement!

"I will (change jobs or go back to school or whatever you want to do) when the children are grown."   If you have chosen to have children as well as a career, you may be tempted to use your children as an excuse for not moving forward with your own life. I am not suggesting that every woman must work to be fulfilled, or that every woman must have a college degree. Nor do I mean to imply that women are not supposed to stay home with their children as long as they feel it is appropriate.

If, however, your children are school age, and you know they are independent enough not to need you at home full time anymore, can you really justify postponing your own growth for another 10 to 15 years? You may need to attend night school, work at a part-time job, or start a business in your home, to accommodate the needs and schedules of your children. Or you may create any number of other creative alternatives that will allow you to accomplish your dream. The important thing is not to let your children become an excuse for not pursuing your goals, if the real reason lies within yourself.

"I am confused, and don't yet know my life's purpose."
Often, we insist on knowing all of the details of the situation we are moving into before we are willing to take a step into it. Part of our growth process is learning to trust—to trust the Universe, to trust that only good things come into our lives, and to trust ourselves. As we recognize and follow our inner guidance, we will be called upon to simply have faith, even before we know all of the details—to trust that our Higher Self knows all.

When you feel confused, you can either use this feeling as an excuse to stop your progress, or you can ask yourself, "Do I know any part of what I am to do next? Perhaps even a shadow of the right activity?" Act on what you know—and the rest will fall into place, as you follow your inner guidance.

A Proven Way to Overcome Excuses

Once you recognize that you are allowing an excuse to hold you back but can't see a strategy for moving past it, I have a powerful tool for you. Simply ask yourself this question: "If I did know how to do this (ignoring the excuses), how would I do it?" We know now that just asking the question will begin the process of mental searching for the answer. "If this excuse were no obstacle, what would I do next?" Your brain knows the answer—it just awaits your questioning to reveal it to you.

If you accept the answers that come to you at face value, looking for solutions instead of more problems or limitations, you will soon have a strategy that will take you far beyond your excuses and into the Land of Possibilities. Once you have visited this exciting land, you will not want to return to the limited world in which you formerly allowed yourself to live.

Now you have learned the true origins of resistance: procrastination and excuses. And you are now beginning to transform the behavior that had been delaying your good into a powerful tool for self-discovery, enabling you to forge ahead on your path. One other obstacle remains to be overcome on your path to fulfillment: the need to "make a living" and deal effectively with money in your life.

To handle those money issues once and for all, please turn to the next chapter.

Action Steps from 9 to 5

1. Think about a task or a change in your life that you have been resisting. Is there something you know you need to do, but you keep sabotaging your efforts to begin? Are you ready to discover the reason for your resistance and begin making progress? The following steps will help.

   A. Observe yourself from a detached, nonjudgmental, third-person perspective. Notice how your resistance is affecting your life and what the underlying reason for it may be.

   B. Consult your Higher Self for its insight.

   C. To start the momentum going, take one small step toward the activity you have been resisting.

   D. Support yourself as you progress.

2. Have you begun to make a change, but are now encountering resistance from other people in your life? The following principles will help you deal with that resistance:

   A. The other people in your life are simply reflecting your doubts and fears. Look at them carefully, decide how you will deal with them, and continue on.

   B. Realize that other people may become uncomfortable when you threaten their comfort zone. As a result, they will try to drag you back into that familiar place. Look at their resistance as a gift, designed to strengthen your commitment to your goal.

   C. If the attacks continue, consider distancing yourself from the person(s) for a period of time to give them (and you) time to adjust to the new situation.

D. Remain focused on your inner guidance at each stage. Check in whenever you encounter resistance to be sure you are still following your highest path.

E. Learn to center yourself, first by withdrawing and later by centering in the midst of resistance.

3. Do you regularly put things off that need to be done? Are you always cramming to prepare for things at the last minute? Here are some tips to help you overcome Habitual Procrastination:

A. Ask yourself if you are using procrastination to mask a fear, such as fear of failure or fear that you will not meet previous standards. Or, is it that you just lack self-discipline or the ability to concentrate?

B. Spend a few minutes each day on your postponed task; increase the time you spend on the task each day.

C. Keep a log and learn to judge time accurately.

D. Discover your own natural body rhythm, and do your most challenging tasks when you feel the most energetic.

E. Remove distractions from your work environment.

F. Reward yourself for each step taken toward your goal.

G. Be willing to ask questions if you are uncertain how to proceed.

H. If you are usually punctual, but find yourself procrastinating on a particular task, go within and see whether your Higher Self has a message for you to do the task a different way or to just let it go. What appears to be "procrastination" may be inner guidance in disguise.

4. Are you holding back your progress toward making needed changes by using one or more of the excuses discussed in this chapter (or others)? If so, you can do an exercise, either in your journal or on a piece of paper, to defuse your excuse.

A. State the change you would like to make (for example, changing jobs).

B. Beneath that, state what your excuse is (that is, I can't change jobs because I'm too old).

C. On the left side of the paper, list the benefits or "payoffs" to you of using that excuse (for example, it allows me to avoid making changes that are frightening; I don't have to think about my unhappiness because my excuse gives me a reason for it).

D. On the right side, list what you are losing out on by using your excuse (for example, fulfillment, more money, challenge).

E. Then, complete this sentence: "Now I can see that what is really holding me back is_____" (fear, for example).

F. If you are ready to overcome your excuse, finish the exercise by writing and saying to yourself the following statement: "I am now ready to look beyond my excuses that had previously held me back, and to even move through the underlying (fear), so that I can make the changes that will help me be the best I can be. I deserve the best, and I choose to have the best in my life right now."

9

The Dollar Sign

"Finding and creating your life's work will bring you more abundance than any other single action you can take."

—Sanaya Roman

No OTHER ISSUE arouses stronger emotions, opinions, and power struggles than money. Most of us want more than we have. In fact, our "ideal income" is nearly always about 10 percent above what we currently earn. (For those of you who do not desire more money, there is a special section for you at the end of this chapter.) We investigate "get rich quick" schemes, various investments, and spiritual principles such as tithing. And yet we observe poverty, lack, and struggle all around us.

What is this thing called money? What is its proper place in our lives? And how can we get to the point where, instead of just "making a living," we can design our lives for abundance?

What Money Is

Money, of itself, is a neutral substance. It is a symbol used to represent value. We use it as a medium of exchange. We exchange it for food, clothing, and other items and services.

Money is also a symbol for energy. We set the price of an item according to the amount of energy it represents. Henry David Thoreau put it this way: "The cost of a thing is the amount of what I call life which is required to be exchanged for it, immediately or in the long run."

Unfortunately, we often make the mistake of trying to possess money, to hoard "our share." We forget that it is a symbol, that we are just caretakers of it. Instead, we seek it for its own sake—instead of for the energy it represents. We begin to love money and fail to heed the Biblical admonition that the love of money is the root of all evil. Some of us even use money to measure the status of a job, event, or person—or the level of their own personal satisfaction.

Once we realize that money symbolizes energy, we approach it differently. Rather than hoarding it, we realize that it must be used and circulated. It is not a thing or a possession, but an expression of the connectedness of each of us to the other. It can in fact be used as a spiritual tool for the transformation of our world. Its effect depends entirely on how we make it and how we use it.

Where Money Comes From

Do you want a new job because you believe it will give you more money? If that is the *only* reason you wish to change jobs, you will very likely be disappointed—no matter how wonderful your new opportunity sounds. If you believe your job is the source of your income, you will always be disappointed. There will never be enough.

"But," you say, "you just said a moment ago that the cost of things is measured by the amount of energy expended for them. If I am not being paid a salary that represents the energy I invest in my work, why shouldn't I change jobs?"

Perhaps you ought to. But first, examine the reason you aren't receiving an adequate salary. Do you believe in a God (or a world) that withholds money from you? Do you believe you must work hard to earn even a small pittance? Or do you not love yourself enough to believe you deserve the best?

On the one hand, money is a measure of energy or life exchanged for it. Changing jobs may result in more money coming to you. But if you don't change your underlying beliefs about money, your financial situation will not change significantly. You will either create more bills to pay—thus closing the gap between your current income level and your new salary—or you may sabotage yourself, lose the job, and end up back where you started.

Are you ready to move beyond the consciousness of survival, of just "getting by," and into abundance? If so, let's examine some of the beliefs that may be limiting your supply of the good things in life, and transform them into a powerful belief system of abundance. Then, once beliefs of abundance have replaced your beliefs in lack, your outer experience will change as well.

Money Misconceptions

"There's never enough money."   Do you have a basic belief that lack is the natural state of things? If you have lived much of your life in survival, never having quite enough to go around, you may have subconsciously adopted this belief.

The truth is that abundance is the nature of the Universe. All we need do is look to nature to illustrate this principle. The stars in the sky, the grains of sand on the beach, the limitless beauty all around us—all illustrate that there is an infinite supply of everything. And that includes money.

The question we must ask ourselves is this: Are we willing to accept *more than enough* money into our lives? If we have lived from paycheck to paycheck all of our adult lives, it will take a mental adjustment to become comfortable with more than what is needed to meet our monthly expenses. Action Step 2 and the later section in this chapter about conditioning yourself for abundance will assist you in making that adjustment.

"Time is money."   Whatever you do for your livelihood, one of the key resources you have to give (as well as to use) is your time. If a new product will save us time, the salesperson tells us that "time is money"—and that if we buy their product, we will save not only time but money as well. Some of us bill our time on an hourly basis. For us, any time occupied by distractions is money lost. If we can do two things at once, we have saved time—and therefore money. Or so it seems.

But there is a more basic issue behind this statement. Do we measure time by quantity only, or by quality as well? The quality of our lives is established one moment at a time. If we devote our entire attention to saving time, believing it will ultimately enhance our wealth, what do we do to the quality of each moment? We often lose our focus and are unable to stay centered in the now. We are too busy thinking about what we will do next and, as a result, focus almost entirely on the future.

What if, instead of measuring success by the level of efficiency in our lives, we assessed success by how much we enjoy each moment? While time does bear some relationship to money, fulfillment and abundance will elude us if we are continually seeking to "save" time, but fail to enjoy the moments we have.

"It is more spiritual to be poor."　Some of us are afraid that if we attain wealth, we will be less "spiritual." We may have a belief that if we are spiritual, we cannot also be wealthy. Or perhaps we are afraid that we will change our values in the process of accumulating wealth, so that spiritual things are no longer important. Let's examine each of these ideas in turn.

Those who believe that being spiritual cannot include wealth often cite the Biblical passage that it is more difficult for a camel to get through the eye of a needle than for a rich man to enter into heaven. This passage does *not* mean that rich men (or women) cannot get into heaven. Rather, it refers to the unwillingness of the rich man in the parable to give up everything he had for the sake of his spiritual quest. If we remain attached to the material things we have, they will become an obstacle to our spiritual growth. The spiritual person can have possessions and money, while simultaneously knowing that if he lost it all tomorrow, it would not make a difference in his level of happiness.

If you are parents, don't you want your children to have the richest, most abundant life possible? So, too, with the Universe.

Since God has created all of the abundance in the world, doesn't it stand to reason that God also intended for us to partake of the abundance in every respect, including money? One of the challenges we each face in the New Age is to learn to integrate spiritual principles into the earthly plane. Learning to handle money with pure intent is part of that task. Remember, money of itself is not evil—only the attachment to (or love of) it.

As to the second fear—that being wealthy will change us— we always have a choice as to whether or not to change. Haven't you known wealthy people who are the most down-to-earth, loving individuals you have met? Wealth need not change people. Many of us worry about such things as being taken advantage of, the added taxpaying responsibility that results from wealth, or what people may think of us if we become wealthy—all long before we have begun to accumulate any level of affluence! Part of our growth is to let today's challenges be sufficient for today, and know that we can deal with tomorrow when it comes.

"Money is power."   Do you aspire to obtain wealth because of the influence you would have over others? Or the power you would have in your own life to buy what you want? We refer to our "buying power" and say that "money talks." But is it really the money that brings the power? Or is it something else?

At one level—the level of economics—money does embody a certain type of power. She who has the most money can buy the most goods and services. But power, in its truest sense, does not come from money—or anything else outside of ourselves. At the end of life, he who has the most toys may not win—despite the sentiment on the popular bumper sticker. Rather, he who has fulfilled his life's purpose and has the deepest sense of awareness wins in the truest sense. Which kind of power do you want?

If you want money solely as a means to obtain power over others, you are certain to lose any wealth you may ultimately attain. Why? Because we always, ultimately, reap the result of what we have sown by our actions. If we have accumulated money ruthlessly to gain power, someone with more power will arise to take it from us.

For lasting wealth, we must act from clear, pure motivation, with the highest good of all in mind.

"Money is like water—it slips through your fingers."   Some of us believe that even if we made more money, we could not keep it—it would just slip through our fingers. Yet we must acknowledge that there are many wealthy people in our world. So there must be a key to attracting money into our lives so that it will stay. We will examine 10 of these keys later in this chapter.

Money, like any other substance, must be magnetized to us in order to "stick." We have learned that money simply represents energy. As we work at an energy level to attract money, while also conditioning ourselves to receive it and eliminating any contrary beliefs, we will soon find that money stays with us and begins to accumulate. These principles of manifesting are discussed later in this book.

"Making a lot of money would require me to do things I don't think are right."   There are people who make money through unethical practices, of course. But there are far more who accumulate wealth through providing a product or service that has served or benefited others, or through perfectly legitimate investments. Money's impact depends entirely on our use of it, and what we give in exchange for it. If we want wealth, we can have it—without compromising our values.

"The best things in life are free—so why seek money anyway?" As we explore these money misconceptions, I am encouraging you to balance your ideas about money. Money does not have to be sought for its own sake—but it ought to be enjoyed and used to enhance our lives. Granted, many of the wonderful aspects of our lives on earth do not cost money: the love of our family, peace of mind, etc. But having money in our life, and using it wisely, can allow us to live in a more abundant, enjoyable fashion. Money can be a tool for investing in our future as well as meeting our present needs. And why not use it to live abundantly?

"Money is a good servant, but a lousy boss." When money is sought as the end, rather than the means, to a desired aim, it can begin to rule you. You become willing to do whatever is necessary to accumulate money—even if it harms others or is illegal.

Money is designed to serve you, to be used as a tool to obtain abundance in the form that best serves you and others. What is important here is to keep it in perspective—to ensure that your priorities are in proper order so that your life and work are in balance and harmony.

"My job is my source of money." Many people erroneously believe that their monetary supply comes from their paycheck. Your money comes from the Universal Source—God—not from your job. Your job is just one of many channels *through* which money comes to you. Once you understand this important principle, you can release your attachment to receiving a certain amount of money from your job. You are then free to receive from many directions, and to make a job change—if and when it is appropriate—for loftier reasons than simply increasing your income.

Once you have realized that God is your source, you must then be careful not to fashion God as your Divine Parent and endow Him/Her with the same ideas and practices about money that your parents had. If your parents doled out money to you very sparingly, and only gave it to you when you were "good," you may have a tendency to think God does the same thing. In truth, it is the pleasure of the Universe to give you that which you desire. Recognize when you are modeling God after your earthly parents, and release those images for one of a loving, giving God who delights in providing for you.

"Money doesn't grow on trees." This cliche has given rise to the idea that making money must be hard work, and that money is in short supply. In fact, it is a remnant of the Old World thinking that no longer serves us. When we are following our life's purpose, we find that money comes to us easily and abundantly. And we need not sacrifice and labor and slave to "earn" it.

"**Money is security.**" If you believe money is security, then you will feel insecure when you don't have enough of it. You will endlessly strive for more money, hoping that once you have attained the next increment of money, you will finally feel secure. When you do achieve a level of abundance, you will then live in constant fear that you may lose it.

Security is not found in money. Security is an inside job. We must learn to feel secure in our Self, regardless of outer circumstances. Then it does not matter whether we have money or not: We will always be secure and at peace.

By recognizing and examining our beliefs about money, we have taken the first step toward creating abundance in our lives. Next, we begin to apply 10 important principles to attract money to us and create the wealth we desire.

Ten Principles for Attracting Money

1. Discover and follow your life's purpose. By discovering and following your life's purpose in your work—and thereby doing what you love—you will attract greater wealth than ever before. As the recent book by Marsha Sinetar puts it, when you do what you love, the money will follow.

Countless interviews in the media with wealthy individuals reveal one common thread: These people love what they do for a living. One author, Srully Blotnick, became fascinated with how wealthy people create their wealth. His 20-year research study of a large cross-section of middle-class workers showed that those in his sampling who had achieved wealth did so in two stages. In stage one, these workers made their major investment in themselves (rather than in traditional investments), by becoming completely absorbed in their work. They did not necessarily follow a traditional career path, but followed their inner urgings and shifted their approach, as and when appropriate. After years of relatively modest earnings, they accumulated wealth and then reached stage two, in which they made more traditional investments.

Only 8 percent of those studied attained wealth, following these two stages. The other 92 percent—those who failed to achieve wealth—fell short primarily because, according to Blotnick, they pursued stage two investments and "get rich quick" schemes first, hoping to save up enough money to eventually do what they loved.

Are you still working at a job you dislike, simply because it pays well, you can save a little bit, and you might be able to do what you enjoy someday? If so, beware—you may be heading down the path of the 92 percent that never achieved wealth. As you follow your life's purpose, you will attract wealth at higher levels than you ever could by working day after day at a job you dislike, trying to save as much as you can for a "greater later."

You will also discover that wealth does not necessarily come from working one's way up the corporate ladder. Instead, you will be led to follow your inner voice, on a path that may lead you to move from one company to another in rapid succession, or to stay for a period of years in one company. We must be willing to shed our old ideas about how wealth is generated, and let our Higher Self show us new, creative ways that work for us in the New Age.

You may find that your increased abundance does not come immediately upon discovering and beginning to follow your life's purpose. But it will come. Recognizing the natural cycles of money (discussed below) will enable you to progress through each cycle in turn, knowing you are on the path that leads to growth and abundance.

2. Focus your energy. Many people in my seminars, when asked what they do for a living, name at least two things. "I am a data processor *and* I have my own flower-arranging business"; "I work part-time for my husband *and*, the rest of the time, I pursue my passion—photography."

The problem with this dual focus is the Dilution Effect. If you compare the intensity of the amount of light contained in a room with that same amount of light concentrated in a laser beam, the difference is phenomenal. The laser is so concentrated that it now replaces the scalpel in some types of surgery. As you focus your energy on one thing, that kind of intensity can result in your life.

Your impact on the world will multiply, as will your ability to attract money, if you choose *one* activity or livelihood to focus on, and pursue it with all of your heart.

I, too, used to fit the dual focus pattern. During high school, in addition to my schoolwork, I also worked at a retail store part time *and* was very active in my church and several school choirs, not to mention the time involved in private piano lessons! During college, I studied voice *and* also worked part-time as a legal secretary the last three years, in addition to a heavy academic load. Most recently I have been practicing law *and* doing writing, seminars, and consulting, to varying degrees, since passing the bar exam four years ago.

Now, for the first time in my life, I am focused on one thing: assisting people in discovering their life's purpose and enjoying their work. I recently learned the reason why I had always felt it necessary to be doing two things: I was taught to "always have something to fall back on." And by always having two avenues of income, it appeared that I would never be in the position of being without money.

The problem was, I continually diluted my energy. Although I made reasonable sums of money from both my law practice and my consulting business, neither one of them seemed to grow and thrive the way I knew they could. My law practice was my "Plan B" if the consulting business failed, and vice versa. But there is a principle in the Universe that says "If you have a Plan B—just in case Divine Guidance doesn't work—you will probably get a chance to use it!" Once I got rid of my "Plan B" and was willing to rely entirely on my inner guidance, no matter what, I experienced tremendous surges of money, clients, opportunities, and energy. And I attribute it to the power of focus.

The Universe abhors a vacuum. So if the one activity on which you choose to focus does not work out as planned, the Universe will assist you in filling it with a new endeavor. There is no need to fear that failure will be the result of focus. We can trust that only good comes to us. There is every reason to expect levels of abundance unsurpassed in your previous experience—once you focus your energy.

3. Cultivate and maintain a consciousness of abundance. Wealth begins with a belief that there is plenty of everything for all of us. As we observe nature—the stars, the sand, the animals and plants—it is apparent that abundance exists in the Universe. But we must take a step beyond simple observation: We must believe that abundance exists *for us*, and that we can experience it if we choose to do so.

Have you had an opportunity to be around wealthy people? (I hope so, if wealth is one of your goals. One way to know you are very close to creating something for yourself is if you begin attracting people who have already achieved what you want! And you know the value of role modeling from chapter 4.) Wealthy people share one common characteristic: a sort of ease of movement, a comfort in dealing with money and things in the world that many of us lack. This is the embodiment of an abundance consciousness.

This abundance consciousness, once developed, will reflect in everything we say, do, and think. Once we realize that abundance exists and can be ours, we expect it at every turn. Rather than "knowing" that there won't be enough money to pay the bills, we rest in the assurance that there is always more than enough. No matter what the appearance, as we hold to that conviction, we will see it manifest in our lives.

How do you talk about money? Do you expect money to come to you in unexpected ways? If there is something you want to do or buy and the money does not appear to be available, are you convinced enough of the Universal abundance that you can state your belief: "I know that it is the desire (which, incidentally, means "of God") of my heart to go to this trade show, and that the plane fare and other expenses are easily taken care of now." As you do so, you set in motion the forces necessary to fulfill your desire. There is great power in your word!

I challenge you to notice your conversation about money over the next week or so. Are there areas in which you can talk about money with more of a sense of expectancy, from a clear conviction of the abundance that is yours? As you do so, you will in turn attract more wealth to you through the Law of Attraction (more about that in a later chapter).

4. Maintain an attitude of gratitude. One way to cultivate an abundance consciousness—and also to attract more money—is to develop an attitude of gratitude. That is, to find something in every situation for which to be thankful.

Do you already have such an attitude? Before you answer, consider how you respond to a compliment. Do you genuinely thank the person for the compliment, or do you change the subject or negate the compliment. That is, if someone says something to you such as: "that coat looks nice on you," do you respond with something like: "what, this old thing"? Beginning in an area as simple as acknowledging compliments graciously can start the process of developing an attitude of gratitude.

This principle is broader than positive thinking or being polite. It means that in *every* situation, you must learn to be grateful. Until you consciously apply yourself to do this, you may not realize how negative and ungrateful you had previously been. And don't just do this during times of abundance! The phases of apparent lack in your life are exactly the times when using this principle is most critical.

One teacher recommends an exercise to assist you in developing this vital attitude. For 21 days, you are not to allow yourself to voice any complaint—about anything. Instead, your response to any situation must be, "God, that's great!" If, during the 21 days, you slip and do complain, you then start over for another 21 days until you are successful. This simple (but not necessarily easy!) exercise can transform your outlook on life.

Another tool that can help you be thankful in every situation, no matter if you label it good or bad, is to say to yourself, in the midst of your situation: "This too is God, this too is for good, and I demand a blessing from it right now." So if you were just fired from your job, or were criticized for the work you did on your last report, or your boss (whom you thoroughly enjoyed working with) was just transferred to another state—say this simple statement to yourself. By using this declaration, you acknowledge to yourself that there *is* only good in your world, and you open yourself to receive the blessing that is on its way from this apparently "negative" situation.

5. Recognize the many forms of wealth. As we develop our consciousness of abundance and our attitude of gratitude, we will begin to appreciate wealth in many forms besides money. Simply discovering and fulfilling our life's purpose creates wealth in the form of personal fulfillment. The love of our family and the companionship of our friends is another form of wealth. We may begin to measure our accomplishments not by what we have done or how much money we have made, but by how content and full of the joy of life we are.

You have a valuable net worth, whether or not it reflects in your bank account and investments. What do I mean? I am referring to your knowledge, skills, abilities, and experiences. Every time you provide a service or product to someone, you are exchanging your life energy for the money you will receive. If you have incurred a debt to finish college and either obtain a degree or learn a trade, or have borrowed money to start a business, you still have a valuable net worth. The investment you have made in your future is simply waiting to be translated into monetary terms as you begin to earn money in the field of your choice. So I encourage you to widen your perspective on wealth—you have more than you thought!

6. Bless your bills. That's right, I said to *bless* your bills. Too often, we curse them—and wonder why we try to make money when we just have to pay bills with it. Have you ever thought about the fact that our bills represent the trust that our creditors have placed in us? It would be entirely possible to do business on a 100 percent cash basis, where you couldn't buy anything unless you paid for it upon delivery. But to facilitate trade and commerce, we are often allowed to take an item or receive a service and pay for it later, when we receive a bill. Viewed in this way, our bills are a tremendous gift to us, not a burden.

If you find yourself in debt, whatever the apparent reason, it is important that you not condemn yourself. Debt, too, can be a measure of people's trust in you. I believe excessive debt can reflect a lack of trust in the Universe. Do you ever use credit cards to pay for something because you aren't sure whether you will have money to cover it in time? If so, you are missing out on many opportunities for the Universe to provide for you. The Universe always acts in the perfect time—although its timing is sometimes different from the way we have planned it to be! So as you expand your trust in the Universe and its ability to provide for you, you will need to incur debt less and less.

Your debt may also represent situations or people in your past that you have not yet forgiven. Look into your past and see if there are people you need to forgive. If there are, begin doing so. You may wish to engage in direct conversation with them, or you may simply work on yourself. The real work most likely needs to be done on you, anyway, so another way to do your forgiveness work is to go into a basement or isolated bedroom, sit on a chair, and face an empty chair. Imagine the person you need to forgive is sitting in the empty chair, and begin to express all of the feelings you would like to tell them. Vent it all! You will notice your anger, resentment, and bitterness begin to melt away in this process. As the strong emotions dissolve and you can forgive the people who have 'wronged"you in the past, your debt will dissolve as well.

7. Understand and use the laws of manifesting. Just as there are physical laws concerning money management, there are also spiritual laws of manifesting it. By understanding these principles and using them as you seek to draw abundance to you, you will attract it more quickly, and it will satisfy you more.

The first of these principles is to seek the *essence* of what money can bring you, rather than insisting on a particular amount or that it come through a particular channel. What is it that you think more money will bring to you? Freedom? Peace of mind? Power? Success? Is there anything you can do right now to begin to create that quality in your life? Once you have done that, then begin to ask the Universe for the essence of the object you desire, rather than the object itself.

One woman had an annual need for several thousand dollars to finance her children's private school. Every year for several years, the money had been provided to her right at the time it was needed. One year, however, she became concerned because the deadline for paying tuition was fast approaching, and she did not yet have the money. It was then suggested to her that she ask for the essence of what she wanted—that is, having the tuition paid for—rather than asking for the money with which to pay for it. She did just that and was soon offered a job teaching at the school, a fringe benefit of which was that her children could attend there at no charge. So she received the essence of what she wanted—her children's tuition payment—but not the actual cash.

Second, work at an energy level, not just at the level of effects. As you use exercises such as those at the end of chapter 10 to attract what you want, you will discover that there is more involved in attracting abundance into your life than just the mechanical steps of getting a raise, saving money, and managing your investments well. There is a very real energy in money, and you can attract it to you by working at the level of energy.

Finally, realize that there is a natural time lag between the birth of your desire and when it manifests on the physical plane. Things rarely manifest instantly on the earth plane. Usually, some waiting is involved. So be patient with the manifestation process, and keep your eye on your desire during the period of dormancy while your desire blossoms into a beautiful flower.

8. Give some away.   Our final three principles for attracting money are three basic premises of financial management that are also spiritual principles. The first of these principles is the recommendation that you give away some portion of what you earn. Tithing, as it is sometimes known, is a practice whereby the first 10 percent of your income is given back to the source of your spiritual nourishment. Many people believe tithing is designed for the sole benefit of the churches to whom tithes are paid. In fact, nothing could be further from the truth. (And remember, I am not a minister, so I have no vested interest in making that statement!)

The principle of tithing is designed to benefit *you*, the giver, in at least two ways. First, it helps you develop your abundance consciousness. How? Because if you give a portion of everything you receive away, it gives your subconscious the message that there is plenty—enough so that you can give some away. Second, tithing has a tremendous side benefit: you receive back in multiples of what you have given. If you give $10, you will receive back at least $100. It may not come all at once or all from one source, but you will see at least a tenfold return. Wealthy people often attribute their wealth in large part to some form of tithing, or giving away a share of their earnings.

You may not be comfortable with the 10 percent figure, or even with the concept of tithing. If not, think of tithing as giving a percentage of your income away to a worthy cause. It might be to a church, to a fund or society whose work inspires you, to a speaker you've heard, or to facilitate the work of an organization or cause that has assisted you or in whose work you believe. Start with 5 percent, or 2 percent, if that is more comfortable for you. Once you see how it works, you will want to increase your percentage!

There are those who say suggest that if you are self-employed, you might calculate your tithe on your profits, rather than on your gross receipts. I believe that whether you are on a salary or self-employed, your tithe (or the percentage you give away) ought to be a percentage of the *gross* you receive (that is, before your payroll deductions if you are on salary, and before expenses if you are self-employed). It is easier to calculate, and it gives you the opportunity to experience the greater circulation of 10 or more times your gross, rather than your net. (This is not to suggest that you ought to give just to receive, but multiple return is a natural by-product of giving, so why not open yourself to the highest possible level of good?)

9. Live on 70 percent of what you earn. The second of our three money management principles is to live on 70 percent of what you earn. What do you do with the other 30 percent? The first 10 percent we have discussed: you give it away. The second 10 percent% could be used for payment of debts. This will ensure that you are making continuing progress toward reducing your outstanding indebtedness (assuming you don't incur more each month than you are paying out)!

The third 10 percent, then, could be put into a savings account or invested to build up a capital reserve. Did you know that only 3 out of every 100 people in America have any degree of "financial security"—savings, investments, and means of generating money other than Social Security—by the time they reach age 65. And even among the higher income professions (law, medicine, etc.), only 5 out of 100 do not have to depend on Social Security at age 65. Most people simply postpone starting a savings plan and focus on their day-to-day needs and immediate pleasures, hoping that "someday" things will change. The time to begin is now!

One of the dilemmas I faced as I began to learn the principles of handling money was this: How can I justify saving up a "reserve" when one of the things I want to learn right now is the ability to trust the Universe for supply? I came to three conclusions. First, learning to trust the Universe does not mean that we must always be in lack or in need. As we accept our abundance, we will have greater opportunities to trust it, either for greater sums of money or for new ways to use it. This got rid of my closet belief that I had to have next to nothing in order to learn to trust.

Second, I learned that a savings account is one way to reaffirm the fact that we have more than we need, as well as to multiply the abundance of others as the bank or other institution uses our money to draw interest. It can also be used as a magnet to draw more to us, and to help us get comfortable handling larger and larger amounts of money.

Third, I learned that money must have something to do. If we have a "wish list" of things we will do when our abundance manifests, it speeds the process. One of the most creative suggestions I have read for using this principle in the context of savings was given by Bob Mandel in his book, *Two Hearts Are Better Than One*. He suggests that just having one savings account for "emergencies" sends a message to the Universe that it had better send us an emergency so we can put that money into circulation. We don't need to create those situations! So he suggests having several savings accounts, each with a specific purpose. When he and his wife discovered this principle, they opened a travel account, a cash flow account, a financial independence account, a large purchase account, and an investment account. This gave the money several things to do, and also gave the Universe several channels through which to funnel its abundance to them.

What do you want to do with your wealth? What are your financial goals? If you get that raise in your job, what will you give that additional money to do? You may wish to prove this idea of multiple savings accounts for yourself. But at a minimum, begin to be a wise steward of your monetary supply by setting at least 10 percent aside for capital reserve accumulation. And make a list of what you want to use the money for. Then you will be one of the 3 or 5 out of 100 who reaches their retirement age in abundance, rather than lack (not to mention experiencing abundance along the way as well)!

10. Establish a consistent giving and receiving cycle.   Giving and receiving are equally important in creating wealth; neither is more "holy" or less selfish than the other. Until we learn to be a gracious receiver, all of the giving in the world will not create the level of abundance we are destined to experience.

The Universe mirrors back to us exactly what we believe, think, and do. "As you give, so shall you receive," as the Bible puts it. So if we are consistently late in giving money away or paying bills, we will receive late as well. If we pay our bills early, and include a little bit extra above our minimum payments, we will receive early and with enhanced abundance.

One way to practice receiving is to decide you will graciously receive everything that you are offered during the next month, regardless of whether it is something you think you can use. If you can't use it, you have an opportunity to pass it along to someone else and practice giving. You will notice a wonderful flow beginning to occur.

Just as there is an ebb and flow to the tides in the ocean, there are similar cycles with money. We can learn to stay centered and confident regardless of which cycle our current money situation is in. When we are in the ebb, or deficit, times, our challenge is to continue giving, to understand the message behind the experience, and to work at the level of cause to increase our openness to abundance. During the flow times, when there is more than enough, we may need to consciously keep our expenses down to a certain level to ensure that they do not always increase to meet or exceed the incoming flow.

Sometimes we encounter a "flat" period, in which neither ebb nor flow is occurring. To begin the cycle once again, it us often helpful to examine our own energy. Are we stifled in our job, and find it reflecting in a flat space in our finances? Or perhaps there is a relationship that has stagnated, and our money simply mirrors it? Or an area in our physical health that needs to start moving? Once we deal with the cause behind the financial effect, the flow can resume.

These 10 principles will begin your process of attracting the abundance and wealth you want in your life. And because they are spiritual concepts, not just financial planning tips, they will lead you not only to financial abundance, but to lasting abundance in every area of your life.

Supporting Yourself During Career Transition

Many people are reluctant to make a job or career change due to the fear that they won't be able to "support themselves" during their transition. In my seminars, I have found this to be the number-one reason why people are unwilling to change.

I recommend two alternative approaches to this situation. The first is for people who are truly miserable in their current jobs but who are uncertain about their purpose or the appropriate next step in their career path. To remove the distraction of the current situation, I often recommend that they find a temporary job with low stress and relatively low responsibility, and quit their present job. This allows them to pay their bills during their period of transition and also frees their attention to concentrate on their purpose and goals.

For those who do not wish to follow that approach, I simply suggest that they reexamine their concept of God. Although God is always constant, our concept of Him/Her/It can change as we grow.

So I urge you to ask yourself these questions: Do you truly trust the Higher Power in the Universe to sustain you? Do you believe in a God that delights in giving to you, or in a God that withholds and judges? By realizing that you (most likely) have never had to go without food, never been without clothes and shelter, and never been separated from God, you can begin to recognize that you will always be cared for. And you can let go of the fear that a transition will threaten your life support. God always supports us, and if we are being led into a new job or career, it is the Divine Urge within us to do so, trusting that our financial and material needs are always met.

We now know that following our life's purpose can only lead to one result: greater supplies of money and abundance than ever before. So we need not fear poverty or lack of support as we forge ahead through our transition.

Conditioning Yourself for Abundance

If you have not experienced financial abundance in your life thus far, you may subconsciously fear it because it is unknown. You feel that you may not know how to play the game if there isn't "more month left at the end of the money"! Or you may associate some pain with having money that causes you to subconsciously sabotage your efforts to increase your wealth.

To lessen these fears and prepare yourself to receive more, I offer several steps you can take to condition yourself for abundance. At their essence, they involve changing your old beliefs about money into empowering beliefs that will align your conscious and subconscious desires to create what you want. These steps are outlined in Action Step 2 at the end of this chapter. Please take the time to go through these steps for yourself if you wish to prepare yourself to receive more.

Creating wealth is another area in which we are called upon to balance our male and female energies. Some of us grew up without much structure around money, and have never kept a budget. Others among us are so structured and tied to a budget that we watch every

penny. Between these two ends of the continuum lies a balanced perspective. As we balance our structured, male approach to money by
letting go of some of the structure, and counterbalance our female
side by learning how to budget and invest our money, we will attract
abundance more quickly—and be able to sustain it.

Handling Abundance: The Traps of Wealth

As you focus on fulfilling your life's purpose through your work and
apply the other principles for attracting wealth, you will soon find
yourself experiencing the abundance you have desired. You will then
face new challenges and issues that were not present before, such as
how to diversify your investments, enjoy your money, manage your
money effectively, and find the highest uses for it.

A key question to ask as you face these new issues is: "How can
I best use my money in this situation to fulfill my life's purpose?"
Asking this question before making any decision to spend or invest
will help keep you from getting "caught up" in your wealth. It will
keep you in balance and will also ensure that your money is put to
its highest and best use.

It is critical that as you begin to accumulate monetary wealth,
you continue to recognize the source of your abundance—God—and
that you continue to trust in God's consistent supply. One trap of
wealth is a tendency to think you are self-sufficient, that you have
created all of this money by yourself and no longer need to rely on
God. You will be tempted to put your security and trust in your
money, rather than in the Source of your wealth. If you fall prey to
that trap, you will find it difficult to sustain your wealth or to enjoy it on a consistent basis.

Another trap of wealth is a false belief that once you have
achieved wealth, you will always have it. You will continue to be
challenged to deal with unexpected events—or even crises—to keep
you on your growing edge. The ebb and flow will continue, with
varying degrees of intensity, whether you are wealthy or poor. Do
you have the ability to bounce back from discouragements, such as

the stock market crash of 1987, or the failure of a business in which you have invested heavily? Can you continue to trust God to sustain you, no matter what?

You will also be tempted to rely on experts for investment and tax advice, as well as how to proceed in your business and manage your wealth. While such experts have their place, you are ultimately accountable for the management of your wealth. Are you willing to consistently trust your inner guidance as the decisions you have to make become more complex?

These and other challenges face you once you have achieved the abundance you desire. For those who have decided to follow their life purpose and who have created wealth, these new challenges are simply the next step on an ever-unfolding process of growth.

The Value of Voluntary Simplicity

Many of us who have consciously chosen a spiritual path elect not to create wealth in our lives or, once we have created it, elect to relinquish it for a life of voluntary simplicity. Voluntary simplicity refers to an inner and outer singleness of purpose and avoidance of excess clutter and distractions in our lives. Living in voluntary simplicity involves setting clear priorities for ourselves, giving up some things for the sake of that which is more important, and deliberately organizing our lives to more directly live out our purpose.

Marsha Sinetar studied a number of people who have chosen such a life, and chronicled their experiences in her book, *Ordinary People as Monks and Mystics*. She found that everyone in her study was quite frugal with money, whether they had a little or a lot of it. They valued time more than money, choosing to eliminate the activities they had done out of obligation in order to have more time for quiet reflection and personal growth and exploration.

The most difficult part of choosing a life of voluntary simplicity is often surrendering our attachment to what others may think and whether or not they will approve of our choice. Also challenging is the frequent relinquishment of what we consider the comforts of modern life. Many people who elect voluntary simplicity retreat to the mountains or to a log cabin in the woods, with no electricity or running water. Others design their simple life within the structure of being a corporate president or homemaker. Whatever form the outer trappings take, the objective is nearly always one of inner growth, expanded awareness, and a desire for new meaning, to live a life of choice rather than obligation.

Whether you choose to fulfill your purpose through abundance or through voluntary simplicity, the critical choice is to follow that purpose and to let it be a golden thread that unifies and permeates every area of your life.

Now that you have faced your fears and your patterns of resistance and procrastination, are willing to move past your excuses, and are reformulating your beliefs about money, it is time to deal with the day-to-day issues. What are the issues you deal with from 9 to 5 as you begin to carry out your purpose? That is the subject of the next three chapters.

Action Steps from 9 to 5

1. Have any of the Money Misconceptions listed in this chapter held you back from experiencing the abundance you consciously desire? Does simply recognizing that you have these beliefs help you to move beyond them to create different beliefs in abundance?

    For each of the Money Misconceptions that fit you, design an opposing affirmation that you can use to replace your old belief and enhance your abundance.

2. **Condition yourself for abundance.** The following steps will help prepare you to receive more in your life. You can write your responses to these steps (which I have drawn from Tony Robbins) either in your journal or on a piece of paper.

    A. First, list all the things you are losing out on because you don't have enough money.

B. Then, list what you associate with money (good or bad).

C. Next, list all the different things you were taught about money, whether positive or negative.

D. Note conflicts between number 2 and number 3; ridicule the statements listed in number 3 to reprogram them. You can do this by writing, after each of the negative statements, another ending for it. For example, if one of your beliefs was: "Always have a 'nest egg'," you might write after it: "If you want to be forced to use it!" Or if you believe that "Money doesn't grow on trees," you might follow it with: "It grows on my positive beliefs."

E. Finally, list the benefits you will have when you have financial freedom. Visualize more than mere financial sufficiency; imagine financial abundance!

   Do you want wealth and abundance more now than when you began? Reinforcing the benefits you will receive from financial abundance, after ridiculing your old negative beliefs about wealth, will help condition you to receive all that you desire.

3. **Visualization of Abundance.**

Relax your physical body and clear your mind of distractions, using your favorite relaxation technique. Now, step into the future, when you have created the wealth you desire. Notice how far into the future you had to go.

   Look at your wealthy self. Do you look any different than your current self? More assured perhaps? More at peace?

   Where do you live? Notice every detail of your home. See yourself walking in the front door and taking a tour through every part of the house, looking on it with great pride and gratitude. Notice who else lives there with you, if anyone. Are you married? Do you have children? How do they feel about living in this abundant environment?

   How do you spend your time now that you are wealthy? Do you work? At what kind of a job?

What do you exchange your money for? That is, what do you buy with it?

Get a very clear picture of your wealthy lifestyle. Now, draw that lifestyle closer and closer to the present moment, until it is clearly in focus *right now*. Make it as bright and large as you can imagine. Clearly impress it upon your conscious and subconscious mind. Make an agreement with both parts of your mind that you will all cooperate to create this lifestyle as quickly and easily as possible, for the highest good of all concerned. And come back into the present moment, into this room.

As you repeat this exercise over and over, making your vision of wealth very clear in every detail and bringing it into the present moment, you will very soon find yourself creating it in the physical world.

PART FOUR

The Issues From 9 to 5

10

Dealing With Stress
and Boredom

*"To grow spiritually, you do not need to create a perfect environ-
ment, have no negativity around you, or retreat from the world.
You are here to learn how to be your Higher Self in the midst of
the kinds of energies that are present on earth."*

—Sanaya Roman

STRESS AND BOREDOM are two of the greatest obstacles we face
as we seek to integrate our life purpose into our daily work. We
experience situations of overload in which too many demands are
coming toward us. We can't cope—let alone be civil to those around
us! So we often watch the clock and hope we can tolerate the situation for the rest of the day.

On the other hand, perhaps we work on an assembly line or in
some other kind of job that involves the same monotonous activity
every hour of every day. Or we don't have enough to do to keep us
truly busy for the time we are expected to work. How do we effectively deal with these two types of situations and use them to empower us, rather than distract us from our quest for fulfillment?

STRESS

What Is It?

Stress seems to be a necessary part of life in the '90s. We rush from
here to there, trying to "get it all done" at work so we can beat the
traffic and rush home to relax. We shove ourselves into high gear to

177

meet the conflicting demands of our work and home life. And the only reward we get is more of the same tomorrow. Is there any way out?

I believe there is. To begin with, we can always choose our response to any situation. Stress, which is often defined as a condition or situation requiring some kind of behavioral adjustment, simply poses a greater challenge than some other situations. Rather than automatically generating the classic "fight or flight" response (increased blood pressure and heart rate, etc.), we can use some simple techniques to respond more positively to stressful situations.

Indeed, we must retrain ourselves to approach such situations differently. Otherwise our physical health will continue to deteriorate, and heart disease, cancer, and other debilitating illnesses that result from stress will become more and more frequent.

Sources of Stress

Many factors contribute to the severity of the stress we experience. Such diverse things as our motivation to work, our beliefs about life, and our level of self-esteem determine whether we can "roll with the punches" in our daily lives, or instead, experience stress on a regular basis.

1. Alignment of Job and Life's Purpose. One of the most common reasons people experience stress at work is because their job and life's purpose are out of alignment. That is, they are working for some reason other than to fulfill their life's purpose. As a result, their work has no meaning or direction for them, and they experience stress when anything occurs at work that disrupts the "routine" that they have become comfortable with.

Why do you work? Is it just to generate an income? Because you feel you have to? Or because you are making a contribution and fulfilling your life's purpose through your work? If you are working to fulfill your purpose, events that may otherwise be stressful are seen as opportunities to grow and to apply the principles you have learned about working with purpose.

2. Disempowering Beliefs. Another factor contributing to our stress is the beliefs we have developed that make stress more likely to occur in our lives.

    A. Victim Thinking. Many people disempower themselves (and thereby increase their stress) by seeing themselves as victims of circumstances at work. This kind of Victim Thinking says that ''I have no control over my experience—things just happen to me. My life is controlled by forces outside of myself (such as God, my family, my boss, my friends, my upbringing, my disease, the government, or any one of a number of other 'powers that be'). And I often get the short end of the deal.'' Despite the helplessness that obviously results from Victim Thinking, it is attractive to many people. Why? Because to the Victim Thinker, there is always someone to blame— and the thinker doesn't have to do anything to change. ''I can't lose weight—my parents were both fat and it's in my genes.'' ''I'll never amount to anything—I grew up in a poor family.''

    To the Victim Thinker, stress is perceived to be the result of too many external demands, as in: ''*They* did it to me;'' ''*They* expect too much;'' ''I can't do all of these *things*.'' The problem is that as long as we believe that someone else causes us to have certain experiences, we have given all of our power to that person or situation. There is no way for us to change that experience—unless the other person leaves or stops behaving a certain way!

    If our stress results from multiple demands, it is not the fault of our supervisor, or the barrage of customers who just came in the door, or the people whose calls cause the telephone to ring off the hook. Our stress reaction to the situation is the result of our choice to work in that job *and* our choice to react in a certain way to the situation that has arisen. The path to freedom lies in realizing that no one else truly has that kind of power over us; that we choose our experiences and our reactions; and that we can change them.

    B. Inflexibility and Resistance to Change. Inability to be flexible and unwillingness to welcome change also contribute to our level of stress at work. Are you rigid and inflexible, insisting that things be a certain way, or else? Do you insist on always being in control? Always having things your way? Simply harboring these attitudes automatically increases your level of stress.

Now, more than ever, change is a "given" in life. Change is accelerating at an unprecedented rate. And we must be prepared to deal with change in every aspect of our lives. Each of us chooses either to move with, or against, the natural flow of life. If we refuse to change, we create stress. If, instead, we choose to flow with life's ever-changing experiences, we can begin to enjoy each day. We see life as an exciting adventure and find new levels of satisfaction in each new experience.

Successful people know that each new change holds an opportunity for growth, a chance to experience new dimensions of life. As a result, they embrace change. They don't just tolerate it—they may even seek out opportunities to create change because of the opportunities it holds. The more you can learn to adopt a resilient, flexible, playful perspective on your job, no event or situation can faze you or disturb your enjoyment.

C. Low Self-Esteem.   Our self-image—who we think we are—can also have a significant influence on how much stress we experience. If we have a low self-image, believing we are not worthwhile as a person, we tend to clutch things, to hold on to what we have, and to be excessively concerned about our individual rights, needs, and feelings. Our focus is entirely on ourselves, and we have a great fear of losing what is "ours." Whenever anyone questions or decision or action, we view it as a challenge—and the natural result is stress.

Once we begin to develop into an expanded concept of ourselves and to value ourselves more highly, we naturally experience less stress. We learn to listen to and trust our inner voice; to take responsibility for our actions and choices; to recognize our oneness with other people and enhance our sense of caring. There is less need to be territorial once we trust the Universe to take care of us. So simply pursuing faith in a Divine Being, in whatever tradition we are comfortable, will of itself change our outlook on life and reduce our stress level.

Tools to Deal With Stress

Once we understand what stress is, have recognized the beliefs that contribute to stress, and have begun to change them, we can complement that process by using certain techniques for dealing with stress on a daily basis.

But first, just a note here about a close relative to stress: nervousness. Nervousness about a project, task or situation is simply one manifestation of fear. We become nervous because we are afraid our efforts will be rejected, or we will be ridiculed by the other person, or will otherwise not be able to "handle it" (whatever "it" may be in that circumstance). The first step to dealing with nervousness is to transform the underlying belief, as discussed in chapter 7. Next, if we still experience the reaction of nervousness, we can simply take a few deep breaths, tense and relax our muscles, give ourselves a "pep talk," and proceed into the situation with confidence. As we go through the situation, we will have the remarkable experience of successfully handling a situation that had appeared ominous only moments ago.

The following suggestions do not deal with nervousness, but with the stress that results from overstimulation on the job, whether it is due to excessive responsibility, too many demands imposed simultaneously, or similar situations. Using these tools will help you reduce stress in your life.

1. Lifestyle Surgery (Again). Often when we are experiencing on-going stress, we need to reevaluate our entire lifestyle. How did we get to the point where all we are doing is running from one activity to the next? Are we happiest with a bustling schedule, or would we prefer to have more unscheduled time in our life?

Many times, we feel stress because we constantly overcommit ourselves. Beneath our overbooked schedules lies an issue waiting to be resolved. Do we consciously choose a very busy lifestyle, with its accompanying stress, so that we don't have to face our anger at our ex-spouse, or the dissatisfaction we feel in our career or our life?

If we continue to repeat this choice, its ultimate outcome is workaholism: working excessively long hours, becoming so involved in our work that we have no time left for our family, ourselves, or dealing with the issue that lies beneath our behavior. Meanwhile, even the smallest upset during the day causes us to become unduly angry. We overreact and thereby increase our stress level.

Action Step 1 at the end of this chapter gives you some simple steps to performing "lifestyle surgery" to reduce your stress level. Then, you can begin to pace yourself and build "breathing room" into your schedule so that unexpected events do not push you to your limit.

2. Centering in the Midst of Stress. Often, when we are in the midst of a stress reaction, we have momentarily forgotten our purpose and have gotten "caught up" in the stimuli coming at us. What we must immediately realize is this: *there is always a better reaction than stress.* One of the most effective ways to come back to "center" —that peaceful place within us—is to use one or more of the following centering techniques when you are right in the middle of the situation:

- Post reminders of your life's purpose and goals in conspicuous places in your work area, and look at them during these challenging times. This will help you to look beyond the temporary situation and remember why you are in that place, doing what you are doing.

- If you can, shut your office door or go to a quiet place (a stairwell or closet, if necessary!) where you can enjoy a few moments of calmness. Then, take a few moments to use one of the centering exercises found in the Action Steps at the end of this chapter. These visualizations will restore your perspective and allow you to become peaceful, calm, and centered no matter what is going on around you.

• Ask yourself this question: Is this situation worth the energy I am expending reacting to it? In other words, is this a situation that can be changed if I become angry, upset, and stressed—or will my emotional and physical upset be the only real result? Many times, if we can realize that our reaction is way out of proportion to the situation and won't change the situation, and that we are the only one who suffers, we can stop our stress reaction before it overcomes us.

3. The Power of the Witness. Another way to defuse a stressful situation (or to avoid getting into it in the first place!) is to simply return to our old friend, the Witness. As we observe ourself, without attachment or judgment, we will notice when we create a stress reaction. We can begin to see what situations trigger that reaction. Then, rather than beating up on ourselves because we "did it again," we can simply interrupt the pattern. Soon, we will interrupt it sooner and sooner, until we remain calm and don't even think to react with a "fight or flight" pattern.

4. Detached, Present-Tense Focus. In today's multi-sensory society, we are constantly bombarded with stimuli and expected to process many things simultaneously. We are taught to divide our attention between two or three activities so that we can "get the most done in the least time." This technique is sure to lead to stress—if not constantly, at least occasionally.

Learning to focus our attention on one thing at a time can greatly reduce the number of potentially stressful situations in our life. If, while you are trying to finish a distribution report, two customers walk in, the phone starts to ring, and a salesperson approaches you with a question, you might be tempted to respond with stress from overload of stimuli, right? Most of us encounter similar situations regularly, whatever our job. The key is to finish one thing, giving it our full attention, before shifting our attention to the next.

Here again, if it is possible for you to close your door, have your calls held, and post a "do not disturb" sign while you are finishing an important report, you will finish the report much more quickly and avoid encountering multiple demands until you are ready for them. But what about the situation where you don't have your own office, or you are in a retail sales or receptionist job, where you are expected to deal with demands as they arise?

Studies show that people in support, clerical, and similar positions experience far more stress than high-level executives or professionals. Why? Because they lack the ability to control the flow of stimuli to them. They can't close their office door or have their calls held—they are responsible for answering the phone, or greeting the customers. Here are some hints for lessening the stressful aspects of such jobs:

- Prioritize your tasks. Know which are the most important to be accomplished that day, and be sure those get done— even if others must be postponed due to "interruptions" or unplanned events.

- Bring your own unique style and personality to each customer contact, each phone call, each task you do. Remember that when you answer the phone, there is a human being on the other end—one who doesn't know that you have five other tasks going on simultaneously. The way you answer the phone often gives the caller his/her first impression of the company. If you can smile, be friendly and courteous, and enjoy the interchange with each person, that first impression will be favorable. In addition, you will be perceived as professional in your job, and you will tend to enjoy the calls more as well.

- Strive to focus on one call, one customer, one task, at a time. This will prevent you from being overwhelmed by all of the other demands being placed on you (which you can't do simultaneously anyway).

- Take a break from your job at least every two hours. If nothing else, walk around the office or store, or best of all, walk outside and get some fresh air. This simple pause in your routine will calm you and allow you to return in a refreshed, revitalized frame of mind. Otherwise, stress builds up in your body and mind and detracts from both your health and your effectiveness.

- Be sure to interact with your co-workers and with the customers on the phone and in the business, rather than narrowing your focus to your task 100 percent of the time. That is, while you ought to have a complete focus on your task while you are doing it, intersperse a brief conversation with a co-worker or take a personal interest in a customer or client. One recent study in a manufacturing plant showed that production decreased when a new air conditioner made it impossible for the workers to talk to each other. Achieving a balance between your tasks and your personal interaction in your work day will increase your enjoyment of work and decrease your stress.

- If the demands you are facing each day are more than you can deal with, share your concern with a supervisor and ask for assistance. If necessary, see a counselor or trusted friend for their input. Value yourself enough to speak up when, despite mustering all of the stress-reducing tools you know, you are unable to cope. Asking for help is far better than suffering in silence.

5. The Importance of Physical Health. The impact of stress is felt chiefly in our physical bodies. Therefore, the magnitude of that impact will depend to some extent on the condition of the body that is experiencing the stress.

We will discuss in chapter 11 some basic principles of physical health that will increase your energy level. Many of those same techniques will also help you become more resilient to stress. Perhaps the most important of those is the suggestion that you do at least 20 minutes of aerobic exercise three to four times a week (or daily, if you experience stress on a continuing basis). Without exercise, the adrenalin that is produced by the fight or flight response will be stored in your muscles, resulting in fatigue and blocking of your arteries. If accumulated, more serious physical problems can occur. Frequent exercise allows the adrenalin to be dispersed from the muscles and stimulates the endorphins (our natural tranquilizers). Try it—you'll be amazed at the difference in how you feel!

6. Breaks and Rewards.   To function at our best—as well as maintain our focus—we cannot concentrate on one task or activity for hours on end without a break.

Whether we are hourly workers, managers, professionals, or entrepreneurs, breaks are vital. They help interrupt the accumulation of stress at both the physiological and the psychological levels They restore our focus and help us regain our perspective.

Taking time out is one kind of break. Rewarding yourself for no particular reason is another: buy yourself some of your favorite flowers; take a walk in the park; listen to an outdoor concert; get an ice cream cone in the middle of the day; or any other activities that make you feel special. You can then return to the working routine with a fresh reserve of energy.

Breaks during the day are not the only breaks we need. An occasional "well" day—a day at home just for us—or a weekend spent in bed, can do wonders for our inner child. And vacations, at least once a year, must become a part of our lifestyle, even if we own our own business. Otherwise, we may achieve the monetary and business growth goals we have set for ourselves, but not have the energy, motivation, or physical health to enjoy them. So I encourage you to build some personal time, some breaks of varying duration, into your work and life. They will pay handsome dividends in the long and short run.

7. Be Teachable.   There is always more to learn. If we think we have already learned everything there is to know, we resist any input that is contrary to what we "know"—and we experience stress. Workers who are relaxed and enjoy their jobs and lives are in awe of the beauty and wonder of the Universe. They are always willing to explore something new, whether it is a new job task, a new theory or technique, a new play or art opening, or the simple beauty to be found in a walk in the woods. Simply adopting a teachable attitude will decrease your stress level and increase your satisfaction as well.

8. Refuse to Worry.   Worry is a waste of energy. Worry is also a statement that you do not believe in a good and abundant Universe. Have you ever watched a child go through his/her day? Small children do not worry about where their next meal will come from, what they will do tomorrow, or whether things will turn out well. They simply trust that their parents will take care of everything. And that is what we must do with the Universe.

Worry prevents us from keeping our focus in the here and now. It causes us to put our attention on the future instead. Have you ever noticed how many of the newspaper headlines are based on things that *might* happen? ("Economic forecast looks grim"; "After recent earthquake in San Francisco, the chances of an earthquake in our city have increased by 40 percent," etc.) The press thrives on causing us to worry about what might happen—and makes sure we know about all of the terrible things that have happened. But how often do you read about positive events, such as news of a good deed done, or a trend in an optimistic direction?

We must continually challenge ourselves to create positive headlines for our own lives. This means focusing on what we did well today, rather than what we did poorly; knowing and stating that our needs are taken care of (even if we are between jobs or don't yet know where our income or next meal will come from), rather than despairing and complaining. Refusing to worry and stating the positive has two striking effects. Not only does it change our outlook on life, but it also encourages others and uplifts the entire energy field around us. That, in turn, results in more positive energy, and improves the quality of life in every direction. We need more of that, don't you agree?

Henry David Thoreau states this point well in his book, *Walden*:

> *The true husbandman will cease from anxiety, as the squirrels manifest no concern whether the woods will bear chestnuts this year or not, and finish his labor with every*

day, relinquishing all claim to the produce of his fields, and sacrificing in his mind not only his first but last fruits also.

As we place our trust in the Universe, knowing that everything is taken care of and dedicating ourselves to our life's work, we open ourselves to receive even greater good, in often unexpected ways.

9. Bring Fun Into Your Work. Laughter and enjoyment are natural stress relievers. When we are enjoying ourselves and can laugh at our predicaments, our stress immediately subsides.

In today's workplace, where the Fulfillment Ethic predominates, fun at work is an absolute right that each of us has. We deserve to enjoy what we do, as well as to experience deep fulfillment from it. I am not saying that you must be constantly clowning around and inefficient in your work. But there are many little things that you can do to "lighten up" at work so that you and those around you experience greater enjoyment. Some examples follow (and I'd love to hear your favorites, too!):

- Hang a poster of a picture, cartoon, or poem in your work area that reminds you to "Hang in there" or "Thank God It's Today" or any of the many others that are available.

- When an important project turns out to be a major "flop," give it a nickname and joke about it (but use good taste—and at least wait a few days or weeks until the pain of it wears off)!

- Have periodic social get-togethers with your office staff or store department or manufacturing unit. This can be as simple as a Saturday afternoon picnic or an in-house volleyball team. But getting together away from the job creates a camaraderie that carries over into the workplace and often leads to lasting friendships as well.

- Remember the birthdays and other special events (marriages, births, etc.) of the people in the company (or at least in your department). And recognize your coworkers for their accomplishments, too—even the small ones! Take the initiative to plan something yourself if no one else does. Giving of yourself does as much for your own enjoyment as it does for other people!

- When you're having a day when one thing after another seems to come out backwards, incorrect, or late, take a moment to laugh at the Cosmic Humor in the situation. Maybe this just isn't the day to work on that project—but until you realize what is happening and have a good laugh, you may not know to change your point of focus.

- Laugh *with* others at their mistakes and humorous predicaments—but not at them.

- Do something outrageous (like wearing a mask, button, or unusual accessory or clothing, or give someone a ridiculous gift that means something special because of something you have learned about them, etc.). Outrageousness breeds laughter—and thereby enjoyment (as long as it is not done at the expense of the other person).

- Recognize the natural rhythm of the daily routine in your company—and give special nicknames or have special rituals for break time, lunch time, mail time, or the end of the month statement mailing (for example, "It's 'stamp lickin' time"). These "shared secrets" that are only known to you and those who work with you, give the workforce a sense of shared community that tends to enhance their enjoyment of their daily activities.

These and many other ideas that you will no doubt think of can help you lighten your daily load and enjoy your work more.

10. Understand the Natural Flow of Life. Just as money has an ebb and flow into and out of your life, time and activities ebb and flow. You will eventually be able to anticipate many of the busy times before they arrive, and you can then take extra time to do meditation and centering techniques at those times.

One affirmation I like to use for the busy "flow" times is this:

"In the midst of all of the activity in my life today, I am centered and at peace." That affirmation, used in the morning of a prospectively busy day (and every time throughout the day that you think of it) can serve as a simple reminder that you need not let yourself be affected by circumstances. You always have a calm center within you to which you can return, in the midst of any situation.

For many of us, the ebb times, when our activity slows down, are a bit unnerving. Rather than embracing them, we become nervous, jittery, and uncomfortable. One of our tasks is to learn to enjoy these times, and to use them to delve even deeper into ourselves.

Boredom

Stress and Boredom: Two Sides of a Coin

Stress and boredom are actually two ends of a continuum, two sides of a coin. Stress results from overstimulation; boredom results from understimulation. Yet both stress and boredom produce similar effects within us. These are:

- strong emotions (anger, depression, frustration);
- physical disease (heart attack, cancer, etc.);
- alienation from others; and
- feelings of helplessness.

Recent studies show that people who are lonely—another form of boredom resulting from lack of interpersonal stimulation—are less happy in their lives and suffer from more physical diseases than do people involved in at least one close relationship.

But are the causes of stress and boredom really that different? I believe that in many cases, the same underlying beliefs we explored as the basis for stress may also contribute to boredom. If we engage in Victim Thinking, we stay in a job long past the time it was challenging and good for us because it is "their" fault: "I" can't change anything. Inflexibility and resistance to change also takes the form of the Staying Trap: We are afraid of what an unfamiliar situation might be like, afraid we can't cope, so we stay where we are. And low self-esteem also enters into the picture: If we don't think we deserve a better job, we will stay where we are "comfortable," which often means a job that no longer serves or challenges us.

What is Boredom?

The dictionary defines *boredom* as a state of weariness or dissatisfaction. We know that it results from understimulation in our work environment. We have all experienced it at one time or another: We spend the majority of our time when we are bored watching the minutes slowly tick by on the clock, as it moves slowly but surely closer to the end of our shift. I experienced this when I worked in a major retail department store in which every department had to have someone in it, but the night shift was not very busy in many departments. There was simply nothing to do but watch the clock. Is there any way to find meaning in such a job?

Finding Meaning in the "Boring" Job

Following are a few suggestions for making your work meaningful, even when your job is boring.

1. Be Sure You Must "Put Up With" the Boring Job. Why do we put up with boredom? We touched on some reasons in the "Staying Trap Statements" in chapter 3. You may wish to look back there now. Are you hiding behind one of these rationalizations for staying in a job that is boring to you?

Second, examine your job choice carefully. Do you really have to invest your energy in a job that bores you? There are times in our lives when that may be true. At one point in my life, while I was going to school, the department store job I described above was a very convenient channel for the income that supported me. The schedule was flexible, and the pay was good, so I elected to endure the tedium that came with the job. I would not do so in a full-time job. Perhaps you, too, are working your way through school, or are almost to retirement age in a semi-skilled or government job where staying is more attractive to you than leaving, or are otherwise in a position where a boring job serves you. Just be sure that you really do not have an option to change jobs. If you do, consider making that needed change before you stifle your creativity and growth for 4 to 10 hours each day.

2. Derive Your Personal Satisfaction from Hobbies or Other Activities. If you do, in fact, need to stay in a boring job during this time in your life, it is important that you have another outlet for your creativity. Otherwise, you will experience frustration as your natural need for growth and development becomes stifled and stagnant.

One woman in a seminar I gave recently worked in a government job that did not challenge her, but in which she chose to stay until she retired several years later. To give her creativity an outlet, she joined a ski club and became one of its most active members. Thus her needs for creativity were met, yet she could keep the fringe benefits, pay, and other advantages of her government job.

3. Realize the Value of Routine Work in Personal Growth. In some traditions, routine work is work of the highest order for spiritual awakening. Zen monks spend time daily after their morning meditation doing routine work, such as sweeping floors, washing dishes, and similar tasks. These tasks are ideal vehicles for awakening since they perfectly model the natural cycles of growth and decay, birth and death, and order in the Universe.

So if you have an assembly line job, or a position in a medical lab where you view one blood sample after another, or a window-washing or dishwashing job, consider yourself fortunate. You can notice the cycles in your work, approaching it with consistent focus, and can thereby awaken to your spiritual essence. More about that in chapter 13.

4. Concentrate on Keeping Your Focus in the Present. You can remove some of the tedium from a boring task by making a conscious effort to focus in the present moment. Rather than allowing your mind to wander to what you will have for dinner tonight, how long it is until the next break, or other distracting thoughts, gently keep bringing your mind back to the present moment, putting full attention on what you are doing. The process of resuming your concentrated focus can become a way to avoid looking at the clock every few minutes, and can allow you to bring a higher quality to each aspect of your task.

5. Bring More of Yourself to Your Work.   Your unique personality longs to express itself. Let it do so as you bring your special flair to a task, or take a special interest in a customer or client. This will enable you to stay alert and to also feel like you are making a contribution through your work.

Another way to bring your own personal touch to your work is to approach it as an art. When you set up a table in the restaurant where you bus tables, can you set it in such a way that it becomes an inviting, artistic setting? If you work in a stereo store, can you arrange the equipment, records, or accessories in a way that is aesthetically pleasing to the customer? As you arrange the clothing in a retail store, can you make it as appealing as possible to the customer? Whatever you do, if you can bring a touch of artistic flair, or otherwise include your own personality in your work, your mind will forget all about being bored—it will be too busy creating!

6. Make a Game of Your Work.   Is there a way you can find a humorous angle to your tasks? Or start a contest with yourself to count the number of widgets you assemble in an hour? The number of each type of drink you mix during a shift as a bartender? You might pretend you are writing a novel on your profession, and look for the special nuances, personalities, and connections that are unique to your situation.

If you look at blood samples day in and day out, pretend they are Rorschach ink blots—can you see pictures in the blood? Can you make comical images in the soap suds (if you are a dishwasher)? Whatever you do, bring an element of humor to it, and it will pass much more quickly.

In his book, *The Inner Game of Tennis*, Tim Gallwey relates the work he did with AT&T telephone operators to alleviate boredom in their job. He encouraged them to listen for a quality in the callers' voices, such as warmth, irritation, sexiness, vitality, etc. He also recommended that they rank the angry voices on a scale of 1 to 10: how angry were they? These techniques were very effective because they introduced a component of human interest into an otherwise boring job, and enabled the workers to be more productive.

7. Learn Through Your Work.   There is always more to learn. If you can find a way to keep learning through your job, you will experience less boredom. You might think of the work you have chosen as your teacher—what is the "lesson plan" for today? It might involve interpersonal skills, such as how to work with overbearing people, how to receive (or give) constructive criticism, or other "people lessons."

You might need to take the initiative to investigate some aspect of your job that is particularly interesting to you. Doug, a sales clerk in a retail store, decided to learn more about merchandising techniques. He began experimenting with the merchandise in his department, arranging it different ways and highlighting different items, until he devised just the right mix to maximize sales. His department consistently had the highest sales in the store, largely because of his innovative merchandising techniques.

Jane, a hostess in a small restaurant, took an interest in a particular segment of the food industry that fascinated her: franchising. She studied the process of franchising, talked to franchisees and franchisers, and investigated various companies that offered franchise opportunities. She is now very successfully operating a fried chicken franchise. And she learned about that opportunity while doing her independent research, as she followed her inner guidance and did the things she loves to do.

Learning and expanding your horizons can transform a boring job—with its low level of demands on your time and energy—into a wonderful opportunity for growth. It doesn't really matter what you learn, as long as you keep learning!

8. Insist on Excellence. No matter what the pace of your job, insist on the highest standards of excellence for yourself. If you work in a mail room, devise a technique to sort the mail the most efficient way possible—and use it consistently. Be sure you know how to keep waste of packaging materials to an absolute minimum. Learn the names of the people you deliver mail to within the company, and greet them with a smile each morning. If you repair shoes, learn what techniques work with what styles and materials. Learn how shoes are made, and how to fix difficult holes or tears.

The difference between those who insist on excellence in their work and those who just "get by" is obvious: Excellence brings an added quality to a job, a sense of confidence, "knowledge plus" about the job and the company, and a commitment that includes willingness to go above and beyond the call of duty to meet a customer's or boss's needs. Several years ago, Tom Peters and Bob Waterman chronicled a number of key companies who have become very successful by insisting on excellence not only in the individuals in the company, but in the company as a whole. Their findings are outlined in their books, *In Search of Excellence* and *A Passion for Excellence*. Even the most routine of jobs will become a work of art, a personal challenge, if you insist on the highest standards in yourself and others.

Both stress and boredom can become a thing of the past in your work as you apply the principles we have discussed in this chapter. In the next chapter, we address other issues that arise at work every day—and how to approach them effectively and in a way that contributes to your life's purpose.

Action Steps from 9 to 5

1. **Lifestyle Surgery for Stress Reduction**

    A. List all of the activities to which you are committed or which are a part of your daily life. Examples: work, children, organizations, church, exercise, etc.

B. Now, place an "L" next to each one that is contributing to your life's purpose. Place an "E" next to each activity that you enjoy.

C. Draw a pie, and assign a piece of the pie (of appropriate size) to each of these activities that you do each day. This pie ought to reflect your current actual schedule. How much of your time are you spending on "L" activities (that contribute to your life's purpose)? How many on "E" activities (that you enjoy)?

D. Now, draw a pie (or write out a schedule, if you prefer) showing your ideal distribution of time. This pie could reflect the way you would spend your time in the ideal situation. (Be sure to plan some personal time for yourself!)

E. Now, on a third piece of paper, list on the left side the reasons you have, in the past, told yourself you cannot spend your time as you wish (that is, in the way you drew the pie in part d). On the right, pretend that there is no obstacle to designing your time according to the Ideal Pie. From that perspective, address each of the "reasons" you have previously listed, and why they are not true limitations.

Does this help you see some areas where you can adjust the time you spend on certain activities so you can have more personal time, more time for your family, or so that a greater part of your time is spent in activities directly related to your life's purpose? Now, begin to review your schedule based on what you have discovered!

2. Centering Exercise

[This is a three- to five-minute exercise to be used in the midst of stressful situations.]

Close your office door or find a quiet place. Sit quietly, close your eyes, breathe deeply a few times, and focus on a peaceful image in your mind. It might be a tranquil forest, a beautiful beach, or a special moment with your child. Use whatever image represents absolute peace and contentment to you. Breathe in the peace of that setting. Gently release that image for a few moments, then open your eyes, and take that peaceful feeling back into the workplace with you.

3. **Handling Stress in Your Job**

Think about your current job for a moment. Do you experience stress in your work? When does it occur? Can you discern a predictable pattern so that you can begin to anticipate the stressful times and prepare yourself in advance?

Look back over the 10 tools for dealing with stress that are outlined in this chapter. Choose at least one of them to use the next time you experience stress. Note in your journal how that tool works for you. When you find several that are effective for you, train yourself by practicing them regularly, so that using those tools is soon your natural response to success.

4. **Overcoming Boredom.**

Are you in a boring job? If so, ask yourself these questions to begin to overcome your boredom:

A. What other alternatives do I have to staying in this boring job?

B. How would I begin moving toward one of these options now?

C. What cause, organization, hobby, or other activity can I get involved with that will fulfill my need for creativity and help carry out my life's purpose more directly while I am in this job?

D. How can I enhance my moment-by-moment experience in this job? (Examples: focused concentration, bringing more of myself to my job, making a game out of it, learning from my work, and/or insisting on the highest standard of excellence.)

11

Increasing Your Daily Satisfaction

"It is no use walking anywhere to preach unless our walking is our preaching."

—St. Francis of Assisi

IMAGINE FOR A MOMENT that you want to take a trip to Hawaii. You learn about Hawaii, visit travel agents, read all the literature you can find, and even check out some books from your local library to be fully informed about this tropical paradise. You even imagine, in your mind, what it will be like when you get to Hawaii, and some of the things you will do. You have had a fear of flying in the past, but you have even worked through that and are mentally ready to take the flight to Hawaii. So you sit in your living room and enjoy the idea of flying to Hawaii, lying in the sun, eating tropical fruit, and seeing the sights. But you never get out of your driveway, travel to the airport, and get on the plane. No matter how clear you are about your desire, or how much you want to see Hawaii, unless you get on the airplane and go there you will never see it.

Isn't that a lot like many of us? We read all the books, listen to all the tapes, know we should change our experience at work—but we keep going through the same routine, day after day, wondering why it never seems to get better. We are good at learning concepts, but can't quite translate them into practical terms.

You have now read about your life's purpose and how to put it into action. This chapter is designed to help you translate your life's purpose into the practical issues of your working life. Here, as they say, the "rubber meets the road."

Starting Your Day

The first practical issue we each deal with is our initial thoughts upon awakening each morning. It is then that you have an opportunity to start fresh—to design your day just as you choose it to be. How do you set the tone for your day? When you wake up in the morning, what is your first thought: "Good God, it's morning!" or "Good morning, God!" I am referring here to more than just an overall positive or negative attitude (although that is certainly part of it!). How do you *feel* when you wake up?

Morning is one of the times when your subconscious mind is most receptive. Therefore, what you think about when you first awaken sets the tone for your entire day. If you repeatedly wake up with negative thoughts, your subconscious begins to associate a negative state with waking up. And it is hard to start your day off right if you associate pain or obligation with waking up in the morning!

You *can* program (or re-program) your subconscious mind so that you actually enjoy getting up in the morning—whether you ever have in the past or not. Here are three ways to do it.

1. An Affirmation to Start the Day. Think for a moment about your ideal day. How does it start? Do you wake up feeling energetic and vibrantly alive? Excited about what lies ahead for the day? Picture yourself experiencing whatever emotions you would like to experience upon awakening into that ideal day.

Once you have a clear picture of that image in your mind, write out an affirmation that expresses that feeling. It might be as simple as:

"I am full of energy, thankful for the abundance in my life, and vibrantly alive today. I know that only good comes to me, and I gratefully accept it."

Design one that fits your most positive state of being.

Next, program yourself to think of this affirmation as your first thought in the morning. You can also record your affirmation on a tape recorder, write it on a piece of paper and post it where you will see it early in the day, write it on the bathroom mirror, or put it in anyplace where you are sure you will see it immediately upon awakening.

When you wake up tomorrow, look at (or listen to) your affirmation first thing, and then repeat it once or twice until you *feel* it. Don't you already feel more energetic and alive? You have set the tone for the rest of your day to build upon and expand that powerful feeling.

2. Empowering Questions.   A second method of starting your day out powerfully (which I draw from Tony Robbins) is to ask empowering questions. Many of us wake up saying to ourselves, "Why do I have to go to work?" or "I wonder if I'll survive the meeting with Joe today." This type of question does not serve any useful purpose. Any time we ask our brain a question, it does its best to serve us and to find an answer. If we ask why we have to get up, or why we have to go to work, or why it always happens to us, our brain will search all of our life experiences and knowledge and do its best to find answers to those questions. And the answers to such questions do not lead to a greater sense of joy or energy, do they? (In fact, they will often drag us down further!)

Instead, we might ask ourselves, "How can I make today the best day of my life so far?" "What are some ways that my life purpose can be advanced through what I have planned today?" "What am I grateful for today?" Our brain will then start searching for the answers to these questions and will lead us into higher levels of satisfaction and fulfillment in our life.

Here, as with your affirmations, this technique is most powerful if you can really *feel* the answers to these questions. The energy of emotion is what communicates your questions, not just to your conscious mind, but to your subconscious mind as well. Eventually, you will associate these empowering feelings with the act of waking up each morning.

3. Program Yourself for Success.   A third technique for starting your day off right can be used *after* you have gotten out of bed and are going through your morning routine. It is a practice of what I call "programming yourself for success." It involves taking several minutes to repeat your favorite affirmations for the day, and declaring to yourself how you choose your day to be. If you have a particular issue you are dealing with, you can do a special affirmation for it. If you have a meeting scheduled that day that is especially important, you can affirm your desired outcome for it.

This programming process can be done anytime during your morning routine when you have five to ten minutes alone. One of my favorite times to do it is in the car while driving to work! Another person whom I know does this process in the shower. You must make a conscious choice to make time to do this—especially at first, before it has become a habit. I challenge you to try it for just one week and notice what a difference it makes.

Staying Focused on Your Purpose

In a very real sense, you are what you think about. You know by now that you are bombarded with literally thousands of stimuli each day, from a broad variety of sources. You are learning to regulate what you pay attention to and what you ignore. But what about your work area or office? Are there stimuli in your environment at work that remind you about your purpose and your goals—or that distract you from them?

No matter how small or open your work space may be, there are ways to install some reminders that you will see throughout the day of what you are doing here and how you intend to carry out your purpose. Here are some examples of ways to both remind yourself of your commitment during the day and just give yourself an "attitude boost":

- Put something live, such as a plant or some beautiful flowers, in your work area.

- Write your favorite current affirmation on notecards or Post-It notes and tape/stick them on your phone, your

Rolodex, in your lunchbox, in the closet, or wherever you will see them from time to time during the day.

- Personalize your work area with a picture of your spouse, family, or special friend; a postcard of your favorite retreat; or a little saying, object, or memento sitting on your desk or on the counter in your store that is special to you.

- If you have a picture of your ideal job, day, house, mate, or whatever you want to create in your life, put that in a drawer or on the back of a door where you will see it occasionally—and reinforce the image.

- Write your current affirmation on your day's calendar.

- Make up Rolodex cards with affirmations on them, and place them randomly throughout the alphabet in your address file so you see them as you are looking for various addresses or phone numbers.

- Surround yourself with beautiful things (if that is important to you and part of your vision): pictures on the wall, the colors in your office and furnishings.

- Use a commercially prepared set of affirmation cards (or make your own), choosing a different affirmation or quality of being for each day.

You will think of others that suit you (and I encourage you to send me *your* favorites—I love to hear your creative ideas)! All of these suggestions are simple ways to bring you back on track and keep you centered as you go through each day. In part V, we will explore other techniques for maintaining a disciplined focus in your work for maximum satisfaction.

Managing Your Time for Maximum Effectiveness

Each of us has the same amount of time in each day to use as we see fit. Have you noticed how some people seem to get much more done than others in the same amount of time? And how others seem to always be behind schedule, never quite having enough time to accomplish what they had planned?

One of our challenges is to learn to use time effectively, in both the qualitative and quantitative sense. Quantitatively, we must learn to pace ourselves and use the amount of time we have to complete the things we want to do. In a moment, I'll give you some suggestions on how to do that. We have previously explored the qualitative aspect: the challenge of enjoying each moment to its fullest, and judging our success by the level of enjoyment we have on a moment-by-moment basis (rather than by our income level or job title).

Managing our time is another one of the areas in which balancing our masculine and feminine energies is crucial. The masculine side of us encourages us to use the Type A form of time management: scheduling as much as we can into as little time as possible, doing two or more things simultaneously, without enough time to think about being centered—let alone actually do it!

The feminine side of us, on the other hand, is the Type B time manager. She wants to take everything as it comes, not keep a calendar, and do one thing at a time. She is even comfortable doing nothing—that is, having idle time occasionally.

Which of these aspects is strongest in you? Are you sensing a need for balance in your time management style as you begin to fulfill your life purpose? We are certain to approach our use of time differently as we adopt the concept of working with love, of doing everything we do with focus and a view to growth through our work.

1. A Higher Use of Your Calendar. I highly recommend the use of a daily calendar. It enables you to organize your day, to set your priorities, and to keep the commitments you have made to others, as well as to yourself. And it helps you to translate the goals you have set for yourself into daily steps toward their accomplishment. (I began doing this in junior high school, after I missed two choir rehearsals in one week because they weren't written down on a calendar!)

I recommend a better way to use your calendar, however, than you may have considered before—one that involves the use of your subconscious mind as well as your conscious mind. Each night before you leave the office, store, or plant where you work, take about 10 minutes to look at your calendar for the next day. What appointments or meetings do you have? What projects do you have that *must* be done tomorrow? Is there someone you *have to* reach by phone? Take a moment to note those, to mark them conspicuously on your calendar, and to impress them on your subconscious mind as priorities.

One of the best ways to do this is to do a quick visualization of these activities or events just as you wish them to be, with the best result for all concerned. If you wish to connect with one or more people, either by phone or in person, you might imagine building a bridge or other connection of light to them. If you wish to attract more customers or clients to your business, picture your store or office full of people, full of energy and excited about your product or service. Picture it just as you want it to be.

Then list the other activities that you would like to do the next day—the second priorities, if you will. Those are the things that you will allow to carry over into the following day, if necessary, as you see what unexpected events occur in the course of tomorrow. Then see all of these scheduled matters floating away as you release them to the Universe to be taken care of.

This process does two important things. First, it programs your subconscious mind to begin creating the kind of day you want, one in which the most important things will be accomplished. Second, you will find that you get busy signals on the phone less often, find less people gone or busy when you arrive for an appointment, play less "phone tag," and otherwise find things unfolding with a greater sense of order. If you do not take the time to acknowledge the energy connections that are necessary for carrying on your work, you will just move from one activity to another aimlessly, with less satisfactory results.

When you arrive at work the next day, simply glance at your calendar again and reaffirm perfect Divine Order for your day. Your subconscious mind has already been busy setting up the right connections with your clients or customers, suppliers, and other necessary business connections. And your entire day *will* unfold in perfect Divine Order—whether it matches your calendar or not! There is no such thing as an "interruption"—it is just another way in which Divine Order is perfectly unfolding. So you pay attention to that as long as is appropriate, and then return to the task you had been doing.

2. Keep Your Focus in the Present. Too often, in today's results-oriented, busy society, we are continually looking to the future. We want to get through with this, so we can go on to that. We want to get rid of this distraction, so we can complete another project. We concentrate only on being done, and not on the doing.

There is a story about a Zen teacher who was putting the finishing touches on a remodeled kitchen in the Zen Center, when another very wise teacher entered the room and asked, "How are things going?" The first teacher answered, "Things are going fine. There are only a few details to finish up."

The wise teacher answered, looking puzzled, "Only a few details? But, details are all there are."

Truly, whatever your chosen job, details are all there are. The sooner we stop trying to "get rid of" the details in our lives, and to finish this so we can do that, the sooner we will begin to experience peace and satisfaction in the present moment.

When we examined burnout in chapter 3, you will recall that our motivation for success has a great influence on whether or not we burn out. Many people are highly successful by other people's standards but don't feel successful because they constantly compare themselves to others. If this comparison to others continues to influence the person's definition of success, they will never be successful—at least not in their own estimation. They will reach one goal and then be disappointed because someone else can do it better, or have more, and they can't enjoy their successes. There is always more to strive for, more to do, and never enough.

The only way to escape this vicious cycle is to develop a present-tense focus and learn to enjoy each moment. In other words, it isn't just the achievement that counts, but the getting there. "Success is the *quality* of your journey," not the destination, as Jennifer James puts it in the title of one of her books.

One way to do this is simply to let yourself enjoy your successes as they occur. Celebrate yourself, even in a small way, and recognize that you are accomplishing what you have intended to. Another way is to pay full attention to each task that you do, not allowing your mind to wander. This technique is explored further in the discussion of Inner Success in chapter 13.

3. Dealing with Deadlines. Another common challenge concerning the use of time is deadlines. There are two types of deadlines: internally set and externally set. Internally set deadlines are those you have set for yourself—the things you "have to" get done today (even though no one else is requiring it of you). We often set ourselves up for frustration by programming too many of these internally set deadlines into our day, or by setting them unrealistically high.

Externally set deadlines, on the other hand, are the expectations or requirements of others (for example, your boss) with respect to your performance. There is often less flexibility with the time limits of these deadlines than there is with internally set deadlines.

But how do you deal with deadlines?

A. Learn to differentiate internally- versus externally-set deadlines. Once you recognize which type of deadline you are facing, you can more easily determine whether or not it can be changed. (Internally set deadlines are more often subject to change than externally set ones.)

B. Set priorities. Stick to your established priorities as much as possible. This will enable you to decide which deadlines need to be given more importance.

C. Make a contract with yourself. On internally set deadlines, it will assist you to make a contract with yourself to be sure you make *some* progress each day toward your goal. If your goal is to write a book, perhaps you can set a goal to write five pages each day.

Gradually, but steadily, you will reach your goal. One word of caution: don't make your deadlines so rigid that there is no give and take. Allow some space for the unexpected.

D. Resolve deadline conflicts. If externally set deadlines conflict with each other, ask the people making the demands whose priority is to come first. Find out the reason behind the deadline: does the completion of your task trigger someone else to begin their portion of the overall project? Or is your deadline just a timeline internally set by your supervisor that could actually be postponed a few days? And be sure you understand the instructions for the project, so you don't waste needless energy doing something that turns out to be the incorrect approach.

E. Don't be afraid to ask for help. Many times, you cannot do everything—nor are you really expected to. Enlist support from other coworkers or subordinates—or from your boss!

F. Learn from your "mistakes." If you miss a deadline or do not meet the expectation of your boss on a project, take some time afterward to examine the entire sequence of events to see how you can avoid the same situation next time. Look at the event as a learning experience, *not* a failure.

G. Listen to your inner voice. Your inner voice can be an invaluable guide to you in setting priorities and deciding what to do next with respect to what will be in your highest interest in the long run. It can even provide you with insights into the reasons that may underlie your apparent inability to meet certain deadlines. You will do well to check in with it often and heed its guidance.

Increasing Your Energy Level

No discussion of daily issues would be complete without a brief note about physical health. Even the best management of your time will be of little use to you if you do not have the energy to enjoy your life. The following Ten Steps to Enhanced Energy are simple techniques that help me maintain the energy I need in my life. I'm sure they will help you as well.

(Clearly, a complete treatment of these issues is beyond the scope of this book. If you wish more information on these topics, please contact the author or refer to the publications listed in the Sources at the end of the book.)

1. Eating for Energy: The Importance of Balancing Blood Sugar. Our diet has more to do with our energy level than many of us realize. For example, many times the "slump" we feel in the middle of the morning or afternoon is due to a sudden drop in our blood sugar dropping to inordinately low levels. Once we learn to manage our blood sugar level effectively, we can eliminate those slumps in energy.

The best way I have found to regulate your blood sugar—and thereby regulate your energy level—is to eat five or six or small "meals" during the day, each two to three hours apart. The food you eat ought to be a well-balanced combination of complex carbohydrates, proteins, vegetables, fruit, and a small amount of fat. Sugar and salt ought to be eliminated from the diet entirely if possible.

For your mid-afternoon "meal"—the time when many of us feel a regular energy slump—one of the best things you can eat is a big, juicy apple. It has a great deal of natural sugar and will pick you up almost instantly. Another food that works well for many people as an afternoon pick-up is low- or no-fat yogurt, with or without fruit. Find a natural food that works for you at the period during your day that is often your time of lowest energy. Then, consistently use what works for you to regulate your energy.

2. The Nutrition of Natural Foods. As you begin to spread your calorie intake out over the day, also be sure that your diet consists of primarily natural, unprocessed foods. For maximum energy, 70 percent of your diet might consist of "water rich" foods: fruits and vegetables. Eating them raw, or cooking them slightly (such as steaming vegetables or grilling meat) will retain their maximum nutritional value.

3. The Power of Protein.   Despite the recent publicity about the importance of carbohydrates in our diet, protein is at least as important for generating and maintaining energy. Protein has the same amount of calories per gram as carbohydrates (whereas fat has considerably more). Therefore, by choosing the protein foods that are also low in fat, we will consume the same amount of calories as we would if we ate carbohydrates. Protein increases our energy; carbohydrates take longer to digest and therefore use more energy.

The key is to use protein and carbohydrates during the times of day when they will serve us best. For example, if we center our morning and noon meals around protein, we will maximize our energy level when we need it most: during the work day. A lunch consisting of protein and vegetables and/or fruits (for example, chef's salad or fruit plate with cottage cheese) is particularly important, as this will do a great deal to eliminate the "mid-afternoon slump." Our evening meal can then center around carbohydrates to allow us to wind down our day and rest. Just notice the difference between the way you feel after a high-starch lunch (such as a sandwich and french fries) versus a high-protein lunch with lots of raw vegetables (such as a shrimp salad). That simple test will convince you of the wisdom of this principle.

You may choose to include whatever kinds of protein are compatible with your body's needs and desires at this point in your growth. I think red meat as a protein source is acceptable, in moderation, although I do not choose to eat it myself. Other sources include chicken, fish, eggs, tofu, and legumes. Choose those that feel appropriate for you.

4. Fitness from Food Combining.   Another suggestion on the use of food in your life involves food combining. Many people respond very favorably to an eating plan in which protein and carbohydrates are not consumed in the same meal. That is, each meal will consist of vegetables and/or fruits and EITHER a protein or a carbohydrate food—but never both at the same meal. The rationale is that protein needs an acid base for digestion, whereas carbohydrates need an alkaline base to be digested. If we consume them together, they neutralize each other and can cause gas, indigestion, and ultimately illness due to toxic build-up in our digestive tract.

If you wish to try this approach, more information is available in the *Fit for Life* books by Harvey and Marilyn Diamond and also in the books by Doris Grant and Jean Joice, which are listed in the Sources at the end of the book.

5. Vitality from Vitamins. While I am not a "health nut" or "vitamin junkie," I like to think of vitamins as my "food insurance." My schedule is often busy, as yours may be as well. There are days when I don't take the time to eat the right foods at the right time. So I take a natural multivitamin each day just to be sure that my body has what it needs to serve me best. Vitamins cannot make up for substandard eating habits, of course. But if you are committed to sound nutrition and usually eat a healthy combination of foods, with occasional detours from your regimen—vitamins can make up that deficit and enhance your energy.

One vitamin that is particularly helpful in dealing with stress is vitamin B-6. I take 100 milligrams of this vitamin any time I am busy or am experiencing stress, and it is a great help.

A second critical vitamin for counteracting stress is vitamin C. I take extra doses of vitamin C nearly every day, and particularly increase my intake of it if I feel the slightest symptom of a cold coming on. Whereas in my childhood and early adulthood, I had colds regularly during the winter, I no longer get more than an occasional sniffle (which I know is a message that I need to rest and nurture myself). I recommend it!

6. The Cleansing Power of Water. Finally, I recommend that you drink six to eight glasses of water each day. Not only will this cleanse your body and assist it in eliminating toxins, but it serves as the perfect substitute for coffee and carbonated drinks that are less than healthy.

7. The Substance Trap. We live in a world of quick fixes. Many of us turn to coffee to wake us up in the morning, a drink or two of alcohol after work to calm us down, and perhaps a few cigarettes during the day to give us a boost. None of these substances contribute to our long-term health, and in fact they may hinder our ability to experience satisfaction on a daily basis at work. They drain our energy by providing a temporary altered feeling state, and in the case of sugar and alcohol, provide empty calories that pile on the pounds.

What we are often doing is trying to "pace" our energy level by using these substances. Either we are trying to arouse more energy than we feel in that moment, or we are trying to suppress excess natural energy. Ultimately we miss out on experiencing much of our God-given energy.

Even if we do not use substances to pace our energy, we must admit to ourselves that habits such as drinking alcohol, smoking, and consuming too much sugar or caffeine drain our energy. If at all possible, we must eliminate these substances from our diet and life. We will soon find that our energy increases and we enjoy life—and work—much more.

The first step in eliminating our dependence on substances is to become more comfortable with our own natural cycles. These cycles exist on a daily and monthly basis, as well as through the years. As we become more willing to experience our natural energy, we will depend less on substances to pick us up and let us down.

It is often helpful to substitute another beverage or habit in place of the coffee, alcohol, or smoking that we had been engaging in. This serves as a temporary "bridge" or "crutch" as we are learning to eliminate the pattern altogether. For example, we can drink herbal tea or water (hot or cold) instead of coffee, or mineral water instead of alcohol. Or we can eat nuts instead of smoking cigarettes. (Be careful not to substitute one addiction for another, as in substituting candy for alcohol or cigarettes.) Of course, if you discover that you are addicted, you might think about seeking professional assistance or attending an Alcoholics Anonymous, Overeaters Anonymous, or other support group to deal with the problem.

If you feel you cannot eliminate these substances completely, you can at least decrease your intake of them during especially busy or demanding times. This will help regulate the amount of stress in your experience, rather than multiplying it. Whatever substance you may find yourself overusing, you may wish to return to chapter 3 to evaluate whether or not that habit is a compulsive behavior that masks a deeper issue that needs to be dealt with.

8. Energizing Through Exercise.   Another highly effective tool to enhance your energy level is aerobic exercise. Without exercise, toxins build up in your muscles—as does stress. You need to exercise a minimum of 20 minutes at least three times per week (five to six times is better) for maximum aerobic effect. Jogging, walking, swimming, or any activity you enjoy will do—if you do it on a regular basis!

We have all heard this advice time and again, but if you have yet to do it, don't wait another moment! It yields multiple benefits on both the short and long term.

9. Breathing for Life.   Have you ever noticed that when you are experiencing stress or boredom, your breathing becomes shallow? Very often, just when we need air the most for our body's vital functions, we begin breathing shallow, short breaths.

I find it extremely helpful to first, realize when this is happening, and then, to sit tall and take a few deep, slow breaths, from the bottom of my abdomen, holding it in for a moment, and releasing. Doing this just a few times in the midst of feeling stressed or tired will immediately rejuvenate you to continue on in your work or other activity.

10. The Power of Physiology.   How you carry yourself, whether you are sitting or standing, sends a powerful message to your mind about how you are feeling. So does the way you move and the tone of your voice. Compare in your mind, for a moment, a person who is talking at a relatively fast pace, with an excited tone of voice, gesturing strongly, standing tall, and smiling as he talks. Can you guess how he is feeling? Now contrast another man, standing with his shoulders slumped and head down, talking in a soft, monotone voice, with little or no gestures as he talks. He is probably feeling quite different from the first man, right?

You may think that the appearance of these two men is the *result* of their feelings, and that may be. But have you ever considered that we can change our feelings by changing our physiology—that is, the way we stand, gesture, and speak, and the expression on our face?

To illustrate this, imagine for a moment that you are depressed. Really get into the feeling of depression, and stand the way you would stand if you were depressed. Now, lift your head and eyes up, so you are looking slightly above your normal line of sight. Do you feel any different? It's hard to stay depressed and look up, isn't it? Now position your body in the way you would if you were very excited and vibrantly alive. Did your internal state change?

You can use this technique next time you feel less than vibrantly alive. Just try positioning your body the way it would be if you were happy and excited (or whatever emotion you want to experience that is the opposite of the way you feel now). You will very soon find—assuming you can truly capture the feeling you wish to experience in your gestures and physiology—that your internal feelings change, just by changing your physiology.

Using Your Inner Voice in Decision Making

You encounter situations every day in which you must decide between two or more options, beginning with what to wear when you are getting ready for work, to what career will best fulfill your life's purpose. How do you make decisions that work well for you and all concerned?

The most important principle for successful decision making is to follow the path that feels most joyful. Many times we squelch our joy in favor of following the Rules of Life, and never reach that point where we are truly enjoying our life. As we follow the path of joy instead of the Rules, we experience moment-by-moment satisfaction. And our satisfaction is contagious: others feel better and have the courage to follow their own course of joy because we have set an example.

If, for example, your choice of after-work activities is between visiting with a special friend (whom you have not seen for some time), working late, or going home and cleaning out the attic, ask yourself, "Which of these activities feels most joyful?"

I am not saying to abrogate all of your responsibilities because you don't feel like doing them or because they aren't the most joyful option. We must also make space in our lives to fulfill those necessary commitments. But if there is a way to build joy into every activity, your life will become more satisfying.

This simple principle will help you make all of your decisions so that they lead to the fulfillment of your life's purpose and enhance your life experience. And as long as the path of joy you choose does not harm anyone else, you have the highest and most fulfilling code of ethics there is.

The Messages in Your Experiences

Do you realize that each of your life's experiences has a message for you? Just as our interactions with people can serve as a gauge for our work on ourselves, our experiences can provide us with insight into our inner selves. You will recall that in chapter 3, we met Anna, the woman who worked in an accounting job she didn't like and began to have more and more frequent migraine headaches as a result. What Anna failed to realize is that the migraine headaches were a message to her that something needed to change in her life.

Like Anna's migraine headaches, each of our illnesses, pains, and dis-eases has something to tell us. If we will but listen to them, they will lead us to the source of the hurt and enable us to heal.

I used to have a head cold at least once, and usually several times, each winter. Then, as I learned more about the connection between sickness and our inner self, I discovered the source of my head colds. It was not the cold, damp Oregon weather or the time of year. It was simply the only way I could justify taking time off from my always busy schedule to pamper myself. After I realized that, and worked at taking regular breaks and learning my needs for "pampering time" *before* I became ill, I eliminated my need for head colds. And now, all it takes is a slight sore throat for me to realize what my inner self needs—and I take the needed time off.

If you wish to examine your own illnesses and their messages for you, I encourage you to spend time consulting with your Higher Self, asking it to lead you to the meaning of your dis-ease. I also recommend Louise Hay's book, *You Can Heal Your Life*, for more information.

Other types of experiences also have messages for us. For example, if your appliances begin all breaking down at once, it may indicate a breakdown in your connection with your Source. Or it may be a sign of confusion in your life or direction. Whatever your situation may be, there is a message for you. All that is required is that you notice it, seek the guidance of your Higher Self, and hear the message the situation has for you.

Now that we have examined these daily issues and how to use them to facilitate our fulfillment, how can we bring a higher perspective to our work and increase our fulfillment still further? That is what we will explore in the next chapter.

Action Steps from 9 to 5

1. Design an affirmation that describes the way you want to feel and think when you awaken each morning. Make it upbeat, positive, and energizing! It need be no more than two to three sentences, and ought to capsulize you in your ideal state.

   Write this affirmation on note cards, and put them on your refrigerator, coffee maker, bathroom mirror, or anywhere you will see it first thing in the morning. Say it out loud when you awaken, and notice how much better your day goes!

2. Start today to keep a calendar of your day's events and commitments. Just before you leave work tonight, notice what you have planned for the next day. Take a moment to see everything you

have planned unfolding perfectly, with order and mutual satisfaction for all concerned. Then release your commitments to the
Universe for perfect action. Your day will go much more
smoothly!

3. Think of an ongoing conflict you have with someone at work,
    or an ongoing illness you are experiencing. Relax your body and
    get into a meditative state. In your mind's eye, go to a place that
    you perceive as peaceful and safe. Meet your Higher Self there,
    in whatever form It takes. Ask your Higher Self for the message
    in this experience or condition. Ask It any further questions you
    need to clarify the message and the appropriate action for you
    to take. When you have received the information you need,
    slowly come back to the present moment. Then take the neces-
    sary action to allow your healing to take place.

12

The "Other" People at Work

"My true relationship is with myself—all others are simply mirrors of it."

—Shakti Gawain

THE PEOPLE WE ENCOUNTER at work frequently pose the greatest challenge to our effort to be our best Self. They criticize us, or they don't cooperate with us, or they get angry with us—and we react. They may not share our vision, or their values may be different than ours. We are tested to our limit in dealing with customers or clients who are rude or upset, or who can never be satisfied. In this chapter, we will discover how to view the other people in our workplace as a catalyst to assist us in carrying out our life's purpose, rather than a hindrance to it.

Unity of All Life

There are at least two ways of viewing "other" people in our life. One very common perspective is the view that we are all different from each other, each a separate being, engaged in our own activities, and not connected in any way to the other beings on the planet. This view leads to loneliness and decreased joy in our lives, for we miss out on the fulfilling interactions we could have with others.

Alternatively, we can see everyone as connected at a deep level, each a part of the other. We can notice that we bear more similarities to each other than differences. This view is gaining increasing acceptance, particularly in the New Age. As we recognize that we all originate in spirit, and are spirit at our essence, we approach our interactions with others differently. We can empathize with others, and respond compassionately to their human drama, as we notice that their story is much the same as ours. Each of us has a different cast of characters and variations on a theme of events in our lives. But our stories are more or less the same.

Christ stated this principle when he said: "If you do it to the least of these, my brethren, you have done it to me." This principle applies to each act of compassion we do, each small step we take in fulfilling our vision, each smile or act of generosity. Likewise, when we criticize our co-worker for doing such a lousy job, or curse at the driver who just cut us off on the freeway, we are at some level criticizing and cursing at ourselves. And that action/thought, particularly if strong emotion is attached, goes out into the Universe and tends to repeat itself—in our lives! That makes you think, doesn't it?

This consciousness of connectedness must be recognized in a very tangible way in the New Age. One of the ten "Megatrends" noted by John Naisbitt in his book by that name is the shift from a national to a global economy. This means that over the past 30 years, we as a country have moved away from the luxury of operating within an isolated, self-sufficient system bounded by national borders. We now know that we are all part of a global economy. Everything that happens at an economic, educational, ecologic, political, and spiritual level in one country in the world naturally affects what occurs in all others.

For example, the Pacific Rim and the Third World countries have drastically impacted the American economy by offering inexpensive labor, which drives down the price of goods. Their higher quality standards often result in better quality goods, requiring the U.S. to then set higher standards for its goods. An oil shortage in the Middle East results in lines of cars at the gas pumps in the U.S. and other countries. A nuclear leak or error in a weapons test in one country can dramatically affect the environment around the world. Unless we learn to work together and recognize our global interdependence, people in all countries will suffer the consequence of irregular supply and demand, not to mention environmental and other effects.

What does this mean to you in your quest for fulfillment at work? Simply that you can no longer afford to judge the behavior

of others, to view them as separate from yourself, and to simultaneously expect to experience satisfaction in your life or your work. Just
as we are all connected globally in a physical, economic sense, we are
also connected on a spiritual level.

The fulfilled worker recognizes that we are, in truth and in fact,
"one human family." She realizes that each person in her present,
past, and future—including herself—is doing the best they can with
the information, skills, and resources available to them. If they could
do better, they would! They don't intend to isolate other people, or
to be overly critical. Perhaps they are simply expressing, in the only
way they know how, a cry for love.

This is illustrated in the story about a woman who went to the
pharmacy to have a prescription filled. She had been going to the
pharmacy for years, and knew the pharmacist well. Usually, he
would take time to ask her how things were doing for her, how her
grandchildren were, and the like. On one particular day, however,
the pharmacist was exceptionally abrupt, and even rude. He filled her
prescription but did not want to talk. She was puzzled, but decided
to mentally send loving thoughts to him and to not let his behavior
upset her.

She later discovered that his wife had suffered a stroke that
morning and was hospitalized with possible paralysis. This loss so
upset him that he was not his usual self. She felt very grateful that
she had chosen to respond with love, rather than reacting to his anger
by being upset or indignant.

We never know what else is occurring in the lives of those with
whom we work, play, and otherwise come into contact with each
day. Sometimes the compassionate response is simply to ask if something is wrong, and to offer what assistance we can. But if that is not
possible (or if we have done what we can at a human level), there is
much healing power in mentally sending loving, peaceful, positive
energy toward the person or situation. Such energy can heal at deeper
levels than we are even aware of on the physical plane. We can do
this by bringing thoughts of love or peace into our mind, and imagining them radiating toward the person who can benefit from it at
that time.

As we recognize our oneness at a deep level, we open ourselves to experience that connection on a regular basis at work.

The Law of Attraction

Because of our connectedness with others, the people who are in our lives are drawn to us through a principle called the Law of Attraction. Simply stated, this Law says that we tend to attract to us exactly what we are. Put another way, our life experiences tend to reflect our beliefs about ourselves and about life. As Ernest Holmes put it, "At all times, we are either drawing things to us or pushing them away."

The Law of Attraction works in a number of ways in our lives. We explored some of them in chapter 8. We saw that it causes us to attract reactions to our decisions that parallel our level of clarity and confidence about the decision. We learned that our forethought and consideration of the impact of our decisions on the others in our lives can minimize this effect. And we saw that this Law also works by causing us to attract people and situations into our lives that personify, or exaggerate, our doubts or fears about our decisions to make changes in our lives.

This Law also causes us to attract experiences that match our beliefs. Sharon, for example, became puzzled by the things that were happening to her. Every time she sat on a committee or participated in a meeting at the company where she works, it happened. Either she got the most unpleasant task of all to do, or she was the one whose views were rejected or ignored, or she became the brunt of the latest company joke.

These victimizing situations in which Sharon found herself reflect an underlying belief she has. By examining the results she has been creating in her life, we can surmise what her underlying belief might be. Most likely, Sharon has a belief that she has little value as a person—in other words, a low level of self-esteem. Therefore, she "naturally" creates situations in which she is "victimized," no matter what the context.

Once Sharon recognizes her belief that "I am not valuable," she can change it. She might begin to value herself, even in small ways. She could speak her views with confidence and assertiveness in meetings, honor her inner voice and follow its guidance, and congratulate herself for small successes each day. (I'm sure you can think of other ways.) She can begin to cultivate a belief (perhaps by using an affirmation or other technique we learned earlier in this book) that she is a worthwhile, valuable person. That belief will then begin to reflect in her actions, as well as the situations and people she begins to attract into her life. And soon, she will no longer be a victim (or, to put it more accurately, a "volunteer" for degrading or humiliating situations).

The Law of Attraction is working in your life, whether or not you are aware of it. To prove this for yourself, I recommend that, for the next week, you simply observe your experiences. Watch your interactions with people at work. Notice what you are thinking about when you are slighted, or congratulated, or when a degrading or critical remark is said about you in your job. Are you putting yourself down? Loving yourself? Enjoying your work—or just tolerating it that day?

Or what if one of your co-workers is constantly backbiting? Might that backbiting reflect your own feelings of inadequacy or self-criticism? Or does she do this about everyone, and it is simply demonstrating her own feelings of inadequacy and need to get attention? Remember, each of us is always doing the best we can with what we know at each moment. Simply recognizing that can help you come from an attitude of compassion rather than anger or criticism.

Understanding how the Law of Attraction works in our lives can help us realize why we repeat certain types of relationships. It can also assist us in looking beyond the surface effect (whether it is love, fulfillment, or conflict) to make our relationships work better. We will only attract into our lives the people and situations we need to experience to learn and grow. Once we learn the lesson from that person or situation, we no longer "need" to attract it.

Action Step 1 in this chapter will help you begin attracting the type of people you want in your life. Then, in chapter 13, we will reexamine the Law of Attraction and learn how to use it to accelerate our ability to draw situations and things to us.

What We Resist, Persists

One reason we attract people that mirror our dislikes or weaknesses is the principle that "what you resist, persists." The energy in resistance is so strong that it actually draws people to you that match the idea or belief you are resisting.

I had an opportunity to see this principle at work in college in my living situation. Since I was single at that time, I usually had a roommate (or more than one). I had been raised to place great value on keeping my home neat and tidy. "A place for everything, and everything in its place," as the old saying goes. I associated pleasure with a clean house. So what kind of roommates did I attract? Well, they varied, but few of them had the same standards for housekeeping that I did. We often began with an agreement about who would do what among the housework that was needed, but I inevitably ended up doing the bulk of the work.

After a few instances of this, I developed a belief that no one else had housekeeping standards that meet mine. My usual reaction pattern was to become resentful and angry because I got the "short end of the deal." The more I resisted and got angry, the more I kept on attracting the same situation. After all, they "should" help me; they live here too!

Then I realized something. Keeping the house clean was simply not as important to my roommates as it was to me. They didn't get upset if it wasn't clean—and they didn't always think I was wonderful if I cleaned up while they were gone. So I decided to change my belief and attitude about the situation. Since keeping the house clean was important to me, and it wasn't to them, I decided I would stop resenting *them* when they didn't keep our bargain in that department. Since *I* wanted things clean, I would keep them clean to my standards—and would free them to do what was important to them.

I changed my old belief to a new belief that said, "I create an environment that is pleasing to me, and I release my roommates to their highest good." I then started to experience remarkable peace of mind. I was no longer responsible for my roommates' behavior, and I spent much less time being emotionally upset. I had a clean house, and everyone was happy. After I made that shift in belief I began to attract roommates with higher housekeeping standards, too!

So beware of strong resistance. You may unwittingly attract more of the very thing you do not want!

Your Interactions as a Gauge for Growth

If you have a severe "personality conflict" with another person, or if you are frequently criticized or humiliated by others, these people may be reflecting your own beliefs about yourself. The way to deal with these people, then, is not to attack them, but to work on yourself. Once you begin to love yourself, rather than criticizing yourself, you will no longer attract critical people to you.

Once you begin to view your relationships with others in this way, you can use your interactions with them as a gauge of your personal growth. For example, let's say that last month you got upset every time you were around George in the next department, because he constantly teased you about how you really "screwed up" on a major project recently. You soon realize that George was mirroring your inability to forgive yourself and your labeling of the experience as a failure. You then forgive yourself and begin to see what you can learn from the "screw-up," instead of being limited by it. This week, when you go by George's desk and he teases you, you are unfazed. You simply send George love and ignore his remarks. Your current reaction to George's teasing is a gauge that you have dealt with that issue, since it no longer bothers you.

Until you get to the point where the actions of others do not cause you to react, it is wise to avoid taking action (when possible) while you are emotionally upset. When we are in strong emotional states, we trigger those states in others. Thus the energy of all of those around us is upset and magnified if we act on our emotions. Likewise, our positive, loving emotional states will be transmitted to others. So if you find yourself becoming upset, angry, or frustrated in an interaction, you may need to withdraw from it, calm yourself, and finish the conversation later. Soon, as you do the necessary work on yourself, you will be able to handle situations easily that formerly bothered you.

The Challenge of Detachment

Each day, we encounter other people's emotional reactions. This poses a challenge for us: how do we act compassionately and lovingly toward them without getting caught up in their negative energy?

We begin by realizing that it will not help the situation for us to get involved in the other person's drama. The highest gift we can give the person is to stay centered and radiate love in the midst of even the most negative, emotional situation. This helps keep the situation from getting out of control, and also shows the other person an alternative way of reacting in such circumstances. Try this next time someone is mad at you, or others are upset around you. Though it is challenging, it releases incredible energy within you!

Loving Communication Techniques

Effective communication is a crucial tool in dealing with others at work, whether they are co-workers, bosses, or customers or clients. When we communicate with love, all of our working relationships are enhanced. Rather than contributing to the deterioration of a situation, we can often resolve it easily and quickly by being willing to keep the lines of communication open.

The use of "I" statements is one way to communicate more lovingly. If you have a disagreement with someone, or need to resolve an event that happened in which your feelings were hurt, the use of "I" statements rather than "you" statements is extremely effective. That is, rather than saying, "You made me angry at the meeting yesterday," be willing to own up to your own reaction to the situation and say: "I felt angry when you took the credit for my work yesterday." Then, both you and the other person can state the way you feel without accusing the other person or blaming. The situation will be resolved much more quickly with "I" statements than with "you" statements. And such statements leave less room for emotional reactions, too.

Communicating honestly and genuinely is also important when dealing with others at work. People will respect you when you are willing to communicate your feelings and make an effort to keep your relationships working satisfactorily. As we grow and realize our connectedness, we know there is no need to hide from each other, or to harbor hidden agendas. Each of us is growing in different areas at different times. If we overreact to a situation, we can defuse it by admitting that we have some work to do in that area and ask the other's forgiveness.

Often, as you begin to awaken to your life's purpose and integrate it into your daily work, others around you will not share your vision. They do not yet realize that there is a higher perspective to work than the 9-to-5 routine. Your task in this circumstance is to communicate your loving attitude, to carry out your vision, and to serve as an example for those who are ready to grow into their own vision. If you find yourself continually ridiculed or otherwise challenged in your quest, consult your Higher Self. Perhaps you need to find more fertile ground to plant your vision (for example, a new job). Or maybe the ridicule is just as a test to purify your intention. Only your Higher Self knows what you ought to do in your particular situation.

As you develop a genuine caring about the others in your life, your love for them will show in all of your contacts. They will sense that they make a difference to you, and will often return that sense of caring as they interact with you. Even if they don't, you will feel better about yourself and will become known for your genuinely loving attitude. That in itself will raise the consciousness of your workplace.

Balancing Family and Work Commitments

The worker of the 1990s is more and more often a woman, and increasingly the worker has one or more children. Those children's needs frequently conflict with the demands of the workplace. How does the New Worker balance these demands?

There are several common responses. One, of course, is not to have children at all. More and more couples are now childless by choice. A recent study of women entrepreneurs showed that 42 percent had no children. These women have made a conscious decision to focus their attention on their work and their hobbies or desires to travel, rather than trying to balance family and work.

Other couples are waiting until later in their lives to have children. Rather than starting their families in their early 20s, many couples are in their 30s or even 40s before bearing children. This gives the would-be parents an opportunity to establish themselves in a career before bringing children into their lives.

Those who choose to have children and work must develop innovative ways to balance these two demanding parts of their lives. If you have chosen the option of having children, you then have several ways to play the balancing game. One is to try to do both your career and parent roles perfectly. This approach is sure to lead to burnout and frustration. Unless you are superhuman, you will not be able to play both parent and career person perfectly (despite what the popular press says)!

The following suggestions will help you balance your career and family responsibilities:

1. Be realistic. Beginning your commitment to have both career and family with realistic expectations can avoid much frustration along the way. Don't expect it to be easy or to always work smoothly. Remember that you have made the choice to have children out of a deep sense of caring and love, and commit yourself to do whatever it takes to make that balancing act work. Parenting is rewarding, but also challenging.

2. Choose a spouse who complements you. If you are not yet married, but plan to have children in the future, choose a spouse who is equally committed to having children. Also select someone who complements your temperament. If you are an achiever type, a supportive spouse may be a better match than another achiever. The supportive spouse may then be able to work part-time or stay home with the children while you progress in your career.

If, on the other hand, you want children and would like to work at least part-time, but aren't invested in a career, perhaps an achiever spouse would be your best choice. Your spouse can then serve as the primary breadwinner for the family while you are the primary caretaking parent. Whatever your situation, choose a spouse that complements both your personality and your long-term family goals.

3. Choose a career path that is suited to having children. "There is no such thing!" you may be saying. Well, you have already recognized that choosing to have both a career and a family will not be easy. Now what I am suggesting is that you choose your career with your family goals in mind. New laws now mandate parental leave in some states. But how long can you realistically be away from your job without losing the responsibility you have gained, your familiarity with the latest developments in your field, etc.? Will your career allow you to take time off to have children and then return to your job? If not, you may need to consider another career area that will allow you to balance both of your goals.

4. Be prepared to make some sacrifices. You will not be able to do everything in your family *and* everything in your career that you may wish. Balance must become a familiar part of your life. Balanced parenting requires that you choose your priorities, one day at a time. One day your work must come first because you have an important presentation to make or a deadline to meet. The next day, your children take top place so you can attend their school play or tend to them while they are sick. Refuse to feel guilty when you must occasionally give one activity less than your best, due to conflicting demands. You are doing the best you can, given all of the circumstances at that time!

5. Draft your spouse into co-parenting responsibilities. If you are married, you and your spouse have entered into the commitment to have children together. Even in the 1990s, however, where both parents are typically employed outside the home, the mother still does the majority of the child care, cooking, and household tasks. If you are one of these mothers, you owe it to yourself to make arrangements with your spouse to share the child care and household tasks with you—or even to stay home for several months or years as "Mr. Mom" while you pursue your career.

6. Get a housekeeper, nanny, cook, maid, or whatever help you need (and is within your budget). Another choice that can help tremendously with the demands on your time is to hire help with the household tasks and the children. Many of us have been raised to believe that the "good mother" does all of the cooking and cleaning, bakes wonderful desserts and prepares gourmet meals, is always cheerful with her children, and somehow finds time to redecorate the house and still be able to balance a career in there somewhere. Not true!

Today's mother must be willing to acknowledge that it is acceptable to ask for help, both from the family and from appropriate sources outside the family. If your budget is limited and/or your children need an extra incentive to help you with the household tasks, offer to pay them! After all, you will end up paying *someone* to help out. Asking for and getting help is the only way to keep your balance in the face of the challenges of role conflict.

7. Take time off for your child(ren). Obviously, in most cases it is desirable for a mother to take several weeks, months, or even years off upon giving birth. This bonding time is critical to both mother's and child's development. Hopefully, you have chosen a career path that will allow for that time.

When your children are growing, consider taking a day off (or more) now and then to spend with them. When the weekend comes, spend at least part of it with just your children. And no matter how much or how little time you have with your children each day during the week, be fully present with them. They can sense when they do not have your undivided attention. Even a few moments of concentrated attention can be very satisfying for both parent and child.

8. Choose an employer who recognizes the special needs of working mothers. Many forward-thinking employers are now realizing that half of the workforce is women, and that many of those women have children. To attract the best of these workers, they are offering on-site child care, or paying part of these employees' child care expenses as an added benefit if on-site child care is not feasible. As working mothers choose a job, they might research their prospective employer's philosophy on child care and parental issues. While it is not wise to dwell on the issue (or even bring it up on the first interview), it is a factor to consider in the working parent's job selection process. These suggestions, coupled with your own innovative ideas, will assist you in balancing children and career. I would love to hear your suggestions and the ways you have done this balancing act in your own life, as well!

Now that we have overcome the initial stages of discovering our life's purpose and have begun to put it into action, the next two chapters will present some suggestions for the higher levels in our journey.

Action Steps from 9 to 5

1. Think of a type of person who seems to appear in your life over and over again. It might be one of the things you listed in response to clue number 7 to discovering your life purpose (recurring issues or problems) in chapter 2. List as many appearances of that type of person as you can remember, either on a sheet of paper or in your career discovery journal.

Now read over your list. Can you determine what your underlying belief might be that is causing you to create this type of person in your life over and over again? Look for common aspects of each person, and try to state them in a sentence that begins with "I am" or "The world is" or some other general statement of belief.

Are you ready to change that belief and stop attracting this person-type from now on? If so, beneath your statement of your current belief (or on another sheet of paper), write a statement of the belief you wish to substitute for the old belief. Example: if your old belief is: "I am never good enough," your new belief might be: "I am a valuable, wonderful person." Your new belief ought to be an affirmative statement, with as positive a tone as you can muster.

Now, use one or more of the techniques we learned in chapter 6 to replace the old belief with your new one (for example, writing it out as an affirmation on note cards and placing it in numerous conspicuous places; visualizing yourself experiencing your new belief; or surrounding yourself with other people who embody and/or support you in your new belief. Then, watch for your experiences to change and your old pattern to disappear, as the new belief becomes embedded in your subconscious.

2. Are you struggling to balance a family and a career? It may be helpful, just for a moment, to list the benefits and rewards of being a parent. Then, list the benefits and rewards of being a worker. Isn't it worth taking the necessary steps to do this "balancing act" so that you can continue to receive these rewards?

PART FIVE

Keys to Transformation

13

Getting On With It

"And how do you get on with it?
The things that don't get you to God you give up.
. . . Letting go is the act of purification."

—Ram Dass

To FULFILL OUR LIFE'S PURPOSE, both on a daily and lifetime basis, requires a renewed commitment from us in each moment. We must learn to be comfortable with both inner and outer change, and to bring a higher perspective to our work than simply a 9-to-5 routine. This chapter is designed to expand your ability to adapt to change and to help you look at your work in new ways.

Changing Your Beliefs

As you progress on the path of your life's purpose, you will become aware of old beliefs that you did not know you had. They are brought to your awareness when you are ready to deal with them. You know from working with the concepts in this book that your beliefs (which reside in your subconscious mind) are the key to your actions and life experiences. Therefore, to continue to progress, you will need to transform certain beliefs that no longer serve you into positive, life-enhancing ones.

You now have the tools to do just that: your knowledge of the Law of Attraction, and the techniques for goal achievement we learned in chapter 6.

If, for example, you have a belief that no one else ever does anything right, your normal reaction pattern may be to get angry whenever one of your employees or co-workers fails to meet your (extraordinarily high) expectations. You notice that you seem to attract "incompetent" workers. And then you decide that you want to change that belief. So you establish a new belief for yourself. You begin to affirm to yourself, "The other people in my life always do the best they can with the information and skills they have available to them." Or, "I always react lovingly, no matter what others may do." You may use any number of tools to assist you in doing this, including affirmations, visualization, role modeling, and the other techniques you learned in chapter 6.

Next, you emphasize to yourself the reasons why this new belief is necessary: you want to work with competent people, and you want the people who work for you to function at their highest level. You then begin to put your new belief into practice. Tomorrow, you notice that you are in the midst of your standard reaction pattern. But this time, you stop halfway through and realize what you are doing. You realize you have a choice: you can continue to act out this pattern, based on your old belief, or you can change. If you elect to change, you may need to withdraw from the situation at that point and reevaluate your response. Or you may be able to immediately turn to a more loving, compassionate response—such as telling the person you are certain they did their best, and then calmly pointing out the areas that could be improved.

By the next week, you begin to interrupt yourself *before* the pattern begins. Soon, if you continue to practice replacing the old belief and pattern with the new, you will not even think of the old reaction. The new one is installed—and will soon be automatic!

The steps you have just taken to change your belief are:

1. **Recognize your old belief.**

2. **Decide to change.**

3. **Write out a statement of your new, desired belief.**

4. **State the reasons why you want to change.**

5. **Begin to affirm and otherwise reinforce your new belief.**

6. **Interrupt your pattern and install the new belief in its place.**

As you improve your ability to interrupt your old pattern, congratulate yourself—you are making progress! Without beating up on yourself, you can simply recognize your old belief and usual pattern, and begin to change it. Now, continue to reinforce the new belief you have chosen. Visualize yourself reacting the way you *want* to in situations that used to "push your buttons" (that is, learn to respond instead of react). You will soon see changes in a positive direction in your life.

There is a wonderful byproduct of this process. As your new belief becomes more and more a part of you, your life and the people and situations in it begin to change. Our manager who used to believe no one did anything right finds that his/her employees more and more often produce high-quality work and *do* meet his/her expectations. And the ultimate result is a higher level of satisfaction and joy at work for all concerned.

Six Principles to Help You Magnetize What You Want

As you move out into the world to fulfill your purpose, it will assist you to have available some additional tools to accelerate the rate at which you attract your desires. You can also use the Law of Attraction as a powerful tool to magnetize new experiences into your life— such as a new job, resource, person, or more customers for your business.

To use the Law in this way, you must understand some basic concepts about energy. Each of us actually functions on two different levels of awareness as we go through our life experiences. The one which is most familiar to us is the physical plane. This is the level of effects: houses, cars, money, people, things. On this level, it appears that the way one finds a new job is to go to an employment agency, or read through the classified ads in the newspaper and send out letters enclosing resumes, both of which lead to interviews and, ultimately, to a job. But is it really a purely mechanical process? Or is there something more going on beneath the surface?

In truth, we are surrounded by fields of energy—the pure energy with which we become one in the highest states of consciousness. What actually matches a person with a job is not the mechanical steps of resume writing, letter writing, and interviewing. Rather, it is the working of the Law of Attraction. The energy of the applicant, at some level, is attracted to the energy of the employer—even if neither of them is aware of it.

Just as our experiences are the result of the Law of Attraction, so are the things, people, and situations in our life. Once we recognize this, we can use the Law to affirmatively draw to us the things, people, and situations into our life in the form that we want.

It may help to think of this concept much like the law of physics concerning magnetism. Magnetic substances are only magnetic to certain things—and once they come into contact with those things (metallic objects, for example), they draw the object to them irresistibly. In fact, Webster's Dictionary's definition of magnetism includes not only the attraction for iron, but adds that magnetic substances "are believed to be inseparably associated with moving electricity . . ." That same kind of moving electricity, or energy, is at work all around us, influencing everything that we experience.

If you think of yourself as magnetic to people, situations, and things that match your energy, it follows that you attract the mate, job, friends, money, and other people and things that match your present energy level. Once you grow into a new level of awareness, the things and people that used to be quite comfortable and satisfying to you will no longer match. This is one reason why jobs and people and material possessions come into our lives, and later depart from us: the energy attraction is gone.

So how do you use this idea of magnetic energy to magnetize things to you more quickly? By using six principles that work at an energy level (rather than a physical one). To use them, it is helpful if you are already comfortable and somewhat skilled in meditating, as well as in listening to your inner voice. This is because the most important part of magnetizing is the *feeling* of magnetism. Here, much as in achieving your goals, you must involve your deepest emotions in the process for it to be effective.

These six powerful principles for becoming more magnetic to what you want are adapted from Sanaya Roman's book, *Creating Money*.

1. Know that what you are seeking will be a tool for a higher quality you want to express more of in your life.   Stated another way, know how the object you desire will serve your life's purpose or theme. For example, will your new job enable you to express more peace in the world? More compassion? Greater integration of spiritual values into the business world? Whatever it is that you want to express in your life (as long as it does not harm anyone else) ought to be increased or served in some way for the magnetism process to be most effective. Another way to think of this is to imagine that whatever you seek to attract is radiating the quality you wish to increase in your life.

2. Magnetize the essence of what you want, as well as the specific form.   You may know exactly what you want to attract into your life, down to the smallest detail. Even if you do, remember that at the energy level, essences are recognized more easily than specific forms. Therefore, you could magnetize both the essence and the specific form of your desire, to the extent you know it. This is true whether you have a clear image of the form or not.

One way to do this is to use a symbol for what you want, as we did in the Symbol Meditation in chapter 2. You most likely recognized the meaning of the symbol that came up for you in that meditation immediately, as well as some of the kinds of forms that would be likely to create that essence for you. Perhaps you knew that great creativity was part of your symbol, either because of a color or shape or just a feeling. Or you may have sensed great love and compassion. Those are examples of essences. The essence of your desire ought to be clear to you for you to magnetize it most effectively.

3. Ask for what you want or even more.   We have applied this principle in this book by, for example, framing our affirmations to ask for "this or something better." That phrase allows room for the essence of what you seek to manifest in other forms, potentially much greater than the form you have already imagined. Be sure to leave your desire "open at the top," so it can come to you in its highest form.

4. Love and intend to have what you seek to magnetize. This principle first suggests that you send love to your desire. Sending thoughts of love toward what you seek to magnetize will tend to eliminate any fears or doubts you may be harboring about the object. If, for example, you wish to magnetize a new job with more responsibility than your current job, mentally sending love to the essence of that job (that is, responsibility) will eliminate any fears you may have of not being able to handle the added responsibility, or any doubts about your own ability to perform a more fulfilling job.

Pure intent is the second part of this principle. The purer your intent, the faster you will be able to attract things into your life. The intent I am referring to is not the pushy, "I'm going to get mine no matter what" attitude. Rather, it is a calm assurance that you *will have* what you desire in your life. This assurance enables you to overlook apparent setbacks, to keep your eyes firmly on the object you seek, to be persistent, and to see it as already yours. The more you can keep your focus steadily on your desire — and not get distracted by the apparent lack of money, the slowness of your progress, etc. —the more momentum you will build toward having what you seek.

5. Believe that what you are asking for is possible for you to have. One of the voices of your "committee" (the various voices in your head) typically tells you that "you don't deserve this," or "this is too good to be true," or something similar. You must stop listening to your committee, and believe—deeply—that whatever you are asking for *is possible for YOU to have*. This belief becomes an emotionally supported knowing, not just that the thing is possible, but is possible for YOU. That new job you want not only exists out there somewhere, but it is perfect for you. You *can* have it, and no one can do it better than you can. Many of us sabotage our own desires by not taking this step.

6. Get beyond "needing" what you desire; instead, have a certain detachment about it. Have you ever noticed that the people who are single and "can't live without a husband/wife" have the hardest time creating a fulfilling relationship? This is because their perceived need is sensed at an energy level by all of the potential partners they attract, and tends to repel serious commitment. This neediness also reflects in their behavior, which may be overly accommodating, unduly dominating, or in some other way out of balance.

The same is true if we feel something is lacking in our job or career. If we absolutely "have to have" a new job because we can't stand our boss, or because we don't have enough money, we will find it harder to attract a new one that is truly satisfying.

In both of these contexts, the person seeking the new partner or job has a basic sense of incompleteness within themselves. They believe that this void will be filled by someone or something outside of themselves. There is an important message here: *You will never find personal satisfaction and fulfillment in anyone or anything outside of yourself.* You have a physical body and a spiritual essence. All the tools you need to create a fulfilling life reside within you.

Likewise, if you don't feel valuable just for who you are, apart from what you do, no job will ever meet your need. You must change your beliefs about yourself, rather than feeling you "must have" a new job—believing that then you will feel valuable.

Throughout this process, you must simultaneously intend to have what you want, yet not be attached to having it. This becomes easier once you realize you are complete within yourself, and that you don't need anything else to fill the void within you. You can then be willing to let your desire not come at all, or to come in a form different than you expect. You can accept whatever does come as right and appropriate, and, if it is not what you want, learn how you can demonstrate something that fits you exactly the next time. Once we can develop this detachment (or, as the Eastern philosophies call it, nonattachment) from our desires, we see everything in our life as perfect. Ken Keyes calls this the Fourth Center of Consciousness, the Love Center, in which everything that happens simply is, and nothing upsets us. It is a wonderful, freeing place to be. And you can live in that attitude by simply detaching yourself from insisting that things (and people) be a certain way, at a certain time. Instead, you can let them just be as they are. This releases much more energy within you, much like flowing with the river's current instead of trying to paddle your way upstream.

These Six Principles of Magnetism set the stage for magnetizing. The exercise in Action Step 2 at the end of this chapter will allow you to actually experience this process. You can use it any time you wish to experience more in a particular area of your life, or when you wish to change jobs, create more friends, attract a mate, find a new car or house, or any other situation that requires you to connect with the energy of another person or thing.

How to Use The Six Principles

To enable what you want to come to you most quickly *and* in its highest form, I recommend that you use the Six Principles of Magnetism, along with a sensitivity to your inner voice. The Six Principles assist you in framing your desire appropriately for action at an energy level. Listening to your inner voice will enable you to know when to act, when to wait, and how to draw the physical form of what you want to you.

It is helpful to "check in" periodically during the day, and to spend time in quiet meditation, being open to the guidance of your inner voice. Soon, you will be guided to make a phone call to someone, or drive down a certain street or past a certain store, or take the action that is appropriate to attract what you want into your life. You will no longer ignore those seemingly irrational urges to call someone you haven't talked to for months, or to drive a different way to work, once you see that they often lead to new doors opening in your life. And you will know what is best to seek to magnetize into your life at this particular time.

You can also use magnetizing to attract more customers or

clients to your business. If you wish more activity in your business, regularly visualize your store filled with people, all very excited about the merchandise or service you have to offer. Do the magnetism exercise (see Action Step 2) to draw these people to you. And follow your inner guidance if you feel led to place advertisements in a particular publication, join an organization you had not previously thought of joining, offer a special discount or incentive, or take any other action or make other contacts that will contribute to increasing your business.

Eventually, you will learn to "economize" on the use of your energy to magnetize things into your life. That is, you will learn what is the right amount of energy to invest in attracting an object. Small things require only a small amount of energy to attract, if you have pure intent and are properly using the other principles of magnetism. Larger things may require more energy, but perhaps less energy than several months of your entire attention. The amount of energy you invest ought to be in proportion to the size of the object or the pervasiveness of the change.

Enjoying The Process of Change

It is said that the one constant in our lives today is change. Some of it is due to external events, and some is self-generated, as we change our beliefs and use the principles of magnetism to draw new things toward us. Just when you think you have something within your grasp, it changes before your very eyes. Though we often cannot control these external shifts, we can master our reactions to them. And ultimately, change can be your friend, rather than a foe to be overcome.

We learned in chapter 3 some of the indicators that a job or career change is appropriate. In this section, we explore some ways to make positive changes in our lives to enable us to carry out our chosen work, as well as to eliminate what is not working for us.

Whether the change in your life is self-generated or "just happens" as the result of something in the environment, it requires an adjustment. The following steps will help you adapt easily to change in your life:

1. Enter each day with a sense of anticipation. Rather than clinging to an overbooked schedule, resisting any deviation from your routine, begin your day as though you are opening the cover of a brand-new book. In that book are stories and events much greater than you have even imagined. And as you are open to these new experiences, embracing rather than resisting them, you will find your daily life becomes more exciting each day.

2. Don't ignore the subtle urgings of your Higher Self that change is needed. If it is time to apply for that promotion, or get out of that relationship that doesn't serve you, do it! Have you ever had subtle nudgings that you needed to move to a new area or take a certain action, but ignored those urgings? What often happens next is that our Higher Self creates what we call a "crisis" to catapult us into action. We ultimately do what we know we should have done long ago—but only after a dramatic event occurs (such as losing our job or being evicted from our house). Don't ignore the subtle signs you see, waiting for a "crisis" to act.

3. State your willingness to change, and to do whatever is necessary to have the thing(s) you want. Even if the change seems frightening or you don't think you know how to proceed with it, state your willingness to do so. Your willingness sends a powerful message to your subconscious that you are now ready for a new level of growth. And it will begin to attract to you the things you need to make the desired changes.

4. Take the first step. As is the case when accomplishing any goal, simply beginning to move, no matter how small the step, will start the momentum. The other steps will follow in logical sequence, and you will have made the change before you know it!

5. Focus on the positive aspects of the change. Even if there are aspects of the change that frighten you, focus on the benefits of making the change. Will you feel freer, more satisfied, less distracted, or more loving, as a result? The more you center your attention on these positive aspects, the more pleasurable the change will be—and the more motivated you will be to follow through!

6. Reinforce your progress.   As you take each step along the way, support yourself. Notice when you take action that leads you to your goal, and congratulate yourself. Think of special ways you can reward yourself for staying on your chosen path. Those acts of acknowledging your progress will multiply, so that change becomes more comfortable all the time.

7. Have fun!   Throughout the process, have fun. Change *is* an opportunity. It enhances your joy and makes you feel more alive. Since change is a "given" anyway, you may as well enjoy it!

Inner Success

Another key to "getting on with" our life's work is to examine how we define success. Our society places a high value on achievement, progress, upward movement, and material success. Often, we are encouraged to pursue these values to the exclusion of our inner direction and health. Predictably, we are now reaping the fruits of that narrow focus. Cancer, heart disease, AIDS, and other diseases are clear physical consequences of stress, life in the "fast lane," and the pressure to achieve.

Our challenge, in this context, is to carve out a different kind of success for ourselves. I call this Inner Success—a success involving a conscious choice to follow the leading of our inner guidance, expanding our life's purpose to its highest level, and consistently growing in our awareness of life in its many forms.

Inner Success may require us to give up things, people, or ideas that were a part of our life in the past. The one thing it will certainly require of us is a new approach to our life's purpose and our work. The path to Inner Success elevates us to a higher perspective of our work than we have explored thus far. We have laid the foundation for understanding the workplace, discovering our life's purpose, setting goals, and overcoming some of our limitations. Now we are ready to transcend even these concepts to pursue a different, higher path.

This path is best illustrated by the story of the young boy who traveled across Japan to study with a famous martial artist. When he arrived, he met with the master. The master asked him, "What do you want from me?" The boy replied that he wished to be his student and become the finest martial artist there was. He then asked the master, "How long must I study to be the best?"

The master replied, "At least ten years."

The boy thought that sounded like a long time. "What if I study twice as hard as the other students?"

The master replied, "Twenty years."

"What if I practice all day and all night, using twice as much effort?"

"Thirty years."

The boy was very puzzled. "Why is it that each time I say I will work harder and apply more effort, you say it will take even longer?"he asked.

The master replied that the answer was clear. "When you have one eye fixed on your destination, there is only one eye left to help you find your way."

The moral to this story is to "try softer," rather than to "try harder," as we are often taught in today's society. As we follow this inner path, we can "get on with 'it' "—meaning our work on ourselves—as the activities we do naturally eliminate the aspects of ourselves that do not serve us on our way.

The way to Inner Success involves two key aspects: (1) complete focus on your activity, without attachment to the results, and (2) doing everything you do with love.

The Discipline of Focus

Focus, as I am using the term here, means paying complete attention to the activity in the now moment. When you are focused, you are absolutely absorbed in your task, thinking of nothing else but doing the task. There is no drive to hurry, no thought of the future, no distraction—just the doing of the work.

There are three facets to this type of disciplined focus: complete concentration, acting without unnecessary effort, and nonattachment. The first, complete concentration, is derived from Zen Buddhism. Most Eastern religions, including Zen, are designed to teach those who practice them how to develop the ability to meditate and to do everything we do with focus and concentration. Shunryu Suzuki, in his book *Zen Mind, Beginner's Mind*, explains it this way:

> *In order not to leave any traces [of your thought and activity], you should do it with your whole body and mind; you should be concentrated on what you do. You should do it completely, like a good bonfire. You should not be a smoky fire. You should burn yourself completely.*

So if you are writing, completely involve yourself in the process. If you are driving a cab, be fully present.

The concentration referred to is not one requiring great energy and struggle, however. The second aspect of disciplined focus is to act without unnecessary effort. As Shunryu Suzuki states it, "just to do something without any particular effort is enough." When we invest extra effort in a task, it brings an "extra element" to it which dilutes the purity of our actions.

Another way to think of this second element is to ask the question: Do I recognize a "me" being aware of myself doing the thing, or is there such complete absorption that there is no "other" to be aware of myself? You may notice that this view of work appears to contradict the Witness technique that I have stressed so often throughout this book. This is because the Witness technique is simply a gateway to this higher level of work. Whether you use the Witness, prayer, meditation, yoga, or any other tool for awakening and broadening your perspective, they are just that: tools. They are dualistic in nature, since they involve the doer and the doing. Once you have broken your identification with the doer and become one with the Witness, the Witness and that which is witnessed become one.

The phenomenon referred to in psychology as "peak experiences" are an example of this concentration. At those times, the person doing the activity becomes so engrossed in the task that they are no longer aware of their separate self. Such experiences become more and more frequent as you carry out your life's purpose and learn to enjoy each moment of your work.

The third characteristic of disciplined focus, non-attachment, is described by Ram Dass in *Grist for the Mill*:

> *From my point of view, my work is to stay in a place of total involvement in the psychological plane with total non-attachment. I do what I do, and I do it as perfectly as my consciousness allows it to be done, except that I'm not attached to how it comes out. I'm just doing it as best I can.*

If we put many hours into a report solely because we want to impress our boss, we are attached to the result. Instead, if we can put the hours in just because that is what is necessary to do our best on the report, we are moving away from attachment and into disciplined focus.

As we blend these three aspects together in the doing of our work, we experience greater integration and unity in our life than we ever had before. We notice that we no longer segment "this time for meditation" and "this time for eating" and "this time for working"; they all start to be part of one activity.

Brother Lawrence, the insightful Christian monk, had learned this principle well. It was observed of him that during the busiest times in the kitchen where he worked, he still maintained his recollection and spiritual-mindedness. He explained it this way:

> *That time of business does not with me differ from the time of prayer, and in the noise and clatter of my kitchen, while several persons are at the same calling for different things, I possess God in as great tranquility as if I were upon my knees at the blessed sacrament.*

Virtually every tradition embraces the concept of disciplined focus in one form or another. The Zen Buddhists refer to it as satori, or awakening; Christians call it doing God's will; the Krishna term is Karma Yoga; psychologists call it self-actualization or transcendence. Whatever the form, the ultimate goal is the same: using work, performed in the highest way, as a vehicle for understanding life, growing personally, and unifying oneself with God as one understands It.

If you are a cook, approaching your work with disciplined focus, you pay close attention to every detail, as the great Zen master Dogen admonishes:

> *Keep your eyes open. Do not allow even one grain of rice to be lost. Wash the rice thoroughly, put it in the pot, light the fire, and cook it . . . See the pot as your own head; see the water as your lifeblood.*

If you are a manufacturing assembly worker who works with disciplined focus, you ensure that no part is wasted, that you assemble each piece with ease and excellence; and you notice every detail of the assembly as you do it.

Managers who use disciplined focus will concentrate on each task as they do it (rather than getting distracted), implement the best methods for assisting his/her employees to work together effectively and efficiently, and respond without judgment or emotion to his/her employees' and colleagues' suggestions.

Adopting a disciplined focus approach to our work yields many benefits. Our mental discipline increases, much in the same way it does through meditation. We are more productive, since greater concentration results in fewer errors and higher motivation to do our best. No longer is there a separation between our life functions. Rather, we sense a unity among all the aspects of our life, including the various roles we play. We notice details more than ever before, and develop a sense of wonder and awe of our world. We understand the cycles of life and work, and can flow with them instead of resisting or pushing against the natural current.

But disciplined focus is only half of our Inner Success. We must also learn to work with love.

Bringing Love to Work

Kahlil Gibran states a high ideal for us in *The Prophet*, when asked about work. He defines work as "love made visible,"and encourages us to work with love, which he describes as follows:

> *And what is it to work with love?*
> *It is to weave the cloth with threads drawn from your heart, even as if your beloved were to wear that cloth.*
> *It is to build a house with affection, even as if your beloved were to dwell in that house.*
> *It is to sow seeds with tenderness and reap the harvest with joy, even as if your beloved were to eat the fruit.*
> *It is to charge all things you fashion with a breath of your own spirit,*
> *And to know that all the blessed dead are standing about you and watching.*

Do you view your work as love in action—or just "necessary action"? By now, you might notice that you find a greater meaning and purpose in your work than you did before you began this book. Now I suggest that you also begin to bring love into your work so that no matter what you do, it has a special quality to it.

When we work with love, it does not matter *what* we do, but *how* we do it—our attitude toward it—that makes the difference. Once we learn to work with love, what we may previously have thought of as a chore becomes a gold mine of opportunities for learning and growth. Work then becomes a "spiritual classroom," with a different "lesson" for us every day.

Often, the highest form of working with love is to provide an environment of unconditional love in which others can grow. When you love others without conditions or "strings" attached, they will soon realize that nothing they do will change your love for them. This creates a safe, secure place in which they can grow and change —and both of you are able to expand to your highest potential.

How can you do this? You can begin by making a pledge to yourself that in every situation, you will act as lovingly as you can.

As you begin to see your work as an expression of love and caring, you realize it is a vehicle through which you love and serve others. When someone attacks you or criticizes you, they are either reflecting a lack of love within you, or they are feeling frightened or insecure and are crying out for love in the only way they know how. Can you remain loving, centered, and compassionate in the face of such attacks and criticism? As soon as you develop the ability to do just that, the people doing the attacking will sense a part of themselves that they previously did not know when they are around you—their infinite source of love.

By bringing both a disciplined focus and a consciousness of love to your work, you will be able to achieve the most important success of all: the Inner Success that allows you to really make a difference in your own growth and on the planet. And, in our final chapter, we expand that work to its widest extent.

Action Steps from 9 to 5

1. Is there an area in your life in which you know you need to make a change, but you have been resisting? If so, think of at least three steps you can begin to take to make that change. List them in your journal. Also list at least three benefits you will derive from making the change. Focus on these benefits as you begin to take the steps you have listed.

2. **Magnetism Exercise.** This exercise can be used to draw to you, at an energy level, more of what you want in your life.

    Relax your physical body, and clear your mind of distractions, using your favorite relaxation technique. Now, think of something you want in your life. Be very specific about the thing itself, as well as the qualities it will bring to you. If you wish, create a symbol that represents the essence of the thing you desire.

    Now, imagine yourself receiving this thing. Where are you?

Who is with you? How do you feel? Can you now see and feel it clearly? Place this scene of you receiving the object of your desire straight ahead of you in your mind, just a short distance ahead.

Imagine a force field of powerful energy surrounding you. Its source is in your power center, in your solar plexus. It creates a vibration that encompasses you and fills you to overflowing. That force field is irresistibly magnetic to the scene you have just created, and to the object or situation you desire. Imagine your force field radiating forth just the right amount of energy to attract the object of your desire, at just the right speed. Adjust its speed or intensity if necessary.

See all of the events that are necessary to cause this desire to manifest—all of the things that will precede it. There may be many or few. Notice that they are in a straight line, exactly in sequence, between you and your desire.

Now, see a powerful magnetic core, beginning in your solar plexus and going through the center of each of these events, straight through to your desire. See each of the experiences in this stream slowly closing in on each other, like an accordion. When the closure is complete, and your desire is just in front of you, very close, you will experience a "click," a knowingness that it is complete.

Now, let it go, knowing that it is manifesting on the earth plane in perfect time and in the perfect way. Let go of any attachment to it coming in a certain way, time, or through any particular channel. Open yourself to receive it in the highest form the Universe wishes to bring it to you.

Pause for a moment, noticing how you feel. When you are ready, come back to the present moment, knowing that your good is on its way to you now.

14

Beyond 9 to 5: Expanding Your Vision

We are living in a very exciting and powerful time.
On the deepest level of consciousness, a
radical spiritual transformation is taking place.
. . . On a worldwide level, we are being challenged
to let go of our present way of life
and create an entirely new one.
We are, in fact, in the process of destroying our old world
and building a new world in its place.

—Shakti Gawain

As WE HAVE GONE THROUGH this book together, perhaps you have noticed that it has progressed in a pyramid. I have encouraged you to continue pressing onward and upward to ever higher levels of awareness and fulfillment, each building on and naturally emerging from the last. You may have even been frustrated at times: just when you thought you had achieved one level of satisfaction, another level lay ahead to challenge you even further.

You began by becoming familiar with the changes taking place in the workplace of the '90s, from external structures to internal values. Next, you were introduced to the concept of life purpose, and how critical discovering and fulfilling your purpose are to your fulfillment in life and work. You developed some awareness of what your life's purpose is, and you began to set some goals to help you integrate that purpose into your everyday work (including whether or not a job or career change was needed).

Using the methods we explored in chapter 6, you began to make those goals a reality in your life.

I then prompted you to courageously examine and move beyond

251

your fears; your habits of delaying your good, including resistance, procrastination, and excuses; and your beliefs about money. I challenged you to insist on the best for yourself, and by understanding the Law of Attraction, to begin to draw into your life the people, things, and situations that support you and enhance your growth.

We were then ready to bring a higher perspective to some of the issues we face each day, including stress, boredom, time management, our natural energy cycle, balance in our lives, dealing with other people, and listening to our inner voice in decision making. At the next level, we learned to approach our work as a vehicle through which to grow, using the concept of Inner Success.

Now, in this final chapter, we expand our vision one final step as we examine the global implications of our vision, both now and in the future, and the path of business ownership as a vehicle for growth.

A Vision for the Future

Just imagine, for a moment, a world in which each of us has discovered and is fulfilling our life's purpose, and we each approach our work with love, pursuing Inner Success. Everyone is working and living harmoniously with each other. All social and business interchanges are loving and gracious. All needs are met; there is no poverty. There is no need for crime or war: no one thinks of it. There is an obvious, natural flow to each day. And each person pursues his/her own growth by diligently working on the issues in his/her life.

Can you imagine such a world? Does it sound impossible? How do you respond to this vision? If your response is, "It sounds great, but I can't do anything to change the way things are," I encourage you to reexamine that thought.

Fulfilling your life's purpose through your work, as well as every other aspect of your life, is the quickest route to personal and global transformation. Simply by recognizing your life's purpose and doing what you know to do to fulfill it impacts each other person on the planet.

If this sounds a bit far-fetched, let's look at an example a bit closer to home. As a result of reading this book (or through previous training), have you become aware of a pattern you had not previously noticed and were then able to change? For example, perhaps you used to be a Victim Thinker. Once you realized you were choosing to play that role because you weren't valuing yourself enough, you began to value yourself and to assertively state your feelings. Didn't you then find that you no longer attracted situations in which you were the victim? Yes, it is true that you have changed. But the people around you have changed as well, because you took the first step towards working on your own beliefs. This example illustrates the transformation process on a small scale—and that same transformation can also occur on a larger scope as you expand your vision.

The Call to Social Action

One of the natural outgrowths of our life's purpose, and a natural consequence of realizing our connectedness to each other, is a desire to be of service to others; to make a contribution to the world. Whether your life's purpose is to raise a family of integrity, or to promote world peace, or to transform the workplace, its effects are felt throughout the planet. At some point in its manifestation, an inner urge to serve the planet arises in a more direct way. You realize that you are, at some level, responsible for the problems apparent in the world today, and that you can begin the process of changing them. At that point, your vision begins to take on a new form.

Many of us who are awakening spiritually in the '90s enjoy the process of learning, reading, and talking about our newfound insights. We campaign for world peace, and we sing the Peace Song on a regular basis. But then we reach a stage where belief is not enough: we have come to the Point of Action.

At the Point of Action, we move our vision out into the world in a broader way. Henry David Thoreau got to this point when he refused to pay taxes because he did not believe in the war that was being supported by his tax dollars. When his friend, Ralph Waldo

Emerson, visited Thoreau in prison, he asked Mr. Thoreau, "What are you doing in there?" Thoreau answered, "What are you doing out there?"

Along the path of developing our vision, there are many tools to assist us, including visualization, affirmations, and energy work, as well as mental, physical, and spiritual disciplines. After the Point of Action, these tools are no longer sufficient in themselves for the fulfillment of our purpose. We must "move our feet," taking some action, no matter how small, to get our work out. Gandhi put it this way: "Almost anything you do will seem insignificant, but it is very important that you do it."

This means of social change has been termed "spiritual social action." This kind of change is motivated by a desire for change based not solely in material interests, but coming from the deeper perspective of moral or spiritual goals. The key difference between spiritual social action and traditional social action is this: In spiritual social action, the ends (or goals) do not justify the means. Instead, each of our means must embody the essence of the desired end. Each action we take must reflect our purpose; personify our deepest convictions; and take us one step closer to full awareness of our unity with God and with all life.

Perhaps as you have read this book you have questioned the continuing reference to God and the Universe in this, a book on achieving fulfillment at work. "After all," you may think, "what I believe about God has nothing to do with my work or whether I feel fulfilled at work." If you embrace this concept of separateness, of living a compartmentalized life, this may be true for you. But let me suggest that the highest form of religion is the kind that is lived every day, that affects every aspect of one's life.

The American Indians do not make any separation between religion and the rest of their life—their real religion is "living the right way every day." Earlier in this century, psychologist Carl Jung studied people reaching their midlife (after age 40), to determine what factors contribute most to mental health in aging. He found that the people who continued to be vital and excited about life, who aged well, and who had peace of mind, were those who had become comfortable with God, as they conceived it to be. Developing a religion or set of spiritual practices that they could live comfortably with every day was the single most important factor in satisfaction through later life.

In our journey toward fulfillment, we must make peace with God, discover and begin fulfilling our life's purpose, and let it evolve into its natural next stage of social action.

Business as a Spiritual Path

Perhaps you have chosen to own your own business, believing that path to be the most direct way to fulfill your life's purpose. If so, you have a unique set of challenges as you seek to "get on with it" and make your purpose a reality. And you are not alone.

As we begin the 1990s, we are in the midst of an unprecedented surge of entrepreneurship. Why? One reason is that the Fulfillment Ethic has not yet been integrated into many companies' philosophies. Perhaps you can find another company in your field that promotes individual growth and fulfillment. If not, a far more appealing option may be to design a business *your* way: to transform your unique vision into tangible form—a business of your own.

More and more business people who are participating in the current spiritual awakening begin to view their businesses in a new way. They may also seek to integrate consciously chosen values into every aspect of their business. Indeed, entrepreneurs are in an ideal position to implement change: They do not have the red tape and formalized structures of larger companies to limit their ability to act out their ideals. They can be flexible and adaptable to the rapid changes in the workplace. And they are beginning to have a larger and larger impact on all of us.

One example is Ben and Jerry's ice cream company in Vermont. They use only natural ingredients in their products and contribute a set percentage of their profits to charitable causes. The integrity of Ben and Jerry's values, as reflected in these practices, has resulted in incredible growth for the company from a small ice cream parlor in a gas station to a publicly traded company in just a few short years. And they don't have plans to compromise those values, no matter how large the company becomes.

Another model for this higher business consciousness is found in the Briarpatch Network of businesses in San Francisco. These businesses share three values around which they design their business practices: 1) being in business because they love it; 2) finding their chief reward in serving people, rather than seeking large sums of money; and 3) sharing resources (including knowledge of business) with each other as much as possible. They also keep their financial records open to the public. Their focus is on cooperation, rather than competition. (After all, since we each have our own unique life's purpose, there is no need for the concept of competition.)

These are just two examples of bringing a higher perspective to entrepreneurship. For those of you that have chosen this path, I offer the following suggestions. They come primarily from my own experience in small business management, and will enable you to more effectively make your unique contribution through the path of business.

1. Choose a business that carries out your life's purpose.   Whether you offer a service, manufacture a product, or sell one or more products, your business activity ought to directly relate to your life's purpose.

2. Allow your business to grow and change.   Too often, we hit on a strategy or structure that works for our business, and never want to change it when the needs and demands of the business do. Your business is a living organism, with a life cycle just like a human being. Adapting to change, to the ebb and flow of business and the growth that is bound to occur, is absolutely critical to success as an entrepreneur.

3. Bring fun into your business.   Having fun at work is part and parcel of fulfilling our life's purpose. What all of us want more of, as awakening workers, is challenge, creativity, and enjoyment—not just a raise or a longer vacation. Some specific ways to bring fun into work are outlined in chapter 11, and I'm sure you will think of others for your unique enterprise. This gives you an opportunity to be creative and innovative, and allows you to bring to your workplace the personality that is exclusively yours.

4. Establish a mission for your company, with stated values to which your company adheres for its fulfillment. Just as we set goals for our personal achievement, we must also set goals for our business. The company mission statement is the first step to doing that. The Employee's Bill of Rights at the end of this chapter can serve as a model for your own company values. Once your mission and values are specifically stated, all employees ought to understand and "buy into" them, so that everyone involved in the company is cooperating toward a common cause.

5. Keep things simple. Whether you are trying to solve a production problem or deal with a disgruntled employee, the simpler solutions are nearly always best. By relying on your inner voice for guidance, and always keeping your eye on your life's purpose—the real reason you are here—you will never go wrong.

6. Use integrity in all things. You will begin to build a reputation as your business expands. Do you represent honesty or "white lies"? Will you go for the cheapest deal, or the most satisfying interchange for all concerned? If you always tell the truth, and bring integrity to both your means and ends (rather than assuming the end result justifies any means necessary), your business will be built on a solid foundation. Your customers and employees will also tend to share the values you espouse.

7. Don't get locked into tunnel vision. Each day, we need to step back and look at the broader perspective. It's easy to get caught up in doing daily tasks, or worrying about the financial report. Remember why you are in business. And approach each situation with an appropriate (rather than excessive) degree of concern.

8. Trust the Universe for your supply. I hope you haven't gotten into your own business just to get rich. Your business may make you rich, but the desire for wealth is not enough to justify the time and effort it will take to achieve it. The Universe knows your needs. Let it supply you with all you need, whether it is money, resources, clients or customers, or contacts. By using the tools you have learned in this book, you know how to draw what you need to you. So don't get too concerned about the money—it will take care of itself (though you need to monitor it and exercise your good business judgment in its management).

9. Balance your business with the rest of your life. Don't forget about your family, friends, hobbies, and spiritual practices just because you have your own business. Keep your priorities in the proper order, and take vacations as often as you reasonably can. Your business is just one part of your life —not all of it.

10. Be willing to share your good. As you network with other business owners and associates, share what you have. Encourage cooperation instead of competition. We have had enough of the "cutthroat" mentality. It is time to approach our work and our life with love, patience with the natural flow, and a willingness to share instead of trying to "get what's ours." As you share, the Universe and the other people in it will share with you.

Right Livelihood

Whether you elect the path of business or choose to work for someone else, your work will be enhanced by incorporating the concept of Right Livelihood into it. This is a Buddhist notion that contemplates using work as a vehicle for one's personal growth and awakening. Right Livelihood simply refers to work that is chosen consciously and pursued with complete awareness, love, joy, and great care. Ultimately, in the Buddhist tradition, work is a vehicle for enlightenment. As you fulfill your life's purpose, you too will find yourself on the path of Right Livelihood.

One author has listed four elements of Right Livelihood: 1) an area of great passion, 2) something you could do for your entire life,

3) something that serves the community, and 4) something totally appropriate for you. Sounds a lot like life's purpose, doesn't it? When you approach your work as your Right Livelihood, work becomes a way to express your creative self, and you do it with total concentration. It is the "right" thing for you to be doing—and you would rather be doing that than anything else.

Those of you who are spiritual can take this concept one step further and actually commit the fruits of your labor to God, or the Divine Power. As you view your work as your Right Livelihood, seeking Inner Success, work becomes the ultimate act of devotion to your Creator. Every act that you do at work is transformed into an act of worship. As Thoreau put it:

> *The true husbandman will cease from anxiety, as the squirrels manifest no concern whether the woods will bear chestnuts this year or not, and finish his labor with every day, relinquishing all claim to the produce of his fields, and sacrificing in his mind not only his first but last fruits also.*

From this attitude springs a new dimension of work, a unity with one's actions previously felt only during peak experiences. And the joy that one can then experience through work is unparalleled in any other human experience.

The Mirror Effect (Again)

As you initially recognized your life's purpose, you may have conceived it as an area of the planet that needed healing. And you have been going about your work contributing to the healing of that area, whatever it is. This is your calling.

At the same time, however, we must each realize that the planet does not really need healing, or "fixing": we do. Perhaps your purpose is to heal discord among people. Each time you hear about an earthquake, hurricane, or other "natural disaster" (a contradiction of terms), you are touched and take what is natural action for you by sending send money, blankets, food, or other physical assistance. And indeed that is your calling. But the next step is this: You must look within yourself to see whether there are areas within you that are in discord. Is it possible that these outer events simply reflect your own inner conflict, and that once you heal that, the "natural disasters" will be healed too? (Or that you won't be as sensitive to them as you now are?)

The effect is a complete circle that begins with discovery of your life's purpose and getting it out into the world. It ends with the discovery that all of the work involved in fulfilling your life's purpose is designed to heal and transform you.

The Mirror Effect, which we first explored in our discussion of resistance, has mass implications. You were drawn to your life's purpose both to be of service to the planet and to heal yourself. Once your individual healing is complete, your service to the planet and the focus of your life may well change.

At another level, we are at a critical point of healing in the history of the planet. Massive inner transformations are occurring within you and within each of us as we awaken to our spiritual nature and as the workplace reflects the desire for fulfillment and growth. And this transformation is reflected in apparent chaos throughout the world. Why not view this turmoil as a temporary effect of positive change? Rather than becoming depressed or overwhelmed by it, why not rejoice that the pivotal time has finally come? As each of us does our part to heal and to grow, we assist the planet in its evolution as well.

Work in the Future

So where are we heading, as we follow our inner guidance and carry out our life's purpose? I believe we are entering the most exciting time in history. Free of the former barriers to individual fulfillment, we can become what we have always longed to be. We can choose to awaken in the center of a busy metropolis, or we can retreat to the mountains and live a solitary existence. We can be a doctor or a writer, an astronaut or a cab driver, a business owner or a full-time parent.

Workers and the workplace will continue to change. Indeed, it is said that the only constant in life today is change. The workplace of the 21st century will bear only shadows of today's structures. The decentralization trend may increase or decrease, as may innovative accommodations to employees such as in-house child care and computer networking to home offices.

But there is one constant in our life that we must never lose sight of: our spiritual essence. No matter what external changes may occur in the workplace of the future, we must never let those changes distract us from our purpose. The price of compromising our essential life purpose, our reason for being, will always be too high a price to pay for conformity.

As more and more people like you begin to embody the principles in this book and those being taught by many wise teachers today, we will, together, create a new world. The workplace will be populated in increasing numbers by awakening, fulfilled workers, who share several key characteristics:

1. Awakening workers are comfortable with change.   They are flexible, open-minded, and warmly embrace change. Change is not an enemy to be eliminated, but a friend which, once welcomed, becomes the bridge to growth. And they initiate change in their own lives when appropriate. They are unwilling to allow resistance, procrastination, excuses, stress, boredom, or any other limiting factor keep them from being the best they can be.

2. Awakening workers know their life's purpose and are living it. They know what they are on earth to do, and they are working at it with passion. Their life has direction, and they enjoy each new day as the recognize the possibilities for growth and progress toward their goals.

3. Awakening workers follow their inner guidance.   As they move through each moment, awakening workers listen to their inner voice and heed its urgings—even if they do not make rational sense. They know that following that guidance will always create the highest result for all concerned.

4. Awakening workers have a "passionate detachment" about their life and work. They are skilled at using the Witness technique, and they observe themselves in all of their various life activities in a detached, nonjudgmental manner. Though they are passionate about their work, they are not attached to the occurrence of any particular results. They simply do what needs to be done, with conscious focus and love.

5. Awakening workers are comfortable with abundance in their lives. These workers have a belief system that supports abundance, and they are demonstrating wealth in every area of their lives. Though they may choose to live in voluntary simplicity, they recognize that the abundance of the Universe is there for the having. And if they choose material wealth, they easily create it.

6. Awakening workers honor and support themselves and others. Awakening workers recognize the principle that "as I give, so I receive." They honor all others in their lives, responding to them with compassion. They graciously receive the generosity of others. And at the same time, they honor and support themselves and their own growth, knowing that they can only give to others when their own cup is full.

7. Awakening workers create the life they desire by working at both the level of energy (cause) and the level of matter (effects). These workers know that there is more to this world than meets the eye. The cause behind all of our experiences is at a subconscious, energy level. They use magnetism and the Law of Attraction to draw their good to them. Having laid this mental foundation, they then allow their life's purpose to be expressed through actions that their Higher Self leads them to take.

8. Awakening workers use everything in their lives, including their work, as means for growth and further awakening. Finally, these workers recognize the principle of Inner Success. They know that their job, their family, their environment, their health, their money, and everything in their lives is a vehicle through which they can grow in awareness. And they exercise laser-like focus, living in the now moment, with love. They know that their life consists of a series of todays, each of which contributes to the quality of their tomorrow. So they live their todays to the fullest.

I invite you to become one of these Awakening Workers. Your highest calling is to follow your own path and life's purpose to its deepest depths, its widest breadths. As you do so, you will find yourself living the most fulfilling life you can imagine. And you will know, from your own process of growth and experience, that 9 to 5 will never be enough for you.

The Employee's Bill of Rights

1. The employee has the right to choose the career and job that he/she wants to pursue.
2. The employee has the right to enjoy his/her work.
3. The employee has the right to express him/herself creatively in his/her work.
4. The employee has the right to be compensated according to his/her value to the company, as measured in part by the efforts put forth by the employee.
5. The employee has the right to adequate training and adequate facilities to perform his/her job.
6. The employee has the right to be treated as a valuable and contributing member of the company and to have a voice in company philosophy and management.
7. The employee has the right to have a family and a career, and to work in an environment in which reasonable family commitments are accommodated.
8. The employee has the right to receive regular feedback concerning the work he/she performs and to participate in setting reasonable goals for his/her work.
9. The employee has the right to know the financial condition, competitive position, and other relevant information about the company, and to be informed, in advance, of management decisions and other impending changes that may affect him/her.
10. The employee has the right to experience the fulfillment of his/her personal goals through his/her work.

Action Steps from 9 to 5

1. Is there a social application that you have been wanting to explore for your life's purpose? Is there a way you can begin expanding it in that way today?

2. Have you always dreamed of starting your own business but were afraid you would have to compromise your values to do so? If so, make it a point this week to talk to some business owners and to do some independent research into the types of businesses that interest you and the procedures required to get started. If you feel drawn toward that path, design a plan for your business, including the philosophy you will adopt to carry out your life purpose through your business.

18 Commonly Asked Questions

1. Why am I no longer satisfied with the job that made me very happy a few years ago?

There may be many reasons for your dissatisfaction. I find that many people's values are changing as the workplace has shifted from the Puritan Work Ethic to the Fulfillment Ethic. When the Puritan Work Ethic dominated a couple of generations ago, people were expected to persevere in their job, to continue putting in their time even if they greatly disliked their work. The key value was loyalty and longevity.

In the 1990s, by contrast, as the Fulfillment Ethic rapidly proliferates, most people are no longer willing to tolerate an unfulfilling job. They want to make a difference, to use their creative talents in their job, and to develop meaningful relationships with their co-workers. You may be feeling the effects of this shift in thinking in your job. If so, you will want to gain a clear idea of your life's purpose, decide the type of job you want, and develop a plan for making the needed change to that new job. See chapters 1 through 6 for more information.

2. I've always felt like my life had a purpose, but I don't know what it is. How can I discover what I am here to do?

First, realize that at some level you already know what your purpose is. Your task is to bring that information into your conscious mind.

You may wish to begin by asking yourself this question: What would I like to do that both excites me the most, and scares me the most at the same time? The answer to that question will give you an important clue to your purpose.

Another question to ask is this: Is there something I have always wanted to do, but have never had the courage or willingness to admit it to myself and to begin taking action to do it?

You can recognize your purpose by its typical characteristics. It is fun, playful, energizing, and completely absorbing for you. It is uniquely suited to you. When you are carrying out your purpose, time goes by quickly, almost unnoticed. And you are making a contribution to the world and others as you do so.

For more information and techniques for discovering your purpose, see chapter 2.

3. How do I know what kind of a job is best for me?

The only jobs that will fulfill you at a deep level are those that are consistent with your life's purpose, and in some way assist you in carrying out that purpose. Therefore, you must first gain an understanding of what your life's purpose is.

Having done that, you must then evaluate each of the remaining six factors in your ideal job or career: 1) your values, 2) what motivates you, 3) your skills, 4) your past experience, 5) the career area and job description of your ideal job, and 6) the type of environment in which you will work best. For more information and tips on each factor, see chapter 4.

4. I have lost my enthusiasm and energy for my present job. How do I know whether I ought to change jobs?

You may be suffering from burnout. One way to determine whether you are burned out, or just in need of a vacation, is to arrange for a day or two, or a week, off from work. If you have vacation coming, take that. If you have to take it as unpaid leave, take one day (or whatever you can reasonably afford) without pay. After your break, notice how you feel when you go back to work. Do you have more energy? Are you excited about going back with a fresh perspective? Or do you feel resentment and anger at having to return?

If you are truly burned out, you will not feel better or more energetic when it is time to return. You will be experiencing three kinds of exhaustion: physical, emotional, and mental. You may find yourself angry for no apparent reason, and irritable at your family even when they have done nothing to merit such a response. You may have a negative overall attitude.

If you fit this pattern, you might think about leaving your job as soon as possible, taking a temporary job if necessary to pay your basic expenses, but leaving time for some personal exploration. Your burnout situation has a message for you, and it will lead you to a new level of growth if you will let it. For more information, see chapter 3.

5. Is it important to set personal goals? If so, why?

If you want to grow personally, intellectually, financially, and spiritually through your life, goals are absolutely essential. They provide a "road map," if you will, for your subconscious mind. They give your mind a destination toward which to head. Goals make the difference between a life of accomplishment, and a life of unfulfilled dreams. See chapter 5 for more, including how to set achievable goals.

6. I've set goals before, but usually don't accomplish them. Do you have any suggestions to help me achieve my goals?

Many people fail to accomplish their goals because they have not designed them to be achievable. That is, they have not tested their goal by the four characteristics of achievable goals. They are: 1) Be specific, quantifying as much as possible, 2) Be realistic, 3) Make your goal measurable, and 4) Be sure your goal only depends on your personal responsibility for its achievement—not someone else's actions. See chapter 5 for elaboration.

Once you have designed your goal to be achievable, you must then design a plan for its achievement and use one or more of the techniques outlined in chapter 6 to make them happen. Once you do each of these steps, being careful to follow through each day, you will achieve your goals.

7. How do I deal with fear?

First, you must determine whether your fear is rational or irrational. That is, does it make sense to be afraid of this situation (for example, fear of not being able to cope if you take a promotion that involves moving to another state)? Or is it purely irrational (for example, fear of being in a crowd)?

Rational fears respond well to intellectual analysis, using the following pattern. First, ask yourself what would be the worst thing that could happen if your fear came true. Could you cope with that? Then go to the next worst, and so on, until you have exhausted the possibilities. Second, list the things you will miss out on if you don't take the promotion, and the things you will gain if you do. Do you feel better? The fear will not have as much power once you have dissected it in this way. Then reemphasize the benefits from moving ahead, and go toward your growing edge!

Irrational fears usually have a message for you. They are your subconscious mind's attempt to protect you from something. For these, a meditation such as that listed on pages 122 to 123 of this book will help.

See chapter 7 for more information about overcoming fear.

8. Now that I'm an adult, shouldn't I stop experiencing fear?

Surprisingly, the answer is no. As long as you keep growing, fear will continue to be a part of your experience. It will occur every time you step outside your "comfort zone" and try something new.

The key is, how will you respond to fear? Will you resist it, use it to justify avoiding new situations? Or will you embrace it, and realize that it is trying to lead you into a new level of growth and awareness? Once you see fear as your friend, your guide into each new experience, you can easily move through it by dissolving it with love.

9. I seem to always sabotage my efforts to change and grow. Do you have any tips for eliminating self-sabotage?

The first tip I would offer in this situation is to stop beating up on yourself every time this pattern recurs. Self-sabotage is often reinforced by all of the attention you give yourself, negative though it may be, when you detour from your chosen goal once again.

Instead, try to love and support yourself, reinforcing the days when you *do* make progress toward your goals. Spend some time each day repeating orally or writing out the benefits of the new behavior or situation you are creating, and how it will enhance you. As often as you can, use the Witness technique to observe yourself from a detached perspective. (See pages 70–2 and 126–7 for more information.) When you go "off the track," simply notice it, and begin to stop the process earlier and earlier each time. Soon the old, sabotaging pattern will no longer recur.

Second, make a firm decision that your sabotaging behavior has to stop. Write down what you are losing out on by engaging in this behavior, and create a greater pleasure that you will obtain by acting differently.

Finally, get into a meditative state and ask your sabotage to take form and reveal to you the message it has for you. Is it trying to protect you from information that may be surprising, shocking, or painful? If so, be willing to look squarely at that information and use this revelation to change your behavior. For more information, see chapter 8.

10. I often put off making needed or desired changes in my life, or find an excuse to rationalize my inability to move forward. Can you help?

These behaviors are often masking a fear that you have thus far been unwilling to acknowledge. For example, you may be afraid of the unknown, or afraid of "failure." The first step toward making desired changes is to decide how you want your life to change. Write out as specifically as you can the change you want to make. Then, state in detail what you are missing out on by not making that change now, as well as what you will gain if you do change. But don't stop there! Right after you do these exercises, state one step you can take toward your desired situation RIGHT NOW, and do it.

Make a covenant with yourself to do one step, however small, each day toward that change. (For example, if you want to change jobs, spend at least 15 minutes each day looking at want ads, meeting with someone, or scheduling interviews.) It is helpful to set aside a particular time of the day—preferably first thing in the morning—to do this. Those small steps will eventually result in your creating the desired change.

If there is an excuse or situation that seems insurmountable, ask yourself, "If I knew how to overcome this excuse, how would I do it?" You may be surprised at the answers that come to you!

For more information, see chapter 8.

11. How can I enjoy my work and still make more money?

Surveys and studies have repeatedly shown that people who become wealthy do work that they enjoy, rather than tolerating work they dislike and trying to save for the "greater later" to enjoy themselves. Part of the reason this is true is because money of itself is a neutral substance. It is attracted to high energy, excitement, and enthusiasm. Therefore, the more you like your work, the more money you will tend to make doing it. Your energy is contagious to your co-workers and customers or clients, as well as to money itself.

Once you are clear on your life's purpose, and are fulfilling it through your work, you will find that you attain wealth beyond what you had thought possible. See chapter 9 for more information.

12. I have a family to support, so it doesn't seem practical for me to consider changing to a more enjoyable job. How do I meet my financial obligations during my time of transition or self-discovery?

This is one of the most common questions to come up in my seminars. Answering it requires that you draw upon the depths of your creativity and resourcefulness, and test the strength of your commitment to your growth. First, know that there *is* a way for you to make the change you desire. The Universe always supports you as you grow.

Once you are clear on what kind of job you want to move into, ask yourself, "If I knew how to make a smooth transition to this new job, how would I do it?'' Write down the first things that come to mind, even if they seem unrelated. Their relationship to each other will usually unfold fairly quickly, and you can begin to devise a creative transitional plan.

If you are miserable in your job and need to get away from the distraction of the situation to determine what new job is best for you, see if there is a temporary or part-time job you can take, with low stress, to pay your basic expenses while you do your self-examination. Promise yourself it will only be for 30 or 60 days, and meanwhile, put your spare-time energy into designing your ideal job as described in chapter 4.

13. My job is extremely stressful. How can I cope with the stress?

Stress seems to be a regular part of many of our lives today. And much of our apparent inability to cope is due to our failure or refusal to care for ourselves. Examine your lifestyle. Do you smoke? drink alcohol? eat nutritionally? exercise at least three times a week? meditate regularly? What about your beliefs—do you consider yourself a "victim" of your circumstances? Do you see yourself as one with others, or separate from them? A nutritional diet and regular exercise, coupled with regular meditation or relaxation exercises and a positive outlook will do much to reduce stress.

You may also want to look at the source of the stress, and whether you have created the same pattern repeatedly in your life. If there is anything you can do to minimize the stimulus that triggers the stress response in you (for example, delegate some of your work to someone else), do it! If the situation itself can't change, and your lifestyle is fairly healthy, ask yourself if it is really worth it to you to continue working, day after day, in a situation that may be detrimental to your physical and mental health.

Dealing with stress is a broad topic. For more information, see chapter 10.

14. I work on an assembly line, in a very routine, often boring, position. Is there any way for me to enjoy my work more?

If you truly don't have the option to change to a more interesting job, or have elected to stay in a boring job for a limited period of time, there are some techniques you can use to make your work more enjoyable. For example, can you make a game out of it, or find some aspect of it that fascinates you and learn more about it? Can you use the time you are working to daydream, and create an exciting future for yourself (including the plans to make it happen)? Or insist on doing the job the very best you can, keeping your attention on each task so that your skill is honed to its highest capacity? Know that this job can teach you much about the value of focused attention, and may well lead to a more interesting position—if you are open and ready for it! For more information and ideas, see chapter 10.

15. I don't really want to make a lot of money. It is more important to me to make an impact on the world through my work. Do you have any tips for how to do this most effectively?

By doing work that carries out your life's purpose, you have taken a big step toward making a broad impact on the world. Your purpose is the reason you are here, and the world is in some way incomplete until you have made the special contribution you have to make.

It will enhance that contribution if you do everything you do with love. As you realize that we are all one with each other, you know that as you honor and serve others, you honor and serve yourself. So do it the best you know how! Focus on each task with love and complete attention, doing it completely and without undue effort. You will find that the quality of your life, as well as that of the people around you, is enhanced as a result.

Finally, take seriously your call to be "in the world, but not of it." That is, take your work out into the world, creating change where it is needed, and doing your part as an individual to enhance the global consciousness. It might be something as small as recycling your garbage, or something as far-reaching as new legislation. Whatever you feel called to do, do it. And your impact will be broadened each day.

16. No matter where I work, people always criticize me. Should I change jobs to get out of this pattern?

If you have created the same pattern over and over again in different situations, changing jobs probably will *not* eliminate it. The reason you keep experiencing criticism is likely due not to the people around you, but to a belief inside of you that tells you you are not good enough—so you bring people into your life to reinforce that belief.

How do you break the cycle? First, recognize the old belief you have had that no longer serves you. Do you want to change it? If so, begin to love yourself and to reinforce (through affirmations and the other techniques we recommended in chapter 6 for goal achievement) your new, desired belief. Begin to actually believe that you *are* good enough, and that you are always loved and supported. As you begin to internalize this belief, the people who used to criticize you will leave your life. And you will have broken your old pattern.

17. I want to have a career and a family. Do you have any tips for balancing the two?

I offer eight suggestions to effectively balance career and family responsibilities:

1. Be realistic about your choice to have both career and family, and realize you won't do both perfectly all the time.
2. Choose a spouse who shares your plans and goals.
3. Choose a career path that will allow time out to have children, and/or one with a flexible schedule.
4. Be prepared to make some sacrifices.
5. Draft your spouse into co-parenting responsibilities.
6. Get help with the housework and child-care duties.
7. Take time off for your children.

8. Choose an employer who recognizes the special needs of working parents.

For more information, see chapter 12.

18. I own my own business. How can I run that business in a way that enhances my growth and provides a service to the world?

Entrepreneurship is booming in the 1990s. Many of us choose to own our own business so that we can work in a way that creates meaning as well as profit. The following 10 principles will help you run your business in a higher way:

1. Choose a business that carries out your life's purpose.
2. Allow your business to grow and change.
3. Bring fun into your business.
4. Establish a clear mission and values for your company.
5. Keep things simple.
6. Use integrity in all things.
7. Don't get locked into tunnel vision.
8. Trust the Universe for your supply.
9. Keep your business in perspective with the rest of your life.
10. Be willing to share your good with others.

Sources

Chapter 1

Angier, Natalie, "25 and Taking Over: The High-Expectation, Low-Sweat Generation," *Mademoiselle*, August 1989.
Naisbitt, John, *Megatrends*, Warner Books, 1984.
Naisbitt, John, and Aburdene, Patricia, *Re-inventing the Corporation*, Warner Books, 1985.
Yankelovich, Daniel, *New Rules: Searching for Fulfillment in a World Turned Upside Down*, Random House, 1981.

Chapter 2

Anderson, Nancy, *Work With Passion: How to Do What You Love for a Living*, Whatever Publishing, 1984.
Roman, Sanaya, *Creating Money*, H. J. Kramer, 1988.

Chapter 3

Barranger, Jack, *Knowing When to Quit.*, Impact Publishers, 1988.
Pines, Ayala and Aronson, Elliott, *Career Burnout: Causes & Cures*, The Free Press, 1988.
Waitley, Denis and Witt, Reni L., *The Joy of Working*, Ballantine Books, 1985.

Chapter 4

Anderson, Nancy, *Work with Passion*, Whatever Publishing, 1984.
Naisbitt, John, *Megatrends*, Warner Books, 1982, 1984.
Perkins-Reed, Marcia A., *WomEntrepreneuring, Or How to Start a Business—and Succeed!* MPR Ventures, 1988.
Pines, Ayala and Aronson, Elliott, *Career Burnout: Causes & Cures*, The Free Press, 1988.

Robbins, Anthony, *Unlimited Power*, Ballantine Books, 1986.
Wilkens, Joanna, *Her Own Business*, McGraw-Hill, 1987.

Chapter 5

Gawain, Shakti, *Living in the Light: A Guide to Personal and Planetary Transformation*, Whatever Publishing, 1986.
Robbins, Anthony, *Unlimited Power*, Ballantine Books, 1986.

Chapter 6

Robbins, Anthony, *Unlimited Power*, Ballantine Books, 1986.
Waitley, Denis, *The Joy of Working*, Ballantine Books, 1985.

Chapter 7

Jeffers, Susan, *Feel the Fear and Do It Anyway*, Fawcett Columbine, 1988.
Robbins, Anthony, *Personal Power* (cassette tapes) Guthy Rinker Corp., 1989.
Roman, Sanaya, *Spiritual Growth*, H. J. Kramer, 1989.

Chapter 8

Robbins, Anthony, *Personal Power* (cassette tapes), Guthy Rinker Corp., 1989.

Chapter 9

Cameron, Charles and Suzanne Elusorr, *T.G.I.M.: "Thank God It's Monday,"* Jeremy P. Tarcher, Inc., 1986.
Fields, Rick, *Chop Wood, Carry Water*, Jeremy P. Tarcher, Inc., 1984.
Gawain, Shakti, *Living in the Light*, Whatever Press, 1986.
Mandel, Bob, *Two Hearts are Better than One*, Celestial Arts, 1986.
Robbins, Anthony, *Personal Power* (cassette tapes), Guthy Rinker Corp., 1989.
Robbins, Anthony, *Unlimited Power*, Bantam Books, 1986.
Roman, Sanaya, *Creating Money*, H.J. Kramer, Inc., 1988.

Sinetar, Marsha, *Do What You Love: The Money Will Follow*, Paulist Press, 1987.

Sinetar, Marsha, *Ordinary People as Monks and Mystics*, Paulist Press, 1986.

Chapter 10

Benson, Herbert, M.D., *The Relaxation Response*, Avon Books, 1976.

Cameron, Charles and Elusorr, Suzanne, *T.G.I.M.: Thank God It's Monday*, Jeremy P. Tarcher, Inc., 1986.

Fields, Rick, et al, *Chop Wood Carry Water—A Guide to Finding Spiritual Fulfillment in Everyday Life*, Jeremy P. Tarcher, Inc., 1984.

Chapter 11

Diamond, Harvey and Marilyn, *Fit for Life*, Warner Books, 1985.

Grant, Doris, and Jean Joice, *Food Combining for Health*, Thorsons Publishers, Inc., 1984.

Robbins, Anthony, *Personal Power* (cassette tapes), Guthy Rinker Corp., 1989.

Robbins, Anthony, *Unlimited Power*, Fawcett Columbine, 1986.

Chapter 12

Holmes, Ernest, *The Science of Mind*, Dodd, Mead & Co., 1938.

Keyes, Ken, *Handbook to Higher Consciousness*, Living Love Center, 1975.

Naisbitt, John, *Megatrends*, Warner Books 1982, 1984.

Robbins, Anthony, *Personal Power* (cassette tape series), 1989.

Roman, Sanaya, *Creating Money*, H. J. Kramer Inc., 1988.

Chapter 13

Dass, Ram, *Grist for the Mill*, Bantam Books, 1976.

Fields, Rick, *Chop Wood, Carry Water: A Guide to Finding Spiritual Fulfillment in Everyday Life*, Jeremy P. Tarcher, Inc., 1984.

Keyes, Ken, Jr., *Handbook to Higher Consciousness*, Fifth Edition, Living Love Center, 1977.

Suzuki, Shunruy, *Zen Mind, Beginner's Mind*, Weatherhill, 1980.

Chapter 14

Fields, Rick, *Chop Wood, Carry Water: A Guide to Finding Spiritual Fulfillment in Everyday Life*, Jeremy P. Tarcher, Inc., 1984.

Gawain, Shakti, *Living in the Light: A Guide to Personal and Planetary Transformation*, Whatever Publishing, 1986.

Index

ABOUT THE AUTHOR

Marcia A. Perkins-Reed is a nationally known motivational speaker and seminar presenter. She brings to her audiences a combination of 20 years of varied business experience (including owning two businesses of her own), degrees in psychology and law, 10 years in New Thought, and the success and fulfillment experienced by herself and her consulting clients. Those who attend her seminars often experience major breakthroughs in their growth, and gain the invaluable benefit of clarity about their life and work.

Marcia is a living example of the principles taught in this book. After practicing law for four years in Portland, Oregon, she has now made a 100 percent commitment to fulfilling her life's purpose through presenting seminars and writing. She travels throughout the United States and Canada, sharing her message with major corporations, churches, trade organizations, governmental bodies, and similar organizations.

Ms. Perkins-Reed has written three previous books, including *WomEntrepreneuring: Or How to Start a Business and Succeed!* and *The Career Workbook*.

Marcia Perkins-Reed is available for speaking engagements, seminars, training workshops, and individual consulting by contacting:

MPR Ventures, Inc.
921 SW Washington, Suite 805
Portland, OR 97205
(800) 759-7059

HAY
HOUSE

If you would like to receive a catalog of Hay House products, or information about future workshops, lectures, and events sponsored by the Louise L. Hay Educational Institute, please detach and mail this questionnaire.

Thank you for ordering *When 9 to 5 Isn't Enough*. Please fill out this questionnaire to help us serve you better. In return, we will send you a catalog of our current products.

NAME _____

ADDRESS _____

_____

I purchased this book from:

    Store _____

    City _____

    Other (catalog, lecture, workshop) _____

Occupation _____

Other topics you would enjoy: _____

_____